A Constitution *of* Many Minds

A Constitution *of* Many Minds

Why the Founding Document Doesn't Mean What It Meant Before

CASS R. SUNSTEIN

Princeton University Press ❈ *Princeton and Oxford*

Published by Princeton University Press, 41 William Street,
Princeton, New Jersey 08540

In the United Kingdom: Princeton University Press, 6 Oxford Street,
Woodstock, Oxfordshire OX20 1TW

press.princeton.edu

Third printing, and first paperback printing, 2011
Paperback ISBN 978-0-691-15242-4

The Library of Congress has cataloged the cloth edition of this book as follows

Sunstein, Cass R.
A constitution of many minds / Cass R. Sunstein.
p.   cm.
Includes index.
ISBN 978-0-691-13337-9 (hardcover : alk. paper)
1. Constitutional law—United States—Interpretation and construction. I. Title.
KF4552.S86 2009
342.73—dc22
2008014128

British Library Cataloging-in-Publication Data is available

This book has been composed in Adobe Caslon

Printed on acid-free paper. ∞

Printed in the United States of America

3   5   7   9   10   8   6   4

And first of all, the science of jurisprudence, the pride of the human intellect, which, with all its defects, redundancies, and errors, is the collected reason of the ages, combining the principles of original justice with the infinite variety of human concerns, as a heap of old exploded errors, would no longer be studied. Personal self-sufficiency and arrogance (the certain attendants upon all those who have never experienced a wisdom greater than their own) would usurp the tribunal.

—EDMUND BURKE, *Reflections on the Revolution in France*

It has been frequently remarked that it seems to have been reserved to the people of this country, by their conduct and example, to decide the important question, whether societies of men are really capable or not of establishing good government from reflection and choice, or whether they are forever destined to depend for their political constitutions on accident and force.

—ALEXANDER HAMILTON, *Federalist No. 1*

If, as in ordinary language, a preceding generation be called old, this old or preceding generation could not have had as much experience as the succeeding generation. . . . What then is the wisdom of the times called old? Is it the wisdom of gray hairs? No. It is the wisdom of the cradle.

—JEREMY BENTHAM, *Handbook of Political Fallacies*

CONTENTS

PREFACE

When Americans think of constitutional law, they tend to focus on the particular controversies of the day. Does the Constitution protect the right to have guns? Will the Court permit the president to detain suspected terrorists? Is there a constitutional right to have abortions? Should states have to recognize same-sex marriages? Are affirmative action plans constitutional? Questions of this kind are always pressing, but they receive special attention whenever the Court is in a time of transition. In any such period, people ask: What will be the future of constitutional law?

In this book, I step back from current disputes and focus instead on some large and enduring issues. These issues have been with us from the founding. They cut across changes in the Court's composition. They arise in many nations, not merely the United States. The issues involve the roles of traditions, public opinion, and foreign law. I mean, in short, to identify and explore three approaches to the founding document: traditionalism, populism, and cosmopolitanism.

We shall see that in all three contexts, what is at work is a *many minds argument*—an argument that if many people think something, their view is entitled to consideration and respect. Traditionalists insist that if members of a society have long accepted a certain practice, courts should be reluctant to disturb that practice. Some traditionalists go further, urging that even political majorities should respect long-standing practices. Populists believe that if most people believe a certain fact or accept a certain value, judges should show a degree of humility—and respect their view in the face of reasonable doubt. Some populists think that if many people believe something, they are probably right, and elected representatives should defer to them. Cosmopolitans believe that if many nations, or many democratic nations, reject a practice, or accept a practice, the U.S. Supreme

Court should pay respectful attention. Some cosmopolitans believe that if most nations, or most democratic nations, do something, other nations should probably fall in line with them.

Of course the three positions are different, and it is possible to accept one while rejecting the other two. But the structure of the central argument is identical in all three contexts.

Nothing in the Constitution itself rules out any of the three approaches that I shall be exploring. The Constitution does not set out the instructions for its own interpretation, and many approaches fall within the domain of the permissible. But traditionalism, populism, and cosmopolitanism all run into serious obstacles. In the end, much of my argument will therefore be negative and critical. I will try to show why each approach has intuitive appeal—but also why each of them faces powerful objections.

As we shall see, traditionalism is quite attractive in the domains of separation of powers, federalism, and gun rights. In those domains, what has been done in the past is highly relevant to what should be done in the present. But when we are speaking of equality, traditionalism has much less force. In that domain, the present knows more than the past, and the former should yield to the latter. For its part, populism cannot be ruled out of bounds. In many areas of constitutional law, judges should pay respectful attention to the considered judgments of their fellow citizens. But in some of the hardest cases, again in the domain of equality, the judgments of We the People are a product of confusion or bias. When public officials are deciding how to handle a difficult problem, it often makes sense for them to ask what other nations do. But for American constitutional law, cosmopolitanism runs into real problems; for judges, inquiring into foreign law is usually far more trouble than it is worth.

In other times and places, the assessment of the three approaches must be quite different. For example, we can imagine nations in which cosmopolitanism makes sense but traditionalism and populism do not. Indeed I believe that this is true for the question of liberty rights in South Africa and Israel. In South Africa, it would be ridiculous to try to build carefully on the liberty judgments of the apartheid regime. In Israel, it makes a great deal of sense to consult the practices of other liberal democracies. In young nations in particular, such consultation is justified, because they provide a large stock of wisdom.

While the discussion will extend to numerous topics in constitutional law and democratic theory, my main goal is to show when and why many minds arguments are strong, and when and why they are not. If the argument is right, it should have implications for traditionalism, populism, and cosmopolitanism in many domains. Workplaces, religious organizations, labor unions, and state legislatures often ask whether they should do what they have done before, follow the majority, or do what foreigners do. When they ask that question, they run right into some of the central dilemmas in constitutional law.

A Constitution *of* Many Minds

INTRODUCTION

⟿

Jefferson's Revenge

AN OLD DEBATE

In the earliest days of the American Republic, James Madison and Thomas Jefferson offered radically different views about the nature of constitutionalism in their young nation. Madison insisted that the Constitution should be relatively fixed. In his view, the founding document had been adopted in a uniquely favorable period, in which public-spirited people had been able to reflect about the true meaning of self-government. Miraculously, We the People had succeeded in producing a charter that would be able to endure over time. The Constitution should be firm and stable; the citizenry should take the document as the accepted background against which it engages in the project of self-government.

To be sure, Madison did not believe that the Constitution ought to be set in stone. He accepted the Constitution's procedures for constitutional amendment; indeed, he helped to write them. But he thought that amendments should be made exceedingly difficult. In his view, constitutional change ought to be reserved for "great and extraordinary occasions."[1] Madison wanted the work of the founding generation to last; alterations should occur only after surmounting a formal process that would impose serious obstacles to ill-considered measures based on people's passions or their interests. This, then, was a key component of Madison's understanding of the constitutional system of deliberative democracy: A system in which the constitutional essentials were placed well beyond the easy reach of succeeding generations.

[1] The Federalist No. 49 (Madison).

Thomas Jefferson had an altogether different view. Indeed, he believed that Madison's approach badly disserved the aspirations for which the American Revolution had been fought. Jefferson insisted that "the dead have no rights."[2] He thought that past generations should not be permitted to bind the present. In his view, the founders should be respected but not revered, and their work ought not to be taken as any kind of fixed background. In a revealing letter, Jefferson contended that those who wrote the document "were very much like the present, but without the experience of the present."[3] In other words, the present knows more than the past, if only because it is, in a sense, older. For these reasons, Jefferson urged that the Constitution should be rethought by the many minds of every generation, as the nature of self-government becomes newly conceived in light of changing circumstances. We the People should rule ourselves, not simply through day-to-day governance under a fixed charter, but also by rethinking the basic terms of political and social life.

According to the standard account, history has delivered an unambiguous verdict: Madison was right and Jefferson was wrong. The United States is governed by the oldest extant constitution on the face of the earth. In most of its key provisions, it remains the same as it was when it was ratified in 1787. Many of its terms have not been altered in the slightest. Just as Madison had hoped, the work of the founders endures. For all his ambition, Madison would likely have been amazed to see that well over two hundred years after the founding—roughly the same number of years that separate the birth of the document from the birth of Shakespeare—much of his generation's labor would continue to govern in essentially unaltered form.

Those who emphasize Madison's triumph acknowledge some important qualifications. The most important change may have been the Bill of Rights, added in 1789—but that early catalogue of rights is best understood as continuous with, or as a completion of, the original document. It is also true that significant amendments were made in the period after the Civil War—abolishing slavery, guaranteeing African-Americans the right to vote, and generally increasing the power of the national government over the states. Other constitutional amendments have introduced important changes by ensuring direct election of senators and the president

[2] Letter of Thomas Jefferson to Samuel Kercheval (June 12, 1816), available at http://teachingamericanhistory.org/library/index.asp?document=459.
[3] Id.

and by granting women the right to vote. But to a remarkable degree, America continues to be ruled by the document originally ratified by the founding generation.

The Changing Constitution

Or so it is generally believed. In crucial ways, however, the tale of constitutional stability is a myth. Jefferson has had his revenge—not through formal amendments, but through social practices and interpretations that render our Constitution very different from the founders' Constitution. What I mean to emphasize here is that those practices and interpretations have everything to do with public judgments as they have extended through time. In other words, constitutional change has occurred through the judgments of many minds and succeeding generations, in a way that captures some of Jefferson's hopes. In countless domains, Madison's victory is quite illusory. There have been numerous founders, and they can be found in many generations. Ours is a constitution of many minds.

This point is likely to seem jarring, and not only because of my claim that American history has, to an unacknowledged extent, fit Jefferson's project. The initial problem is that when Americans think of constitutional change, they focus on judicial interpretations, not on the role of their elected representatives or of citizens themselves. This is a major mistake. It is true that in some of its decisions, the Court, not the public, has been a prime mover. In banning school prayer, protecting the right to choose abortion, and striking down affirmative action programs, the Court has gone well beyond the original meaning of the document, and its own judgments have been crucial. What is much less noticed and far more important, and what I mean to stress here, is the extent to which changes in constitutional arrangements and understandings have been a product of ordinary democratic processes, producing adjustments in constitutional understandings over time. Self-government, far more than judicial innovation, has been responsible for those adjustments.

Sometimes the relevant changes do not involve courts at all. Consider, for example, the immense authority of the president in the domain of national security. That authority owes everything to decisions by the president and by Congress, ensuring that the nation's leader has far greater power than originally anticipated. And when the president and Congress act, they are responsive to the public as a whole. The current authority of the president has rarely been assessed by the Supreme Court and is hardly a judicial creation. It is a product of judgments of a variety of persons and institutions and, in an important sense, of We the People.

Sometimes changes in constitutional understandings are initially driven by the elected branches and ultimately ratified by the courts. Consider the large increase, after the New Deal, in the authority of the national government—an increase deplored by many who emphasize that ours is a federal system in which states have a substantial role. The authority of the national government is a product of democratic processes, not of the federal judiciary; the Court's role has been largely to ratify what citizens and their representatives have done. Or consider the rise of the immensely important "independent regulatory commissions," such as the National Labor Relations Board, the Federal Reserve Board, the Federal Communications Commission, and the Securities and Exchange Commission. These agencies exercise broad discretionary power without close control from the president of the United States. The Court has permitted such agencies to exist; but the prime movers have been the president and the Congress, not the judiciary.

True, the Supreme Court sometimes entrenches a new constitutional principle or a novel understanding of an old principle. But even when it does so, it is never acting in a social vacuum. Often it is endorsing, fairly late, a judgment that has long attracted widespread social support from many minds. The ban on racial discrimination, signaled above all by the Court's invalidation of school segregation, attracted strong support in the nation long before the Court acted. The dismantling of racial segregation in the South was eventually produced by the political branches, not the Court.[4]

In striking down sex discrimination, the Court's decisions can be seen as responsive to a social movement that produced what was a kind of Jeffersonian moment—a moment in which large numbers of people rethought previous constitutional commitments. Nor have the (few and tentative) judicial decisions banning discrimination on the basis of sexual orientation come as bolts from the blue. Those decisions emerged from a social context in which such discrimination seems increasingly difficult to defend—in

[4] See Gerald Rosenberg, *The Hollow Hope* (Chicago: University of Chicago Press, 1991).

which We the People have been coming, in fits and starts, to think that gays and lesbians should not be put in jail for consensual relationship, and that discrimination against them, at least by government, is hard to defend. If the Court ever does conclude that states cannot ban same-sex marriage, it will only be after much of the public has already done so.

In 2008 the Supreme Court ruled, for the first time, that the Second Amendment confers an individual the right to own guns for nonmilitary purposes. In doing so, the Court was greatly influenced by the social setting in which it operated, where that judgment already had broad public support. In recent years, there has come to be a general social understanding that the Second Amendment does protect at least some kind of individual right; and that understanding greatly affects American politics. The Supreme Court's ruling in favor of an individual's right to bear arms for military purposes was not really a statement on behalf of the Constitution, as it was written by those long dead; it was based on judgments that are now widespread among the living.

Some people, above all Bruce Ackerman, have urged that the American constitutional tradition includes not merely formal amendments but also "constitutional moments," in which We the People make large-scale changes in our understandings. These changes ultimately have consequences for the meaning of the Constitution.[5] And some periods do produce unusually large alterations in constitutional principles; Franklin Delano Roosevelt's New Deal, which involved no formal amendment, is the most obvious example. After the New Deal, the power of the national government was greatly increased; the president's authority became much broader; there were changes as well in prevailing understandings of individual rights, including diminished protection of freedom of contract and private property. Because it reflected the commitments of many citizens, the New Deal nicely fits the Jeffersonian story I am telling here. Roosevelt's New Deal was not a return to the founding. It was a reflection of the beliefs and commitments of We the People.

But constitutional change is not merely a product of "moments" in which mobilized citizens support large-scale reforms. There is a continuum from small changes, produced in periods of relative stability, to major ones,

[5] See Bruce A. Ackerman, *We the People*, vol. 1, *Foundations* (Cambridge: Harvard University Press, 1993).

produced when crises or social movements call for significant departures. Just as Jefferson hoped, every generation produces a degree of constitutional reform, and it does so because of its new understandings of facts or its new judgments of value. As one example, consider the increased power of the presidency after the attacks of 9/11. President Bush made broad claims about his authority, and he acted on the basis of those claims, originally with strong public support. Notwithstanding some important losses in court, and other defeats in the court of popular opinion, the president's power has, in important respects, grown as a result of the terrorist attacks. Future presidents will benefit from those increases in power.

Nor is constitutional reform limited to unusual periods of crisis, or large-scale rethinking of preexisting commitments. The federal system has some important virtues here. Many minds in California, Texas, or Wisconsin may reach a conclusion—about same-sex sexual relations, about religious liberty, about the role of firearms—that yields an experiment that turns out to have considerable appeal to the many minds of Americans as a whole. Changes in constitutional understandings may be a consequence.

In emphasizing that the American Constitution is a product of the work of many minds, I do not mean to suggest that our constitutional order has fully incorporated Jefferson's plea for popularly driven constitutional change. In keeping with Madison's hopes, our mechanisms of change rarely invoke formal procedures. The public is not asked to reassess the value or meaning of constitutional provisions governing free speech, religious liberty, property rights, and gun ownership, or the allocation of war-making authority between the president and Congress. In addition, much of constitutional change has occurred through an incremental process, not through the large-scale generational rethinking that Jefferson favored. Evolving traditions, rather than sudden breaks, are the usual American way. And those who believe that the original document is fundamentally flawed, or that a constitutional convention would promote a range of desirable goals, will not be convinced by the argument here.[6]

Nor do I mean to deny the occasionally creative role of the judiciary, interpreting the Constitution to fit with its own preferred views. But as a matter of actual practice, the views of the public and its representatives

[6] See the provocative and highly illuminating discussion in Sanford Levinson, *Our Undemocratic Constitution* (New York: Oxford University Press, 2006).

have turned out to be crucial. When we think about constitutional change, we pay far too little attention to the importance of those views.

MANY MINDS

Some of the most important constitutional debates raise a single question: If many people have accepted a particular view about some important issue, shouldn't the Supreme Court, and others thinking about the meaning of the Constitution, consult that view?

That very question will seem jarring to those who believe that the Court's role is simply to announce "the law." If that is the Court's role, then it might seem senseless to ask about the judgments of others— whether those judgments are reflected in long-standing traditions, the current commitments of American citizens, or the views of those in foreign countries. And indeed it is true that on certain understandings of constitutional law, such consultation is senseless. If the judge is supposed to speak for the original public meaning of the document, a long-standing practice or an intensely held public conviction is almost certainly[7] neither here nor there.

Suppose, however, that we reject the view that the Constitution's meaning is settled by the original public meaning. Suppose too that constitutional law is frequently "shallow," in the sense that the document itself and judicial decisions do not offer a deep theory of (for example) free speech, equal protection of the laws, or executive power. As we shall see, there are large advantages to a situation in which constitutional understandings do not reflect a theoretically ambitious account of disputed provisions. Suppose that judges have long refused to accept a particular, controversial account of constitutional principles. Suppose finally that constitutional decisions are often "narrow," in the sense that they focus on the situation at hand, and do not resolve problems that arise in the future. Where, exactly, should judges look, in deciding how to settle difficult controversies?

In the last decade, many people have been interested in "the wisdom of crowds"—the possibility that large groups of people, by virtue of their size and independence, are distinctly likely to give good answers to hard ques-

---

[7] The qualification is needed because we could imagine that the original understanding would require courts to pay attention, on some occasions, to traditions or public convictions. Indeed, the cruel and unusual punishment clause is often seen as an example.

tions.[8] Many minds arguments have been immensely influential in multiple domains, including politics, business, and law. As we shall see, the long-standing debate about the role of traditions turns, in large part, on the weight to be given to the views of many minds. So too with the debate over "popular constitutionalism," embodied in the suggestion that the meaning of the Constitution turns on the judgments of We the People.[9] So too with the heated debate about whether the Supreme Court should consult the judgments of other nations. Perhaps traditions embody the wisdom of large collections of people, and deserve respect for that very reason. And if most people now believe that discrimination on the basis of sex is unacceptable, perhaps they are right. And if many nations have decided against execution of mentally retarded people, perhaps the United States should join them, on the ground that they are unlikely to be wrong.

These propositions cannot easily be evaluated without asking some questions: Why, exactly, are crowds wise? How and when will it be true that large groups will give good answers to hard questions? Why should we be interested in the practices and judgments of many minds? Some of the most interesting answers are *evolutionary*: If many people have accepted a practice over time, the practice has apparently proved itself to be a good one. Other answers point to the value of *diversity* in generating good predictions. Crowds turn out to beat individuals; with any collection of diverse predictions, the collective prediction is more accurate than the average individual prediction.[10] Still other answers are *Madisonian*: In a system of checks and balances, in which government action is possible only if many independent minds agree to it, we might be able to promote both deliberation and liberty.

I shall spend some time here on arguments from evolutionary pressures, from diversity, and from checks and balances. But a different and more formal answer lies in the Condorcet Jury Theorem, which will play a major role throughout my discussion. To see how the Jury Theorem works, suppose that many people are answering the same question with two possible answers, one false and one true. The question may be whether an American or a Russian was the first person on the moon, whether climate change

---

[8] James Surowiecki, *The Wisdom of Crowds: Why the Many Are Smarter Than the Few and How Collective Wisdom Shapes Business, Economies, Societies, and Nations* (New York: Doubleday, 2004).

[9] See Larry Kramer, *The People Themselves* (New York: Oxford University Press, 2005).

[10] See Scott Page, *The Difference* 209–10 (Princeton: Princeton University Press, 2006).

is caused by human activities, whether America's gross national product increased between 1995 and 2000, whether Hank Aaron holds the home run record. Assume too that the probability that each person will answer correctly exceeds 50 percent, and that these probabilities are independent. The Jury Theorem says that the probability of a correct answer, by a majority of the group, increases toward 100 percent as the group gets bigger. The key point is that groups will do better than individuals, and large groups better than small ones, so long as two conditions are met: (*a*) majority rule is used and (*b*) each person is more likely than not to be correct.

The Jury Theorem is based on some fairly simple arithmetic. Suppose that there is a three-person group in which each member has a 67 percent probability of being right. The probability that a majority vote will produce the correct answer is 74 percent. As the size of the group increases, this probability increases too. If group members are 90 percent likely to be right, and if the group contains ten or more people, the probability of a correct answer by the majority is overwhelmingly high—very close to 100 percent. Consider in this regard the usual accuracy of the majority or plurality on the television show *Who Wants to Be a Millionaire?* Because many people are more likely to be right than wrong, and because the errors are likely to be random, it should be no surprise that on most questions, most people get it right.

The Jury Theorem is not widely known, but most people respond to its general logic. Suppose that we are unsure about some question or lack enough information. If so, we might well choose to adopt a simple rule in favor of following the majority of relevant others—the "do what the majority do" heuristic. If we do that, we are implicitly concluding that if most people do something, they are probably right. And when confronted with some hard problem, we might well consult a lot of people, and give careful consideration to what most of them suggest.

Might the Jury Theorem bear on constitutional law? I believe that it does. If we emphasize the arithmetic behind the Jury Theorem, we will have some clues about when many minds arguments make sense and when they fail. More modestly, we might put the Jury Theorem and its arithmetic to one side and make a comparative judgment: Even if all or most people are not likely to be right, it is possible that the average or median answer, from a large population, will be more reliable than the answer of federal judges. This conclusion might depend on the view that some constitutional problems turn on answers to questions of fact; maybe group answers are better than those of a small number of judges. Or the conclusion might rest on a belief that when moral or political issues are involved, the general population is more reliable than appointees to the federal bench—who, for all their qualities of character and intelligence, tend to come from a small segment of a society, limited to lawyers and usually part of a wealthy elite.

Minimalists versus Visionaries

Many people think that where the Constitution is ambiguous, courts do best to attend to long-standing practices, on the ground that those practices reflect the judgments of many people extending over time. As we shall see, this backward-looking approach owes much of its appeal to the arguments of the great conservative theorist Edmund Burke, who emphasized that past practices, even social prejudices, may have a kind of wisdom, outrunning the capacities of isolated people who must rely on their "private stock" of knowledge. Constitutional traditionalism is embodied in an approach to constitutional law that I call *Burkean minimalism*.

Burkean minimalism, it turns out, is simply one kind of minimalism. To make a long story short, minimalists like to rule narrowly and unambitiously. They despise revolutions. Burkean minimalists try to build on past practices, on the ground that the many minds that contributed to those practices are likely to have thought pretty well. But some minimalists, while despising revolutions, reject Burkeanism in favor of *rationalism*. They question traditions. They are entirely willing to ask whether long-standing practices are actually based on sense and good faith, or instead on nonsense and prejudice.

On the current Supreme Court, Justices Ruth Bader Ginsburg and Stephen Breyer have often acted as rationalist minimalists. Because they are minimalists, they are very different from such liberal visionaries as William Brennan and Thurgood Marshall. Brennan and Marshall had a large sense of where constitutional law should go, and they were not reluctant to offer ambitious arguments, whether or not it was necessary to do in order to resolve a concrete controversy. Brennan and Marshall were willing to use their own judgments about the requirements of justice in order to move constitutional law in bold new directions—protecting privacy, banning discrimination, and striking down capital punishment. Brennan and Marshall went so far as to take seriously the possibility that the Constitution requires government to provide the minimal conditions of subsistence, including shelter and an income floor. By contrast, Ginsburg and Breyer seek to build narrowly and cautiously on the Court's own precedents.

In the recent past, one of the most intriguing developments on the Supreme Court has been the emergence of a powerful alliance between two different kinds of conservatives: the visionaries and the minimalists. Justices Antonin Scalia and Clarence Thomas have been the visionaries. In key ways, they are successors to Brennan and Marshall. Their sweeping opinions call for fundamental changes in constitutional law. To date, Chief Justice John Roberts and Justice Samuel Alito appear to be minimalists, with strong Burkean tendencies. They are reluctant to reject the Court's own precedents, and they attempt to rule in a way that preserves them; their opinions tend to be narrow and unambitious.

The conservative minimalists and the conservative visionaries have often made common cause—on abortion, campaign finance law, employment discrimination, student speech, race-conscious policies, and much more. But true Burkeans like to preserve the past. For the long term, the key question is whether the conservative minimalists believe only that precedents should be followed when it is unnecessary to reconsider them—or believe as well that precedents should be followed even when they are challenged head-on. The future of key constitutional principles—involving the right to abortion, affirmative action programs, presidential power in connection with the war on terror, and campaign finance legislation—is likely to turn on the answer.

CITIZENS AND FOREIGNERS

I have referred to a distinctly Jeffersonian view, also with deep constitutional roots, which sometimes goes by the name of popular constitutionalism. Many people believe that the views of We the People deserve a great deal of attention when judges are deciding on the meaning of the founding document. I shall attempt to show that no less than traditionalism, popular constitutionalism is a many minds argument—one that sees truth, or at least sense and valuable information, in the judgments of large groups of people. While the Supreme Court refers to traditions, and while traditions play an unmistakable role in constitutional doctrine, the role of public convictions is more subtle. I shall attempt to make progress in understanding when and why they matter. A particular question is the circumstances under which the Court should respond to the risk or reality of "backlash." As we shall see, it is sometimes proper for judges to hesitate, simply because an aggressive approach would have bad consequences; and sometimes judges should hesitate because the intensely held views of the public deserve respect.

In recent years, the Supreme Court has occasionally referred to the views of foreign courts in hard constitutional cases. In striking down bans on same-sex sexual relations, and in invalidating capital punishment for young people and the mentally retarded, the Court has asked what other nations do. As we shall see, the argument for consulting foreign practices greatly overlaps with the argument for consulting traditions and public opinion. If most nations, or most relevant nations, reject a certain practice, shouldn't the United States pay attention? Many nations, especially those now establishing constitutional democracy, would do well to consult the practices of other nations. In the end, however, I will suggest that the Supreme Court would do best to restrict itself to domestic sources.

Experts and Political Valences

My major goal here is to understand the nature of many minds arguments in constitutional interpretation—their characteristic structure, their foundations, and their characteristic weaknesses. I shall also be exploring the relationship between many minds arguments and the practice of minimalism, by which judges issue narrow and shallow rulings. As we shall see, the connection is fairly tight.

A pervasive issue involves the role of expert judgments in law, and the relationship of those judgments to the (less expert) judgments of the many. The issue is important because judges are supposed to be experts on law, and ordinary people are not. Consider an analogy. There is good reason to think that the regular patrons of a large sports bar, taken as a whole, will know more sports statistics than any given patron. There is also good reason to think that the majority view of such patrons will often be right on questions about baseball. But there is no reason to trust the majority of the University of Chicago faculty (large as it is) on any question about baseball.

We should hardly be shocked if any particular patron at a sports bar, picked at random, turned out to do better on questions about baseball than the majority of a university faculty.

In this light we should be able to see that on legal questions, a small group of judges might do a lot better than a large group of nonspecialists. If judges are asked about the meaning of the Constitution's right "to keep and bear arms," perhaps they would do a lot better than traditions do, or than the public as a whole does. If legal specialists are asked whether the president has committed a "high crime or misdemeanor," their judgments might be far more reliable than that of a majority of the public, whose members might favor impeachment simply because they are upset with the president, or think he did something badly wrong.

Does it follow that on questions of constitutional law, the views of non-experts are irrelevant? The answer depends on the prevailing theory of interpretation. If we think that the meaning of the Constitution is settled by the original understanding, the view of the founding generation matters, and the view of the present does not. If we think that the meaning of the Constitution evolves with judicial precedent, the views of the judges may matter a lot more than the views of the public. But if we think that Jefferson was in some sense correct, traditions and public opinion will matter a lot.

While my focus is not on the conventional "left-right" divisions within the Supreme Court, it is important to see that the three many minds arguments have different political valences. Not surprisingly, arguments from traditions tend to appeal to conservatives, who think that the Court should look backward and conserve. Liberals tend to distrust traditionalism, believing that traditions are often unjust and that the Court would do better to look forward to a more just future. Conservatives have been intensely hostile to the Supreme Court's occasional attention to foreign law; they fear that the Court is yielding some of American sovereignty to practices in Germany, the United Kingdom, and France. By contrast, liberals have been more hospitable to consideration of foreign law; they tend to think that the meaning of the Constitution turns on questions of justice, and that the United States may have something to learn about justice by considering the practices of other nations.

Popular convictions present a more complicated picture. In the Warren Court years, many conservatives endorsed a form of popular constitutionalism.[11] This was a period in which the Supreme Court was quite aggressive in a liberal direction—invalidating mandatory school prayer, desegregating schools, requiring a rule of one-person, one-vote, and creating a right of privacy. In that period, conservatives wanted the judiciary to pay respectful attention to the practices and judgments of We the People. But in the 1920s and 1930s, it was liberals who endorsed popular constitutionalism, asking the Supreme Court to uphold democratically enacted legislation, including minimum wage and maximum hour laws, the National Labor Relations Act, and the Social Security Act. In the modern period, liberals have reacted to the new judicial conservatism by asking judges to be more deferential.[12] In short, it is not easy to read the interest in popular constitutionalism in political terms, and its political valence shifts dramatically over time.

The Plan

The remainder of this book is structured as follows. Part I offers arguments that are necessary conditions for everything that follows. Here I contend that the idea of interpretation, standing by itself, will not permit us to choose among several reasonable approaches to the Constitution. Some people are "originalists"; they believe that the Constitution should be construed to mean what was originally meant. Originalism is certainly a method of interpretation, but it is not the only one. Any particular approach to interpretation must be defended, not merely asserted. Any such defense must pay close attention to the consequences of the approach in question. Traditionalism, populism, and cosmopolitanism are legitimate contenders.

Part II, consisting of chapters 2, 3, and 4, explores traditions. Chapters 2 and 3 focus on Burkean minimalism. Burkean minimalists want to proceed narrowly and unambitiously. They also seek to rule with careful reference to traditions. The Burkean argument is built largely on the claim that longstanding practices are a product of the judgments of many minds, extending over time. Why—Burkeans ask—should judges, with their limited stock of reason, feel free to reject those judgments?

---

[11] Some of the tale is told in Michael J. Klarman, *From Jim Crow to Civil Rights* (New York: Oxford University Press, 2004).

[12] See, e.g., Mark Tushnet, *Taking the Constitution Away from the Courts* (New York: Oxford University Press, 1997).

This question is a good one, but it is not meant to be rhetorical. Chapter 3 investigates the circumstances under which Burkeanism makes sense. Chapter 4 sharpens the focus by asking about the proper understanding of the due process clause—the source of many fundamental rights, including the right to choose abortion and the right to engage in sexual relations. Many judges have argued for a form of due process traditionalism—an approach that would understand the term "liberty," in the due process clause, as limited to rights that our traditions have long recognized as such. We shall see, however, that due process traditionalism runs into serious problems.

Part III, including chapters 5, 6, and 7, deals with populism. Chapter 5 suggests that it is not possible to specify the appropriate judicial posture toward "public backlash" in the abstract. Here, as with selection of a method of interpretation, everything depends on judgments about the capacities of the judiciary and of elected institutions. Chapters 6 and 7 explore two reasons why judges might care about intensely felt public convictions. The first reason, emphasized in chapter 6, involves the *consequences* of ignoring those convictions. The second reason, explored in chapter 8, involves judicial *humility*. Suppose, for example, that judges ruled that states must recognize same-sex marriage, or that the Constitution forbids the use of the words "under God" in the Pledge of Allegiance. If so, there would be a predictable public outcry, and a range of bad consequences might follow. Judges might also ask: If most people believe that our approach to the Constitution is wrong, should we not listen to them? I conclude that in unusual but important cases, judges should indeed hesitate if many people disagree with their initial inclinations.

Because of how much has preceded it, part IV, consisting of chapter 8, can be relatively brief. It focuses generally on constitutional cosmopolitanism and in particular the intense controversy over whether the Supreme Court should pay attention to foreign law in interpreting the Constitution. If the views of many minds are entitled to respect, perhaps sensible judges, within one nation, should listen carefully to the view of judges outside of that nation. Ultimately I shall suggest that this conclusion is right for many nations, but generally wrong for the United States. The larger lesson has to do with specifying conditions under which many minds, captured in international practice, deserve respectful consideration.

The afterword sets out some broad lessons about many minds arguments. Drawing on the study of traditions, public opinion, and foreign law, it explores when those arguments are strong and when they are characteristically vulnerable. That exploration has implications not merely for constitutional law, but also for traditionalism, populism, and cosmopolitanism in general.

PART I

Preliminaries

CHAPTER 1

⌒

There Is Nothing
That Interpretation Just Is

Many people claim that the Constitution must be interpreted in their preferred way. They insist that the very idea of interpretation requires judges to adopt their own method of construing the founding document.

These claims are wrong. No approach to constitutional interpretation is mandatory. Any approach must be defended by reference to its consequences, not asserted as part of what interpretation requires. We can go further. No approach to constitutional law makes sense in every imaginable nation or in every possible world. The argument for any particular approach must depend, in large part, on a set of judgments about institutional capacities—above all, about the strengths and weaknesses of legislatures and courts. If judges are superb and error-free, their excellence bears on the choice of a theory of interpretation. If judges are likely to blunder, their fallibility bears on the choice of a theory of interpretation.

Consider the view, associated with James Bradley Thayer, that courts should uphold national legislation unless it is plainly and unambiguously in violation of the Constitution.[1] Few people now accept this position, which has found no support on the contemporary Supreme Court. Because the Constitution is frequently ambiguous, Thayer's approach would require courts to uphold almost all national legislation—including school segrega-

---

[1] See James Bradley Thayer, The Origin and Scope of the American Doctrine of Constitutional Law, 7 *Harv. L. Rev.* 129 (1893). For the best treatment, see Adrian Vermeule, *Judging under Uncertainty* (Cambridge: Harvard University Press, 2006). Vermeule explores the relationship between Thayerism and many minds arguments in a brilliant essay, see Adrian Vermeule, Common Law Constitutionalism and the Limits of Reason, 107 *Colum. L. Rev.* 1482 (2007). I have been much influenced by Vermeule's work on these topics.

tion in the District of Columbia, sex discrimination in federal employment, affirmative action, restrictions on privacy, and much more. In these circumstances, it should be unsurprising that judges assert their right to interpret the Constitution independently, and do not accept the legislature's view merely because the document is ambiguous. In the last half-century, no member of the Court has been willing to vote to uphold legislation unless the founding document is entirely clear.

But imagine a society—let us call it Thayerville—in which democratic processes work exceedingly fairly and well, so that judicial intervention is almost never required from the standpoint of anything that really matters. In Thayerville, racial segregation does not occur. Political speech is never banned. The legitimate claims of religious minorities and property holders are respected. The systems of federalism and separation of powers are safeguarded, and precisely to the right extent, by democratic institutions.

Imagine too that in Thayerville, judicial judgments are highly unreliable. From the standpoint of political morality, judges make systematic blunders when they attempt to give content to constitutional terms such as "equal protection of the laws" and "due process of law." Resolving constitutional questions without respecting the views of the legislature, Thayerville's courts make society worse, because their understandings of rights and institutions are so bad. In such a society, a Thayerian approach to the Constitution would make a great deal of sense, and judges should be persuaded to adopt it.[2]

Or consider originalism: the view, pressed vigorously by Justice Antonin Scalia, that the Constitution should be construed to fit with the original public meaning of the document.[3] Justice Scalia's view has not attracted a majority of the Court. Perhaps the justices believe that the original understanding, taken at the level of the ratifiers' specific answers to specific questions, would make the constitutional system worse rather than better. Some people believe that taken seriously, originalism would permit race and sex discrimination by the national government, sharply limit protection of speech, and allow state governments to establish official churches. Justice

---

[2] I put to one side the evident fact that Thayerism is not a complete account of constitutional interpretation. We might agree that courts should strike down statutes only when the violation of the Constitution is clear; but how do we know when the violation is clear? To work, Thayerism needs to be supplemented by some kind of account of constitutional meaning.

[3] Antonin Scalia, *A Matter of Interpretation* (Princeton: Princeton University Press, 1998).

Stephen Breyer has rejected originalism in part on the ground that it would produce terrible consequences.[4] In his view, the choice among theories of interpretations depends in significant part on consequences, and the consequences of originalism would be bad.

But imagine a society—let us call it Scalialand—in which the original public meaning of the Constitution is quite excellent, in the sense that it ensures well-functioning institutions and protects a robust set of rights, in a way that fits with a reasonable account of both democracy and freedom. Imagine that in Scalialand, the democratic process is also very fair and good, in part because of the excellence of the Constitution, and that the nation's admirable legislators are entirely able to make up for any inadequacies in the founding document. Suppose finally that in Scalialand, judges, unleashed from the original public meaning, would do a great deal of harm, unsettling well-functioning institutions and recognizing, as rights, interests that do not deserve that recognition. In such a society, an originalist approach to constitutional interpretation would seem best.

Or consider minimalism: the view that judges should take narrow, theoretically unambitious steps, at least when they lack the experience or the information to rule broadly or ambitiously.[5] Some judges are visionaries, and they reject minimalism. They believe that the Supreme Court should rule broadly, not narrowly, and that it is often appropriate for judges to accept an ambitious theory of liberty or equality or presidential power.

But imagine a society—it happens to be called Smallville—in which the original public meaning of the Constitution is not so excellent, in the sense that it does not adequately protect rights, properly understood, and in the sense that it includes understandings about institutions that become obsolete over time, as new circumstances and fresh needs arise. Imagine that in Smallville, the democratic process is good but not great, in the sense that it sometimes produces or permits significant injustices. Suppose finally that in Smallville, judges will do poorly if they strike out on their own, but very well if they build modestly and incrementally on their own precedents, following something like the common-law method. In such a society, a minimalist approach to the Constitution would have a lot to commend it.

---

[4] See Stephen Breyer, *Active Liberty* (New York: Knopf, 2005).
[5] See Cass R. Sunstein, *One Case at a Time* (Cambridge: Harvard University Press, 1999).

Or consider perfectionism: the view, defended most systematically by Ronald Dworkin, that the Constitution should be construed in a way that both "fits" with it and makes it best, and in that sense perfects it.[6] Perfectionists acknowledge and indeed emphasize the duty to "fit"; an interpretation that makes up the Constitution, or violates its terms, cannot claim to be an interpretation at all. Thus perfectionists insist that any view about the meaning of the founding document must take its words seriously and cannot ignore them. Perfectionists add that the obligation to "fit" the law requires judges to take account of existing precedents. A decision is lawless if it disregards previous decisions or makes hash of them. But perfectionists believe that when several interpretations would fit, judges must select the one that makes the document and the existing law the best that they can be.

Consider, for example, the question whether the Constitution forbids an affirmative action plan at a state university, or protects the right to same-sex marriage, or authorizes the Federal Communications Commission to create a "do not call" registry, allowing people to block unwanted telephone calls. Perfectionists believe that in such cases, judges should try to fit existing law while also making it as sensible and as good as possible. For example, any decision about same-sex marriage must respect the Court's decision to strike down bans on same-sex sexual relations, and any decision about the "do not call" registry must respect the courts' general willingness to allow states to require people to respect "no trespassing" signs. Many people reject perfectionism, on the ground that it does not adequately discipline the judiciary, whose understanding of what qualifies as constitutional "perfection" may not be reliable. Perhaps perfectionism would unleash the judiciary, in a way that would undermine both democracy and rights.

But imagine a society—proudly called Olympus—in which the original public meaning of the document does not adequately protect rights, properly understood. Imagine that the text is general enough to be read to provide that adequate protection. Imagine finally that Olympian courts, loosened from Thayerian constraints, or from the original understanding, or from minimalism, would generate a far better account of rights and institutions, creating the preconditions for both democracy and autonomy.

[6] See Dworkin, *Law's Empire* (Cambridge: Harvard University Press, 1985); James Fleming, *Securing Constitutional Democracy: The Case of Autonomy* (Chicago: University of Chicago Press, 2006).

In Olympus, a perfectionist approach to the Constitution would seem to be entirely appropriate.[7]

Is any one of these approaches ruled off the table by the Constitution itself? Recall that each of them firmly respects the document's text. The question is how to construe it. If the founding document set out the rules for its own interpretation, judges would be bound by those rules (though any such rules would themselves need to be construed). But the Constitution sets out no such rules. It does not say that judges or others, attempting to interpret the document, should be Thayerians, originalists, minimalists, perfectionists, or something else. For this reason, any approach to the document must be defended by reference to some account that is supplied by the interpreter. The Constitution is rightly taken to bind judges (and others). If we are engaged in interpretation, we cannot simply cast it aside. But the meaning of the Constitution must be made rather than found, not in the sense that it is entirely up for grabs, but in the sense that it must be settled by an account of interpretation that it does not itself contain.

It is possible to go further. In the end, any approach to the founding document must ultimately be perfectionist in the sense that it attempts to make that document as good as it can possibly be. Thayerism is a form of perfectionism; it claims to improve the constitutional order.[8] Originalism, read most sympathetically, is also a form of perfectionism; it suggests that constitutional democracy, properly understood, is best constructed through originalism. The most sophisticated originalists recognize this point, emphasizing as they do the virtues of originalism in constraining judges and promoting a sensible system of constitutional law.[9] Minimalism is a form of perfectionism too; it rejects Thayerism and originalism on the ground that they would make the constitutional system much worse.[10] It would appear that the debate among Thayerians, originalists, minimalists, and perfectionists must be waged on the perfectionists' own turf. Perhaps the alternatives to perfectionism are all, in one or another sense, perfectionist too.

---

[7] I bracket potential conflicts between Olympian practices and democratic self-government, on the ground that by hypothesis, Olympian judges create no such conflicts.

[8] See Vermeule, *Judging under Uncertainty.*

[9] See Scalia, *A Matter of Interpretation.*

[10] See Cass R. Sunstein, *Radicals in Robes* (New York: Basic Books, 2006), for an elaboration.

Some people might resist this conclusion. Pragmatists, such as Judge Richard Posner, might not always much care about "fit" with preexisting law; on their view, consequences are what matter, and a forward-looking approach, compromising fit for the sake of good consequences, might well be justified under some circumstances.[11] Judge Posner agrees that respect for preexisting law can be justified on the ground that such respect usually has good consequences, but for him, "fit" is important only for that reason and it need not always be respected. Perhaps Thayerians and originalists would compromise fit as well. Thayerians might not much care about "fitting" previous decisions that take an aggressive approach against the democratic process. For some originalists, illegitimate precedents, departing from the original understanding, have little standing, and judges should feel free to reject them if they are wrong. Justice Clarence Thomas, for example, is not greatly interested in preserving previous decisions that are indefensible from the standpoint of the original understanding.[12]

But if we understand perfectionism with sufficient capaciousness, its critics are actually its practioners too. Sensible pragmatists, including Judge Posner, care deeply about fit, if only for pragmatic reasons. An approach to the Constitution that jettisons precedents, or that pays no attention to the document itself, would be difficult to defend on pragmatic grounds. Many originalists, most prominently Justice Scalia, do care about fit with previous decisions.[13] Those who do not, or who are willing to reject decisions that they deem illegitimate, certainly care about fit—but what matters is fit with the original understanding, not with the decisions that departed from it.

The ideas of "fit" and "justification" leave many ambiguities. "Fit" with what? Justified to whom, and by reference to what? But if we understand the two ideas broadly enough, all reasonable views about constitutional interpretation are perfectionist in character. Even those who favor occasional or frequent unhappy outcomes in constitutional adjudication, in the form of judicial decisions that produce particular results that they abhor, believe that the ultimate ending is good rather than bad, in the sense that

---

[11] See Richard A. Posner, *Law, Pragmatism, and Democracy* (Cambridge: Harvard University Press, 2002).

[12] See the discussion of Justice Thomas's views in Sunstein, *Radicals in Robes*.

[13] See the discussion of Justice Scalia's views in id.

it produces more in the way of self-government, or legitimacy, or other important values.

My central goal in this chapter is to show that any particular approach to the Constitution must be defended on the ground that it makes the relevant constitutional order better rather than worse. In defending this claim, I shall also sketch the argument for *second-order perfectionism*—a form of perfectionism that is alert to the fallibility and limits of those who are entrusted with the job of interpreting the founding document. An appreciation of second-order perfectionism will pave the way for an understanding of many minds arguments in constitutional law.

Because of my emphasis on institutional capacities, I shall be focusing throughout on constitutional interpretation by the judiciary. Presidents, senators, legislators, governors, and mayors engage in interpretation too, as do ordinary citizens, making claims about their understanding of the founding document. Consider the war on terror: Constitutional arguments about individual rights have come from many sources, and the members of the executive and legislative branches have hardly thought that the opinions of the Supreme Court exhaust the domain of legitimate constitutional debate. Note too that many political leaders, and countless citizens, have asserted that the Second Amendment protects an individual right to own guns, long before the Supreme Court was asked to endorse that position. From the discussion of Thayerville, Scalialand, and their surrounding communities, it should be clear that there is no reason that citizens and their representatives should be required to adopt the same interpretive method that judges favor.[14]

On the view that I shall be defending, it is fully possible that citizens will adopt first-order perfectionism, emphasizing their own moral and political judgments, while judges will settle on a second-order variety, attempting to constrain their own moral and political judgments. We might believe, for example, that citizens and their representatives can interpret the Constitution to require states to permit same-sex marriage, or to ban affirmative action, or to provide broad protection to gun ownership and property

[14] The idea of constitutional interpretation outside of courts is explored from various angles in Fleming, *Securing Constitutional Democracy*, and Cass R. Sunstein, *The Partial Constitution* (Cambridge: Harvard University Press, 1993).

rights, without thinking that judges should interpret the Constitution the same way.

Of course it is also possible that citizens do not need constitutional ideals, or constitutional text, to press their preferred views. Perhaps their own ideals will do the trick.

ON THE VERY IDEA OF INTERPRETATION

Does the idea of interpretation, standing by itself, require acceptance of any particular approach to the Constitution? Many people believe so.[15] But their arguments are implausible.

In ordinary life, we do tend to interpret words by asking about the speaker's intentions. If a friend asks you to meet her at "the best Chinese restaurant in town," you will probably ask what, exactly, she had in mind. You will not ask what Chinese restaurant you like best, or which Chinese restaurant is preferred by your favorite restaurant critic. On one view, legal interpretation is not fundamentally different; some form of originalism is built into the concept of interpretation.

This idea is tempting but mistaken. When speakers' intentions are what matters, it is for pragmatic reasons, not because of anything inherent in interpretation as a concept or a social practice. We ask about the intentions of the speaker because and to the extent that the goal of communication will go badly, or at least less well, if we do not. When a friend asks me to meet her or to do something for her, I am likely to ask about her intentions, because I want to meet her or to do what she would like. Or consider communication within some hierarchical organization. If a supervisor tells an employer what to do, it is right to think that in ordinary circumstances, the employee ought to ask: "What, exactly, did my supervisor mean by that?" (The qualification "in ordinary circumstances" is necessary because even subordinates sometimes ask about something other than speakers' intentions; everything depends on the role of the subordinate.) The employee asks this question, if he does, for pragmatic reasons. Employees should generally follow the instructions of their supervisors, and the practice of following instructions, in hierarchical organizations, usually calls for close attention to subjective intentions.

[15] See, e.g., Saikrishna Prakash, Radicals in Tweed Jackets: Why Left-Wing Law Professors Are Wrong for America, 106 *Colum. L. Rev.* 2207 (2007).

But it is easy to think of cases in which interpretation does not operate by reference to speakers' intentions. In fact some of the most committed originalists, including Justice Scalia himself, contend that what matters is the original public meaning of the document, not intentions at all.[16] They defend their interest in the original public meaning, as opposed to the original intentions, on the entirely plausible ground that public meaning is objective, not subjective, and that what matters is the standard understanding among the Constitution's ratifiers, not what the authors "intended." After all, the ratifiers, and not the authors, turned the Constitution into law.

Of course those who make this claim insist on originalism, but they do not care about subjective intentions. I am not saying, and do not believe, that the original meaning should be taken as binding. I am saying only that a prominent understanding of originalism—as involving public meaning rather than intentions—should be enough to demonstrate that attention to subjective intentions is hardly built into the very idea of interpretation.

In fact many of those who emphasize the original meaning tend not to argue that their approach is what interpretation necessarily is, but to adopt a form of second-order perfectionism.[17] They stress the risks associated with judicial discretion; they focus on the goal of democratic self-government. Consider the illuminating suggestion by Randy Barnett, a firm defender of originalism: "Given a sufficiently good constitutional text, originalists maintain that better results will be reached overall if government officials—including judges—must stick to the original meaning rather than empowering them to trump that meaning with one that they prefer."[18]

Of special importance here is Barnett's emphasis on the need for a "sufficiently good constitutional text," understood in light of the original meaning. If the constitutional text, understood in that light, is really bad—if it is hopelessly undemocratic, or if it entrenches the few at the expense of the many—the argument for sticking with the original meaning would be pretty weak. (Why should we stick with the original meaning of a really bad text?) Many originalists contend that their preferred approach justifies

---

[16] See Scalia, *A Matter of Interpretation*.

[17] See Antonin Scalia, Originalism: The Lesser Evil, 57 *U. Cin. L. Rev.* 849 (1989). See Vermeule, *Judging under Uncertainty*, for illuminating discussion of the considerations involved in the selection of a theory of interpretation; I have been much influenced by that discussion here.

[18] Available at http://legalaffairs.org/webexclusive/debateclub_cie0505.msp.

the constitutional system, by making it the best it can be, and of course fits
with it. And prominent originalists are concerned too to show that their
approach fits not only with the document but also with a great deal of
existing judicial doctrine, or at least with those aspects of it that seem
least dispensable. Few originalists are willing to concede that under their
approach, racial segregation is constitutionally acceptable—even though
nothing in the original meaning bans segregation by the national government, and even though it is not easy to show that the Constitution bans
segregation at the state level. Under the original understanding, the Constitution does not ban sex discrimination, but few originalists happily agree
that their approach would allow the national government to prohibit
women from working for the federal civil service, or would freely allow
states to discriminate against women.

On the contrary, originalists tend to say nothing about the difficulty in
squaring their approach with foundational commitments of our current
constitutional order, or to insist that the difficulty is not so severe, because
originalism already embodies those commitments. It is noteworthy that
most of those who stress original meaning find it necessary to stress these
points about consequences, and do not rest content with, or even make,
the claim that their approach is built into the very idea of interpretation.

To be sure, that idea does impose constraints. There is nothing that
interpretation just is, but there are some things that interpretation just isn't.
Even if it would be good, pragmatically speaking, to substitute the best
imaginable constitution for our own constitution, the substitution cannot
count as interpretation. But the idea of interpretation does not compel any
form of originalism. Indeed, it is perfectly conventional to find domains in
which interpretation occurs without the slightest reference to either original intentions or original meaning.

Suppose that the Supreme Court is interpreting a precedent—say, its
own decision to invalidate separate-but-equal, *Brown v. Board of Education.*
What are the implications of *Brown* for racial segregation at a federal
prison, where racial tensions are running very high and where prison officials reasonably fear that integration would produce violence? In answering
that question, the Court is most unlikely to ask about the subjective intentions of Chief Justice Earl Warren, the author of the Court's opinion in
Brown. The Court is equally unlikely to inquire into the subjective intentions of those who joined the opinion. Perhaps there is no such intention

with respect to the question at hand. Perhaps it is not accessible even if it exists. In any case the Court will show little interest in it, less because it is inaccessible than because it is not controlling and perhaps irrelevant even if it is accessible. Nor will the Court pay attention to the original public meaning of its own decision in *Brown* (whatever that might mean!). Judicial interpretation of precedents has little to do with original intentions or original meaning. In dealing with the meaning of *Brown*, the Court makes an independent judgment about how best to fit and to justify its own prior ruling.

My conclusion is that originalism is merely one approach to interpretation. The question is whether it is the right one. That question requires attention not to the concept of interpretation but to the consequences of the recommended approach—to whether it would make our constitutional order better or worse.

FIT AND JUSTIFICATION, ELABORATED

Evidently building on judicial approaches to precedents, Ronald Dworkin contends that interpretation requires an effort both to fit and to justify the existing legal materials.[19] As we have seen, the requirement of "fit" calls for fidelity to the material that is being interpreted. The requirement of justification means that when more than one possibility "fits," the judge must bring forward what seems to be the best principle that accounts for the existing materials. Dworkin believes that the ideas of fit and justification—captured in his notion of "integrity"—reflect the nature of interpretation in many domains. Dworkin may even believe that as a social practice, interpretation *is* a search for integrity in his sense. Let us consider in more detail the ideas of fit and justification in connection with constitutional law and the appropriate judicial role.

Suppose that a nation—say, Iraq—has ratified a constitutional provision that forbids any denial of "equality under the law on the basis of sex." Suppose that the government adopts a height and weight requirement for its security forces and that the requirement turns out to have a harmful effect mostly on women, because women tend to shorter and lighter. Suppose, finally, that if the government is forced to justify the height and

---

[19] See Dworkin, *Law's Empire*.

weight requirement on the ground that it sensibly screens for ability to do the job, it will not find it easy to do so, because no clear evidence shows that size is associated with good performance in the security forces. If the requirement is challenged as a denial of "equality under the law," what should the Court do?

On Dworkin's view, the Court should give a "moral reading" to the constitutional provision, in the sense that the Court should generate the best moral principle that accounts for it.[20] Offhand, we might imagine a reading that reads the clause to ban only one thing: explicit discrimination on the basis of sex. Call this the "antidiscrimination" principle, which would not permit government to exclude women, as such, from the security forces, but which would accept apparently neutral height and weight requirements. By contrast, we might imagine a reading that calls on government to justify itself in convincing terms whenever it has imposed a significant and distinctive burden on women. Call this the "anticaste" principle, which might well require courts to strike down height and weight requirements notwithstanding their apparent neutrality. A possible approach for courts is to identify the opposing principles and to choose the one that is better; perfectionists would ask courts to adopt this approach.

But consider another possibility. Perhaps the Court prefers the anticaste principle as a matter of abstract theory, believing that it makes better sense of the guarantee of equality under the law. Even if so, the Court might select the antidiscrimination principle, on the ground that it ensures that judges will not be forced to undertake inquiries for which they are ill-suited. The Court might believe that judgments about whether a job requirement is sensible are extremely hard to make. It might also believe that if judges attempt to make such judgments, they will often blunder. In short, judges might adopt the antidiscrimination principle even though they prefer the anticaste principle on moral grounds.

If courts reason in this way, are they attempting both to fit and to justify our (legal) practices? In one sense, the answer is clear: They are. But even in this mundane example, their perfectionism is second-order, not first-order. It is because of a sense of their own fallibility that they are refusing to adopt the morally preferred account of equality. Judges know that they

[20] See Ronald Dworkin, *Freedom's Law: The Moral Reading of the American Constitution* (Cambridge: Harvard University Press, 2001).

may err, and their practices are affected by their knowledge of that fact. Second-order perfectionism, with respect to an equality guarantee, can hardly be ruled out of bounds.

Now imagine that the government has argued not only that the antidiscrimination account is the better one, but also that the Court should uphold sex discrimination so long as it is minimally rational—as long as the underlying practice is not utterly senseless and self-evidently indefensible. For the equality guarantee, the government argues that the Court should proceed as it would in Thayerville. In my view, that would be an unfortunate reading of an equality guarantee in Iraq or elsewhere, because it would undermine that guarantee so severely, and because most nations, including contemporary Iraq, are not Thayerville. But in the end, that view must also be sensitive to the capacities of judges, and it must be defended with close reference to them. Suppose that judges, deciding sex equality cases, would produce worse-than-random decisions. If so, we may be in Thayerville, and perhaps the rational basis test would be desirable after all.

Or suppose that the government argues that in Iraq, courts should be originalists. They should ask about the original understanding of the sex equality guarantee. If the antidiscrimination principle is required by the original understanding, they should accept that principle; so too if the original understanding supports the anticaste principle. Perhaps there is no original understanding on that question. But if there is, judges might consider accepting it, on the ground that in view of their own fallibility, and the importance of democratic self-government, the constitutional system will be better if they follow the original understanding than if they do not.

To be a bit more systematic: An approach to the Constitution might impose two kinds of costs. It might impose decision costs, by complicating judicial judgments, and it might impose error costs, by producing bad outcomes. Without making the ludicrous claim that these ideas should be understood in purely economic terms, we can insist that judges would do well to consider the decisional burdens of one or another approach to the founding document. Those burdens, or costs, might be faced by judges or by others, including legislators, members of the executive branch, and citizens themselves, who must pay the cost of uncertainty. A Thayerian approach to the Constitution would certainly impose low decision costs, simply because it would mean that legislation would be upheld unless it is in unambiguous violation of the founding document.

But it is also important to consider the number and the magnitude of errors. If judges uphold sex discrimination whenever it is rational, they would (in my view) permit a large number of serious errors. It is for this reason that in the United States, it would make no sense to accept sex discrimination so long as it is "minimally rational." We may be in Smallville; we may be in Olympus. But we are certainly not in Scalialand or Thayerville. To be sure, people disagree about whether certain outcomes count as errors at all. Judges may agree that the choice among interpretive approaches depends on the consequences, but they might disagree about whether certain consequences are good. If one or another approach would mean that the Constitution protects no right of privacy, does that count against that approach—or in its favor? We might imagine reasonable disputes about that question.

The broadest point is that no approach to interpretation is dictated by the very idea of interpretation. Originalism is certainly a candidate; it cannot be rejected in the abstract or on a priori grounds. The question for originalists is whether their approach would make the American system of constitutional law much worse than it now is. The same question must be asked of Thayerians and minimalists.

I now proceed to explore these questions in the particular context of many minds arguments. A central point is that because of their own fallibility, judges know that any reasonable approach to interpretation must discipline their own judgments, and do so in a way that accommodates social learning over time. To the extent that many minds are allowed to affect constitutional meaning, judicial self-discipline is indispensable. Traditionalism is a good place to start.

PART II

*

Traditionalism

CHAPTER 2

⟿

Burkean Minimalism

Consider the following cases:

1. For over fifty years, the words "under God" have been part of the Pledge of Allegiance. Some parents object to the use of those words, arguing that under current constitutional principles, the reference to God must be counted as an illegitimate establishment of religion.

2. Margaret Jones and Janet Smith have lived as a couple in Arizona for over a decade. They now seek to marry, but Arizona law forbids them from doing so. They contend that the Constitution bans Arizona from denying them a marriage license. Arizona responds that throughout American history, marriage has been limited to heterosexual relationships.

3. For over seventy years, the Supreme Court has permitted Congress to create "independent" regulatory agencies—agencies whose heads cannot be removed by the president simply because he disagrees with them. A newly elected president is alarmed by the views of his predecessor's appointees to the National Labor Relations Board—and he wants to fire them. Responding to the president's wishes, the Department of Justice now attacks the notion of "independence," arguing that it is inconsistent with the constitutional decision to vest executive power in "a President of the United States," and not in anyone else.

4. The president of the United States has long engaged in "foreign surveillance" by wiretapping conversations in which at least one of the parties is in another nation and is suspected of being unfriendly to the United States.[1] The practice of foreign surveillance has been upheld by several

---

[1] In federal courts, the authority to engage in such surveillance has been asserted for thirty-five years. United States v. Clay, 430 F.2d 165 (5th Cir. 1970). The practice of "national security surveillance" has

lower courts, which see that practice as falling within the president's "inherent" authority.[2] Ordinary citizens, subject to such surveillance, object that as originally understood, the Constitution did not grant such "inherent" authority to the president.

Each of these cases presents a conflict between time-honored practices and what is said to be the best interpretation of the Constitution. Those who challenge the practices contend that the best interpretation must prevail. A predictable response is that when interpreting the Constitution, courts should be closely attentive to long-standing practices, and must respect the judgments of public officials and ordinary citizens over time. On this view, constitutional interpretation should be conservative in the literal sense— respecting settled judicial doctrine, but also deferring to social traditions.

Those who make such arguments adopt an approach to constitutional law that I shall call *Burkean minimalism*. Burkean minimalists believe that constitutional principles must be built incrementally and by analogy, and with close reference to long-standing practices. Like all minimalists, Burkeans insist on small steps rather than earthquakes; they are suspicious of visionaries. But they also emphasize the need for judges to pay careful heed to established traditions and to avoid independent moral and political arguments of any kind. On this count, Burkean minimalists should be distinguished from their rationalist counterparts, who are less interested in long-standing practices and more willing to require some kind of independent justification for those practices. Rationalists ask: *What is the reason for the tradition?* Hard-line traditionalists are skeptical about that question.

Burkean minimalists usually defend themselves by reference to a many minds argument. They ask: If many people have accepted some practice in the past, shouldn't we defer to them, rather than exercising our independent judgment? If many people have believed that same-sex marriage and suicide should be banned, or that the president should seek Congress's permission before going to war, shouldn't we show respect for their collective judgment? The most interesting traditionalists endorse the wisdom of

---

been traced to a decision of the Eisenhower administration in 1954. See Morgan Cloud, The Bugs in Our System, *New York Times*, January 13, 2006, at A21.

[2] See United States v. Truong Dinh Hung, 629 F.2d 908, 912–16 (4th Cir. 1980); United States v. Buck, 548 F.2d 871, 875-76 (9th Cir. 1977); United States v. Butenko, 494 F.2d 593 (3d Cir. 1974); United States v. Brown, 484 F.2d 418, 426 (5th Cir. 1973); *In re* Sealed Case, 310 F.3d 717 (FISA Ct. Rev. 2002).

established practices, built on the judgments of the many, and stress the potential recklessness of theories, built on the judgments of the few.

In the nation's history, Justices Felix Frankfurter and Sandra Day O'Connor have been the most prominent practitioners of Burkean minimalism, in the sense that they have tended to favor small steps and close attention to both experience and tradition. As we shall see, Burkean minimalism can be used in diverse ways. Some judges freely permit the democratic branches to reject traditions but are unwilling to overturn traditions on their own. Other judges believe that democratic changes to long-standing practices must receive careful scrutiny from the courts. Burkeanism might therefore be used as a *shield*, enabling government to fend off attacks on traditions, or instead as a *sword*, allowing ordinary people to challenge questionable innovations.

Burkean minimalism is a form of conservative constitutional thought, but many conservatives reject it in favor of two alternative approaches. We have seen that originalists, including Justices Antonin Scalia and Clarence Thomas, believe that the Constitution should be understood to mean what it meant at the time that it was ratified. As against Burkeans, originalists insist that departures from the original understanding are illegitimate even if those departures are long-standing. In their view, that understanding is the lodestar, not time-honored practices.

The second alternative is conservative perfectionism. Conservative perfectionists believe that judges must respect the Constitution's text and structure, but where these are ambiguous, courts are entitled to adopt the interpretation that makes best sense of the document, or casts it in the best light. In other words, conservative perfectionists adopt a method akin to liberal perfectionists such as Dworkin, though they favor results that their liberal counterparts would not approve. Conservative perfectionism is responsible for the attack on affirmative action programs,[3] the effort to strike down restrictions on commercial advertising,[4] and the movement to protect property rights against "regulatory takings" (including laws protecting the environment).[5] Conservative perfectionists are not greatly concerned with

[3] See, e.g., Grutter v. Bollinger, 539 U.S. 306, 378 (2003) (Thomas, J., dissenting) (invoking principle of color-blindness as basis for attack on race-conscious admissions policy).

[4] See, e.g., Cent. Hudson Gas & Elec. Co. v. Pub. Serv. Comm'n, 447 U.S. 557 (1980).

[5] See, e.g., Penn Cent. Transp. Co. v. New York City, 438 U.S. 104, 138–50 (1978) (Rehnquist, J., dissenting) (calling for greater protection against regulatory takings). On the difficulty of finding historical support for this position, see John F. Hart, Land Use Law in the Early Republic and the Original

the original understanding of the founding document, and they are entirely willing to renovate long-standing practices by reference to ambitious ideas about constitutional liberty.

Justice Thomas, for example, has argued that the free speech principle broadly protects commercial advertising, even though he has not compiled evidence that the original understanding supports his position.[6] When the Supreme Court struck down maximum hour and minimum wage legislation at the start of the twentieth century, it practiced a form of conservative perfectionism.[7] More recently, Chief Justice William Rehnquist showed an occasional interest in conservative perfectionism.[8]

What unifies Burkean minimalism, originalism, and conservative perfectionism? The simplest answer is that all three disapprove of those forms of liberal thought that culminated in the work of the Warren Court and (on occasion) its successors. All three reject liberal visions of constitutional law; all three reject the idea, prominent in the late 1960s and early 1970s, that the Supreme Court should protect traditionally disadvantaged groups from political majorities. All three approaches are at least skeptical of *Roe v. Wade*,[9] the effort to remove religion from the public sphere, and the attempt to grant new protections to suspected criminals. The three approaches count as conservative simply because of their shared doubts about the rulings of the Warren Court and the arguments offered by that Court's most enthusiastic defenders.

But there are massive disagreements as well. For example, Burkean minimalists have little interest in originalism. From the Burkean perspective, originalism is far too radical, because it calls for dramatic movements in the law; it is unacceptable for exactly that reason. Burkean minimalists prize stability. They are entirely willing to accept rulings that do not comport with the original understanding when a decision to overrule them would disrupt established practices.

Meaning of the Takings Clause, 94 *Nw. U. L. Rev.* 1099 (2000) (arguing that on the original understanding, regulatory takings did not offend the clause).

[6] See, e.g., 44 Liquormart, Inc. v. Rhode Island, 517 U.S. 484, 522–24 (1996) (Thomas, J., concurring in part and concurring in the judgment) (arguing for broad protection of commercial advertising).

[7] For evidence, see, for example, Lochner v. New York, 198 U.S. 45 (1905), and Adkins v. Children's Hospital, 261 U.S. 525 (1923). The Court's opinions spoke in terms of the ideal of liberty, rather than in terms of the original understanding, established traditions, or clear precedents.

[8] See, e.g., *Penn Cent.*, 438 U.S. at 138–50 (Rehnquist, J., dissenting).

[9] 410 U.S. 113 (1973).

Burkean minimalists also treasure our constitutional traditions, extending over decades and even centuries, and see those traditions as the product not of a particular canonical moment, but of countless decisions by many actors. On this view, the American Constitution owes its content not to a national judgment in 1787, but to a kind of spontaneous order, reflecting the acts and judgments of diverse people at diverse moments in history—including not merely Abraham Lincoln and Woodrow Wilson and Franklin Delano Roosevelt and Martin Luther King, Jr., but also and far more importantly, ordinary people, expressing their commitments in many domains. To Burkean minimalists, originalism looks uncomfortably close to the French Revolution, seeking to overthrow settled traditions by reference to an abstract theory.

Nor do Burkean minimalists have any enthusiasm for conservative perfectionism, which they consider arrogant and far too rationalistic. In the Burkean view, societies should not trust the theory-building efforts of federal judges: theories are contested and unreliable, and they might well misfire. To be sure, Burkeans are willing to build on existing law through analogical reasoning, and in some cases, this process might allow Burkean minimalists to make common cause with their perfectionist adversaries. Conservative perfectionists and Burkean minimalists might agree, for example, to protect at least some kind of individual right to own guns and to strike down rigid affirmative action programs. But insofar as conservative perfectionists are willing to invoke ambitious accounts (of, say, property rights, presidential power, or color-blindness) to produce large-scale departures from existing practice and law, Burkean minimalists have no interest in their enterprise.

Some conservatives, no less than some liberals, are visionaries with respect to the Constitution. They believe that rightly understood, the document embodies a social vision that will have a large effect on American life, one that will require us to change our practices in major ways. Conservative visionaries think that the Constitution forbids affirmative action programs and campaign finance restrictions, that it is inconsistent with (many) gun control laws, that it requires strict limits on congressional power, that it affords far greater protection of property rights than the Court has yet granted.

Burkean minimalists distrust visionaries above all. They think that political life builds on the past, not on ambitious visions. In constitutional law, they are especially skeptical of visions, believing as they do that judges should pay close attention to what many minds have accepted, not what theories counsel.

I have three goals in this chapter. The first is to identify the ingredients of Burkean minimalism. The second is to offer a reconstruction of Burkean minimalism that is not sentimental and that does not reflect ancestor-worship, but that speaks in pragmatic or consequentialist terms. The best argument for Burkeanism is that respect for traditions is likely to produce better results, all things considered, than the alternatives. This pragmatic approach has the advantage of showing why Burkeanism makes good sense in some contexts but none at all in others.

It may well be right, for example, to build separation of powers doctrine on established practices, but also to approach scientific questions, such as those involving climate change or the nature of matter, on the basis of the newest theories rather than the old ones. By keeping the eye on the pragmatic ball, we can see that in law and politics, Burkeanism operates as a kind of rule of thumb, one that might be justified in important domains. And if this view is correct, it is necessary to rethink the long-standing opposition between Burke, defender of the common law and great critic of theories, and Jeremy Bentham, critic of the common law and enthusiastic defender of theory, in particular utilitarianism, which argues for an approach that will have the best consequences.[10] On certain assumptions and in some areas, Burkeanism can be understood as a way of promoting utility or at least good consequences—if only indirectly.

My third goal is to make progress toward answering a simple question: under what assumptions and conditions would Burkean minimalism be most appealing? With respect to racial segregation in the United States, there has long been a strong argument for a non-Burkean or even anti-Burkean approach, exemplified by *Brown v. Board of Education*,[11] which struck down racial segregation. Perhaps *Brown* can be defended as minimalist, because it built on a long line of precedents, and did not come as a bolt from the blue. But even if *Brown* is understood in that way, it is not easily characterized as Burkean, because it disrupted the well-established

[10] See Gerald J. Postema, *Bentham and the Common Law Tradition* (New York: Oxford University Press, 1986).
[11] 347 U.S. 483 (1954).

institution of segregation, accepted by many people over time, in the name of a set of ideas involving equality on the basis of race.

Brown was issued by the Supreme Court, not by the American public as a whole. But even so, *Brown* can be taken as a Jeffersonian moment. By 1954, the American public was no longer committed to racial segregation, and there can be little doubt that most of the nation and its leaders rejected it. Indeed, segregation had become something of a national embarrassment in the midst of the Cold War, in which the United States was seeking to win the world's hearts and minds in its struggle with the Soviet Union. We can see *Brown* as a case in which national experience, including moral growth over time, led to an understanding of the Constitution's equality principle that would not have been possible a few decades earlier.

The most committed Burkeans insist that Burkeanism makes sense in all political domains, including those domains that consist of constitutional law as elaborated by federal judges. A more qualified approach would suggest that Burkeanism is easiest to defend when traditions are truly long-standing, and in that sense supported by many minds, and when the relevant institution, loosened from traditions, has a great deal of power. Rejecting these positions, I shall suggest instead that the case for Burkean minimalism is most plausible for federal judges when three conditions are met: (1) originalism would produce unacceptable consequences; (2) long-standing traditions and practices are trustworthy, or at least trustworthy enough, by virtue of having broad support; and (3) there is great reason to be skeptical of the rule-elaborating and theory-building capacities of federal judges. Because these conditions are often not met, rationalist minimalism is often preferable.

Minimalisms

Shallowness and narrowness. There are different forms of minimalism, but all of them favor small steps over large ones. This preference operates along two dimensions.

First, minimalists seek rulings that are *shallow rather than deep*. Shallow rulings attempt to produce rationales and outcomes on which diverse people can agree, notwithstanding their disagreement on the fundamental issues. For example, people vigorously dispute the underlying purpose of the free speech guarantee.[12] Should the guarantee be seen as protecting democratic self-government, or the marketplace of ideas, or individual autonomy? Or consider the Constitution's religion clauses. Should these be understood as an effort to recognize the dignity of the private conscience, or to minimize religious strife, or to make self-government feasible, or instead to increase social utility? Minimalists do not hope to resolve these disputes. They seek judgments and rulings that can attract shared support from people who are committed to one or another of these foundational understandings, or who are unsure about the foundations of constitutional principles.[13] Minimalists want judges to decide cases without taking stands on the deepest questions in social life.

The minimalist preference for shallowness is rooted in three considerations. First, shallow decisions simplify the burdens of decision; they make it much easier for judges (and others) to resolve disputes. To say the least, it can be extremely difficult to decide on the foundations of an area of constitutional law; shallow rulings make such decisions unnecessary. Second, shallow rulings are likely to prevent errors. A judicial judgment in favor of one or another foundational account may well produce significant mistakes; shallowness is less error-prone, simply by virtue of its agnosticism on the great issues of the day. If several foundational accounts, or all reasonable contenders, can converge on a rationale or an outcome, there is good reason to believe that it is right. Third, shallow rulings tend to promote social peace at the same time that they show a high degree of respect to those who disagree on large questions.[14] Consider a judgment, about the religion clauses, that can be accepted by those with different religious convictions, or with no religious convictions at all. In a heterogeneous society, it is generally valuable to assure citizens, to the extent possible, that their own deepest commitments have not been ruled off-limits. By accomplishing this task, shallow rulings reduce the intensity of social conflicts.[15] This practical point is supplemented by the fact that those who seek shallowness are demonstrating respect for competing foundational commitments.[16]

---

[12] See, e.g., Frederick Schauer, *Free Speech: A Philosophical Inquiry* (Oxford: Oxford University Press, 1990).

[13] See Cass R. Sunstein, Incompletely Theorized Agreements, 108 *Harv. L. Rev.* 1733 (1993).

[14] John Rawls, *Political Liberalism* 147–48 (New York: Columbia University Press, 1993).

[15] See the discussion of "modus vivendi" liberalism in id. at 146–49.

[16] Of course some such commitments are rightly placed out of bounds as a foundation for constitutional law; consider the commitment to slavery or to oppression of religious minorities.

The difference between shallowness and depth should be seen as one of degree. Supreme Court opinions offer reasons, after all, and reasons require a degree of depth. No one favors an opinion that announces, "Because we say so." The point is only that minimalists seek reasons that are minimally contentious and that can attract support from people who are unsure about, or who disagree on, the larger issues.

Minimalists also favor rulings that are *narrow rather than wide*. Narrow rulings do not venture far beyond the problem at hand. They attempt to focus on the particulars of the dispute before the Court. When presented with a choice between narrow and wide rulings, minimalists generally opt for the former.

Consider in this light Chief Justice John Roberts's suggestion, during his first year on the Supreme Court, that one advantage of unanimous decisions from the Court is that unanimity leads to narrower decisions. In his words, "The broader the agreement among the justices, the more likely it is a decision on the narrowest possible grounds."[17] After all, the nine justices have highly diverse views, and if they are able to join a single opinion, that opinion is likely to be narrow rather than broad. This, in the chief justice's view, is entirely desirable, as he explained with an aphoristic summary of the minimalist position in constitutional law: "If it is not necessary to decide more to dispose of a case, in my view it is necessary not to decide more."

As with the difference between shallowness and depth, the difference between narrowness and width is one of degree rather than kind. No one favors rulings limited to people with the same names or initials as those of the litigants before the Court. But among reasonable alternatives, minimalists show a persistent preference for the narrower options, especially in cases at the frontiers of constitutional law. In such cases, minimalists believe that justices lack important information; they do not have a full sense of the many situations to which a broad rule might apply. Minimalists fear the potentially harmful effects of decisions that reach far beyond the case at hand.

With respect to the war on terror, for example, the Court has favored narrow rulings, refusing to say anything about the president's power as

---

[17] Hon. John G. Roberts, Jr., Chief Justice, U.S. Supreme Court, Commencement Address at the Georgetown University Law Center (May 21, 2006).

commander-in-chief and generally leaving a great deal undecided.[18] In the domain of affirmative action, many of the Court's rulings have been particularistic and focused on the facts, arguing that while one program is unacceptable, another one might not be.[19] Or consider the "undue burden" standard in the area of abortion[20]—a standard that is rule-free and that calls for close attention to the details of the particular restriction at issue.

Minimalists insist that wide rulings will produce errors that are at once serious and difficult to reverse—a particular problem when the stakes are high. Hence narrowness might be especially desirable in any period in which national security is threatened. Justice Frankfurter's concurring opinion in the *Steel Seizure* case, invalidating President Truman's attempt to seize the nation's steel mills, offers the most elaborate discussion of the basic point.[21] Justice Frankfurter emphasized that "[r]igorous adherence to the narrow scope of the judicial function" is especially important in constitutional cases when national security is at risk, notwithstanding the country's "eagerness to settle—preferably forever—a specific problem on the basis of the broadest possible constitutional pronouncements."[22] In his view, the Court's duty "lies in the opposite direction," through judgments that make it unnecessary to consider the most delicate questions of constitutional authority.[23] Thus the Court has an obligation "to avoid putting fetters upon the future by needless pronouncements today."[24] Justice Frankfurter concluded that "[t]he issue before us can be met, and therefore should be, without attempting to define the President's powers comprehensively."[25]

In many domains, sensible people take small steps in order to preserve their options, aware as they are that large steps can have unintended bad

---

[18] See Hamdi v. Rumsfeld, 542 U.S. 507 (2004); Rasul v. Bush, 542 U.S. 466 (2004); see also *Ex parte* Quirin, 317 U.S. 1 (1942) (refusing to decide whether the president has inherent power to create military commissions). A partial exception is Hamdan v. Rumsfeld, 126 S. Ct. 2749 (2006), in which the Court addressed a number of issues. Even in *Hamdan*, however, the Court did not say a great deal about the president's power as commander-in-chief, even if it implicitly resolved certain issues against him. See Cass R. Sunstein, Clear Statement Principles and National Security: *Hamdan* and Beyond, 2006 *Sup. Ct. Rev.* 34 (2006).

[19] See, e.g., Adarand Constructors, Inc. v. Pena, 515 U.S. 200 (1995); City of Richmond v. Croson, 488 U.S. 469 (1989). Notably, the Court has converged on a kind of rule, at least for educational institutions: one that forbids quotas and point systems but permits case-by-case judgments that include consideration of race. *Grutter*, 539 U.S. 306.

[20] See Planned Parenthood of Southeastern Pa. v. Casey, 505 U.S. 833 (1992).

[21] Youngstown Sheet & Tube Co. v. Sawyer, 343 U.S. 579, 594–97 (1951) (Frankfurter, J., concurring).

[22] Id. at 594.

[23] Id. at 595.

[24] Id. at 596.

[25] Id. at 597.

consequences, particularly if they are difficult to reverse. People take this approach in deciding, for example, where to live and whether to marry. Something similar occurs in law, where wide rulings might produce outcomes that judges will come to regret. This point derives strength from a special feature of adjudication, which often grows out of particular disputes based on particular facts. Unlike legislators and administrators, judges cannot see a broad array of fact patterns. Lacking information about a range of situations, judges are often in a poor position to produce wide rulings.

These are points about the risk of error, but there is an additional problem. For any official, it can be extremely burdensome to generate a broad rule in which it is possible to have much confidence. Narrow decisions, like shallow ones, might therefore reduce the costs of decision at the same time that they reduce the costs of error.

There is a further point. Minimalist rulings leave a great deal of room for democratic discussion and debate. If the Court issues a shallow and narrow ruling about some issue of liberty or equality, it will not commit the nation to a great deal. Participants in the political process can continue to debate the foundational questions. Other problems remain to be resolved. Minimalist rulings therefore give many minds an opportunity to contribute their own knowledge to social problems. For this reason, minimalism can claim important virtues in a nation committed to democratic self-government and alert to the fact that no one, and no court, has a monopoly on wisdom.

Costs of decisions, costs of errors, and unpredictability. In the abstract, of course, narrowness and shallowness are nothing to celebrate. Narrowness is likely to breed unpredictability and perhaps unequal treatment. It might even do violence to the rule of law, if only because it leaves so much uncertainty. Here is a big problem for Chief Justice Roberts's call for consensus and narrowness: 9-0 decisions, converging on a narrow ruling, may actually prevent the predictability that the chief justice seeks, because narrowness leaves many questions undecided.

In some areas, moreover, predictability is crucial. If the basic rules of property and contract are unclear, people will not be able to conduct their affairs with the certainty that these areas of the law demand. People need to know what they own, and they need to know that their agreements are secure.

Of course there are many analogies. Drivers usually need to know what the speed limit is, and administrators need to know when Social Security Disability claimants are entitled to disability payments, so that the system can run easily without endless conflicts about the basic rules. In constitutional law, schools have to know whether and to what extent they may regulate speech by their students, or discipline students without providing a hearing. Narrow rulings leave educational officials at sea.

Narrow rulings do reduce the burdens imposed on judges in the case at hand, but they also "export" decision-making duties to others in the future, in a way that can increase those burdens in the aggregate. Insofar as minimalists prize narrowness, they are vulnerable to challenge on the ground that they leave too much openness in the system.

To know whether narrowness is good, and how much narrowness is good, we need to investigate the costs of decisions and the costs of errors. Where narrowness leads to high decision costs and many (costly) errors, it should be avoided. Where narrowness reduces the costs of decisions and avoids (costly) mistakes, it may well be the proper approach. We also need to know about the importance of predictability in the area at hand. If ordinary people have to make decisions on a daily basis, and if they do not know what the law is, narrowness can produce disasters. But if decisions are made rarely—say, twice a year—and by few people, the existence of a degree of unpredictability may not be so bad. Any argument for narrowness must acknowledge that in many contexts, width is a very good idea.

Shallowness certainly has its virtues. But suppose that a deep theory is correct, in the sense that it reflects the proper approach to a constitutional provision. Why should judges refuse to endorse the proper theory? Assume, for example, that a certain theory—of free speech, the president's authority as commander-in-chief, property rights—would produce the right foundation for future development. If so, there is good reason for courts to endorse it. Minimalists might leave uncertainty about the content of the law at the same time that they obscure its roots. The best way to evaluate shallowness is also by investigating the costs of decisions and the costs of errors. If any deep theory will be likely to be mistaken, as Burkeans always suspect, then depth is best avoided. If a deep theory is clearly right, judges would do well to accept it.

Burkean Practices and Burkean Judgments

There are many different forms of minimalism; Burkean minimalism is only one. We could also imagine Burkeans who are, along one dimension, not minimalist at all, because they favor wide rulings. But most people who are drawn to Burke also have strong minimalist sympathies.

It is important to distinguish between Burkean minimalism and its more rationalist counterpart, which might be associated with Justices Ruth Bader Ginsburg[26] and Stephen Breyer.[27] Justices Ginsburg and Breyer like to write narrowly and in a way that is focused on the particulars of cases. But they are not Burkeans. They typically demand reasons for practices; they will not rest content with a recitation of history. The central point is that while Burkeans want to base their small steps on established traditions, rationalists scrutinize traditions, and they are willing and even eager to ask whether established practices can survive critical attention.

This difference should not be overstated. No real-world Burkean is likely to refuse to ask, ever, whether a tradition can be defended by reference to reasons. No real-world minimalist is likely to accept every tradition as such, even if that minimalist is a committed Burkean. No real-world minimalist is likely to want to subject many traditions to critical scrutiny, at least not at the same time. Any such effort would quickly produce a departure from minimalism. In practice, there is a continuum from more Burkean to more rationalist forms of minimalism. But it is nonetheless important to distinguish between the two sets of minimalists, because their different emphases can lead in radically different directions.

As it applies to the judiciary, we can understand Burkeanism in two different ways. First, Burkeans might stress actual social *practices*, and

[26] See, e.g., United States v. Virginia, 518 U.S. 515 (1996) (offering a theoretical account of the problem of sex discrimination). It is important to be careful with these comparisons. Justice Ginsburg believes in small steps and has occasional Burkean inclinations. See, e.g., Ruth Bader Ginsburg, Some Thoughts on Autonomy and Equality in Relation to *Roe v. Wade*, 63 *N.C. L. Rev.* 375 (1985) (criticizing *Roe v. Wade* for proceeding too rapidly).

[27] See Breyer, *Active Liberty*. Justice Breyer, no less than Justice Ginsburg, is respectful of precedent and has some Burkean tendencies—as reflected, for example, in his emphasis on the need to proceed slowly and incrementally in the domain of privacy, see id. at 69–74; Denver Area Educ. Telecomm. Consortium v. FCC, 518 U.S. 727 (1996) (Breyer, J., plurality opinion). In this domain, at least, Justice Breyer is skeptical of the use of a priori reasoning to resolve novel questions; and his insistent emphasis on experience and consequences has a Burkean dimension. But insofar as Breyer emphasizes a theoretical account for organizing constitutional law, see *Active Liberty*, at 15-33, his approach is easily distinguished from that of Justices O'Connor and Frankfurter, who had no such account.

see those practices, as they extend over time, as bearing on the proper interpretation of the Constitution. Those who adopt a practice-oriented understanding would be reluctant to invoke a particular conception of the separation of powers to strike down actions that are long-standing—say, foreign surveillance by the president, or presidential war-making without congressional authorization. On this view, judges in constitutional cases should follow a distinctive conception of the role of common-law judges, which is to respect and mimic, rather than to evaluate and challenge, time-honored practices.

In a sense, Burkean courts attempt to delegate power from individual judges to firmly rooted traditions. Consider a prominent example. In voting against judicial involvement in cases calling for the principle of one-person, one-vote, Justice Frankfurter emphasized not only "a uniform course of decision" but also "the equally uniform course of our political history regarding the relationship between population and legislative representation."[28]

More ambitiously, Burkean judges might even question democratic initiatives that reject traditions without very good reason. Perhaps time-honored practices deserve protection because they are time-honored. Consider the Court's ruling that the president may not create military commissions without congressional authorization. In that ruling, the Court's plurality placed heavy emphasis on traditions, concluding that while traditions supported the use of such commissions to try violations of the law of war, they did not support their use to try mere conspiracies to violate the law of war.[29]

Second, Burkeans might stress not social practices but the slow evolution of judicial doctrine over time—and might therefore reject sharp breaks from the judiciary's own past. For these Burkeans, what is particularly important is the *judiciary's* prior judgments, which should in turn be based on a series of small steps, and should avoid radical departures. On this view, current judges should respect those prior judgments, in order to protect settled expectations, to promote predictability, and to show humility in the face of the conclusions of other judges.

There are big differences between an approach that focuses on social practices and one that focuses on judicial decisions. Those who emphasize

[28] Baker v. Carr, 369 U.S. 186, 266–67 (1962) (Frankfurter, J., dissenting).
[29] Hamdan, 126 S. Ct. 2749 (2006).

practices would be skeptical of evolutionary movements in constitutional law *if* those movements depend on the judges' own moral or political judgments, minimalist though they might be. For Burkeans who emphasize practices, it is not legitimate for judges to build constitutional law through small steps—in, say, the area of discrimination on the basis of sexual orientation—that reflect the Court's own judgments over time. But for those who see the case-by-case evolution of judge-made constitutional law as an acceptably Burkean project, judicial steps deserve respect, in part because those steps are unlikely to depart radically from public convictions.

Burke himself emphasized social practices rather than judicial judgments, but insofar as he spoke of and celebrated "jurisprudence," he tended to collapse the two.[30] I do not attempt anything like an exegesis of Burke, an exceedingly complex and not always consistent figure, in this space.[31] My goal is to elaborate Burkean minimalism as an approach to constitutional law without claiming that the approach, thus elaborated, is something to which Burke personally would have subscribed. But let us turn briefly to Burke's views and in particular to his great essay on the French Revolution, in which he rejected the revolutionary temperament because of its theoretical ambition.[32]

---

[30] To the extent that it is an empirical fact that judicial movements turn out to track changes in social practices, the division may not be quite as important as it seems to be. And indeed that does seem to be an empirical fact. For discussion, see Klarman, *Jim Crow*. It is reasonable to doubt, however, whether the committed Burkean should permit constitutional law to evolve with successful movements, rather than simply requiring constitutional understandings to follow long-standing traditions. We should distinguish between the clearly Burkean practice of allowing ambiguous provisions to be "glossed" by traditional practices—in a way that allows elected officials to do as they wish, see *Youngstown*, 343 U.S. at 610–11 (Frankfurter, J., concurring)—and the less Burkean or (better) non-Burkean practice of "updating" constitutional understandings to fit with values perceived as contemporary, see Roper v. Simmons, 543 U.S. 551 (2005).

[31] The literature on Burke is vast, and it would not be productive to offer a list here. See, e.g., Conor Cruise O'Brien, *The Great Melody: A Thematic Biography of Edmund Burke* (Chicago: University of Chicago Press, 1994). An interesting, illuminating, and highly skeptical treatment can be found in Don Herzog, *Poisoning the Minds of the Lower Orders* (Princeton: Princeton University Press, 1998). Within the legal literature, the most influential discussion is Anthony Kronman, Tradition and Precedent, 99 *Yale L.J.* 1029 (1990). My own treatment of Burkean minimalism is altogether different from Kronman's, insofar as I emphasize the limitations of human and judicial knowledge, whereas Kronman attempts, far more ambitiously, to defend "the ancient but now largely discredited idea that the past has an authority of its own which, however circumscribed, is inherent and direct rather than derivative." Id. at 1047. In my view, this idea should indeed be discredited on the ground that it is mystical. The real argument for Burkeanism, and for fidelity to past practices, depends on the proposition, on the surface of Burke's text, that the "private stock of wisdom" will often prove less wise than those practices.

[32] Edmund Burke, Reflections on the Revolution in France, in *The Portable Edmund Burke* 416–51 (Isaac Kramnick ed.) (New York: Penguin, 1999). In exploring the possibility that traditions are a product of many minds, and in spelling out that aspect of Burke's writing, I am deliberately abstracting from the

Burke's key claim is that the "science of constructing a commonwealth, or reforming it, is, like every other experimental science, not to be taught a priori."[33] To make this argument, Burke opposes theories and abstractions, developed by individual minds, to traditions, built up by many minds over long periods. In his most vivid passage, Burke writes:

> We wished at the period of the Revolution, and do now wish, to derive all we possess as *an inheritance from our forefathers*. . . . The science of government being therefore so practical in itself, and intended for such practical purposes, a matter which requires experience, and even more experience than any person can gain in his whole life, however sagacious and observing he may be, it is with infinite caution that any man ought to venture upon pulling down an edifice which has answered in any tolerable degree, for ages the common purposes of society, or on building it up again, without having models and patterns of approved utility before his eyes.[34]

Thus Burke stresses the need to rely on experience and in particular the experience of generations. He objects to "pulling down an edifice," a metaphor capturing the understanding of social practices as reflecting the judgments of numerous people extending over time. It is for this reason that Burke describes the "spirit of innovation" as "the result of a selfish temper and confined views."[35] It is for the same reason that Burke offers the term *prejudice* as one of enthusiastic approval, noting that "instead of casting away all our old prejudices, we cherish them to a very considerable degree."[36]

Why, exactly, would prejudices appeal to Burke? The word itself supplies an answer. Prejudices operate before judgment—they supply answers that antedate reflection. If prejudices are rooted in long-standing practices, it should not be surprising to find that Burke trusts them. Emphasizing the

---

elitist and antidemocratic elements of Burke's claims on behalf of traditions. Consider, for example, Burke's fears of the "hoofs of a swinish multitude." Id. at 449. For a general discussion of this aspect of political thought, with reference to Burke, see Herzog, *Poisoning the Minds*. I am aware that some of the discussion, and in particular the exploration of majoritarianism, might seem jarring to those interested in Burke himself.

[33] Burke, Reflections, at 442.
[34] Id. at 451.
[35] Id. at 428.
[36] Id. at 451.

critical importance of stability, Burke adds a reference to "the evils of inconstancy and versatility, ten thousand times worse than those of obstinacy and the blindest prejudice."[37]

Burke's sharpest distinction, then, is between established practices and individual reason. He contends that reasonable citizens, aware of their own limitations, will effectively delegate decision-making authority to their own traditions, which capture the judgments of many minds. "We are afraid to put men to live and trade each on his own private stock of reason," because of the concern that any one person's stock "is small, and that the individuals would do better to avail themselves of the general bank and capital of nations, and of ages. Many of our men of speculation, instead of exploding general prejudices, employ their sagacity to discover the latent wisdom which prevails in them."[38]

BURKE AND MANY MINDS

Burke's enthusiasm for traditions, as compared to the private stock of reason, can be closely linked to the Condorcet Jury Theorem. Recall that the Jury Theorem shows that if each individual in a group is more than 50 percent likely to be right, the probability that the majority of the group will be right increases toward 100 percent as the size of the group expands. Burke depicts traditions as embodying the judgments of many people operating over time. If countless people have committed themselves to certain practices, then it is indeed possible, on Condorcetian grounds, that "latent wisdom" will "prevail in them"—at least if most of the relevant people are more likely to be right than wrong. The fact that a tradition has persisted provides an additional safeguard here: its very persistence attests to its wisdom or functionality, at least as a general rule.

To be sure, it would be possible to object to this view on many grounds, and I shall be devoting considerable attention to the objections here. Perhaps most of the people who account for the tradition are not more than 50 percent likely to be right. Perhaps they suffer from some kind of systematic bias. Perhaps they are more likely to be wrong than right, in which case the collectivity's chance of being right falls, by Condorcet's own arithmetic,

---

[37] Id.
[38] Id.

toward 0 percent as the size of the group expands. Some traditions (not to mention prejudices) are products not of wisdom, but of some kind of social cascade, in which practices persist not because diverse people decide independently in favor of them, but because people simply imitate other people. Some traditions are a product of a collective action problem or sheer disparities in power, in which some people have imposed their will on others.

These are important objections to Burkeanism in all its forms, and rationalists invoke those objections in both law and politics. Many traditions reflect the independent judgments of fewer people than at first appears. Consider too the fact that recent generations are far larger, in terms of the sheer number of people, than their predecessors. I will return to these problems. For present purposes, my goal is to show that Burke's argument has an implicit Condorcetian logic.

Burke and Judicial Review

In light of his claims about tradition, Burke might be expected to express some skepticism about judge-made common law, perhaps treating it as a form of theory-based intervention by unaccountable officials whose decisions are not rooted in actual experience. But Burke sees his claims as a reason to value rather than to repudiate the common law, which he goes so far as to call the "pride of the human intellect."[39] Burke contends that "with all its defects, redundancies, and errors," jurisprudence counts as "the collected reason of ages, combining the principles of original justice with the infinite variety of human concerns."[40] Of course jurisprudence lacks a simple theory, and it was hardly constructed a priori. But it is a product of experience, and that is its signal virtue.

Burke appears to be seeing the common law as a form of customary law, developing with close reference to actual practices, which it tends to codify. On this view, theoretical attacks on the common law, based on (for example) utilitarianism, show far too much confidence in a theory, and far too little respect for the collective wisdom of entrenched practices. The same might be said of many areas of constitutional law, in which a committed

[39] Id at 456.
[40] Id.

Burkean might distrust theoretical abstractions in favor of the occasionally unruly and apparently self-contradictory rulings that are built on the foundation of particulars.

Burke did not, of course, develop an account of judicial review. English courts lacked (and still lack) the power to strike down legislation, and hence it could not possibly have occurred to Burke to explore the nature and limits of that power. Indeed, Burkeans might be tempted to reject judicial review altogether, perhaps on the ground that judges are too likely to go off on larks of their own. Perhaps little revolutions, of the kind if not on the scale that Burke despised, are a predictable product of an independent judiciary entrusted with the power of invalidation. We could easily imagine a Burkean challenge to the institution of judicial review, seeing it as an invitation to the exercise of abstract reason, used to challenge long-standing practices in the name of a theory.

But for those who sympathize with Burke's arguments, a Burkean account of judicial review is not difficult to sketch. Indeed, Burkeans might well be hospitable to a judicial role in reviewing legislation, at least if that role is understood in a certain way. On the Burkean view, a central role of the courts is to protect long-standing practices against renovations based on theories, or passions, that show an insufficient appreciation for those practices. The goal would be to provide a safeguard against the revolutionary or even purely rationalistic spirit in democratic legislatures. We could easily imagine a highly Burkean understanding of the judicial role, one that would protect the collective wisdom of the past against the momentary passions or theoretical hubris of the present.

Nor is this view foreign to American constitutional law. The due process clause has long been understood in traditionalist terms. In his dissenting opinion in *Lochner v. New York*,[41] in which the Supreme Court struck down maximum hour legislation, Justice Holmes, though not a Burkean, struck an unmistakably Burkean chord when he wrote that the clause would be violated only if "a rational and fair man necessarily would admit that the statute proposed would infringe fundamental principles as they have been understood by the traditions of our people and our law."[42] The application of the Bill of Rights to the states had a great deal to do with Burkean

[41] *Lochner*, 198 U.S. 45.
[42] Id. at 76 (Holmes, J., dissenting).

thinking, especially insofar as it was engineered by Justice Frankfurter. Justice Frankfurter explicitly urged that courts should ask whether proceedings "offend those canons of decency and fairness which express the notions of justice of English-speaking peoples."[43] And the decision to apply provisions of the Bill of Rights to the states has become rooted in a judgment about whether "a particular procedure is fundamental—whether, that is, a procedure is necessary to an Anglo-American regime of ordered liberty."[44]

Of course it would be possible to understand "ordered liberty" in a priori or purely theoretical terms. But in the account that Justice Frankfurter urged, the focus has been on "an Anglo-American regime," which placed the emphasis squarely on an identifiable tradition. Note also that in Justice Frankfurter's hands, the emphasis on tradition itself has a democratic element: if a practice has long been a part of Anglo-American law, then many people have approved it explicitly or implicitly. Many traditions have been constructed by citizens, rather than imposed on them. Burkean opposition to social engineering can be understood in this light.

Much of the time, the Court's modern substantive due process decisions, protecting fundamental rights against government intrusions, have been rooted at least in part on traditions. Justice Harlan's influential approach was based on "continual insistence upon respect for the teachings of history [and] solid recognition of the basic values that underlie our society."[45] More recently, efforts to limit the use of substantive due process have suggested that unless the right in question can claim firm roots in tradition, courts should not intervene.[46] In rejecting the right to physician-assisted suicide, the Court said that substantive due process has been "carefully refined by concrete examples involving fundamental rights found to be deeply rooted in our legal tradition." According to the Court, this approach "tends to rein in the subjective elements" and "avoids the need for complex balancing" in particular cases by fallible judges.[47] Thus the Court's inquiry was framed by asking "whether this asserted right has any place in our Nation's traditions."[48]

---

[43] Rochin v. California, 342 U.S. 165, 169 (1952).

[44] Duncan v. Louisiana, 391 U.S. 145, 149 n. 14 (1968).

[45] Griswold v. Connecticut, 381 U.S. 479, 501 (1965) (Harlan, J., concurring in the judgment).

[46] Washington v. Glucksberg, 521 U.S. 702 (1997) (emphasizing the need to apply the due process clause by reference to established traditions).

[47] Id. at 722.

[48] Id. at 723.

On this highly Burkean and antiperfectionist view, growing out of Holmes's dissenting opinion in *Lochner*, the Court should not strike down legislation merely because it offends the justices' account of reason or justice, or even because it is inconsistent with evolving or current social norms. It is necessary to show a violation of principles that are at once long-standing and deeply held. Of course the Court has often refused to follow this Burkean approach to the due process clause, in a way that has sharply divided Burkeans on the one hand from rationalist minimalists and perfectionists on the other. In striking down bans on same-sex sodomy, the Court explicitly rejected a traditionalist approach, emphasizing modern judgments instead.[49] I will explore these issues in some detail in chapter 4.

Burkeanism and Majoritarianism

This latter point suggests the need to make a distinction between two kinds of Burkean decisions: those that uphold and those that invalidate democratic judgments. As I have suggested, Burkeanism can operate either as a shield to insulate government against constitutional challenges or instead as a sword to support those challenges. By their very nature, Burkeans should be sympathetic to efforts by state and federal governments to defend established practices against constitutional attack. If, for example, states are regulating obscenity or banning same-sex marriages, their decisions might be supported on Burkean grounds.[50] Or consider the separation of church and state. When government is acting in a way that favors a kind of religious belief, Burkeans should not object *if* that form of favoritism has clear support in long-standing social traditions.

[49] See, e.g., Lawrence v. Texas, 539 U.S. 558 (2003). It is possible to read *Lawrence* as a perfectionist decision, accepting a broad understanding of sexual autonomy; see Laurence Tribe, *Lawrence v. Texas*: The "Fundamental Right" That Dare Not Speak Its Name, 117 *Harv. L. Rev.* 1893 (2004), or, alternatively, as a more minimalist decision rooted in evolving social understandings; see Cass R. Sunstein, What Did *Lawrence* Hold? Of Autonomy, Desuetude, Sexuality, and Marriage, 2003 *Sup. Ct. Rev.* 27. In neither case is *Lawrence* easily defended on Burkean grounds. The best effort might suggest that prohibitions on consensual sodomy, while long on the books, were subject to a recent pattern of nonenforcement. See id. Perhaps the committed Burkean would bow to the social practice of nonenforcement and strike down the (wildly infrequent) uses of the law as inconsistent with that practice. But for the Burkean, this is a stretch, simply because it is hard to see prohibitions on sodomy as violative of long-standing traditions.

[50] Insofar as Justice Scalia has emphasized the need to permit traditional morals regulation, he has made strongly Burkean arguments. See, e.g., *Lawrence*, 539 U.S. at 586–98 (Scalia, J., dissenting).

Strikingly, Chief Justice Rehnquist's defense of the use of the words "under God" in the Pledge of Allegiance was an almost entirely Burkean exercise. His emphasis is on historical practices, which argue in favor of permitting the use of those words, rather than on the justifications for those practices. The long-standing practice of public acknowledgement of the existence of God seems to be enough for him.[51] Indeed, Chief Justice Rehnquist's whole view of the establishment clause has a persistent Burkean feature, at least insofar as he would permit public recognition of God by reference not to theories or principle, but by reference to history alone.[52]

The separation of powers might be understood in the same terms. When the president is doing things that presidents have long done, and with congressional acquiescence, Burkeans would be strongly inclined to uphold their action.[53] The central point is more general. If Burkeanism operates as a shield to be used on government's behalf, many Burkeans might endorse a kind of *bipartisan restraint*—on the theory that decisions about whether to change long-standing practices should be made democratically, not by judges. Burke himself was hardly an enthusiastic supporter of democratic processes, but it is possible for Burkean minimalists to vote to uphold long-standing practices while also allowing majorities to change them.

In his dissenting opinion in *United States v. Virginia*,[54] Justice Scalia spoke in exactly these terms. He began by emphasizing that the Virginia Military Institute (VMI) "has served the people of the Commonwealth of Virginia with pride and distinction for over a century and a half."[55] On this view, the longevity of sex segregation at VMI was a good reason for the Court to stay its hand. In Justice Scalia's view, the Burkean point provides a cautionary note for judges but not for citizens, who need not be Burkean and who are entirely free to conclude "that what they took for granted is not so, and to change their laws accordingly."[56] Justice Scalia concluded

---

[51] See Elk Grove Unified Sch. Dist. v. Newdow, 542 U.S. 1, 26–33 (2004) (Rehnquist, C.J., concurring in the judgment). What is striking about Chief Justice Rehnquist's opinion is its nearly exclusive reliance on historical practices, treated as closely analogous to the use of the words "under God" in the Pledge of Allegiance. Emphasizing those practices, Chief Justice Rehnquist makes almost no effort to defend them in principle, in a way that fits well with one understanding of Burke.

[52] See, e.g., *Van Orden*, 545 U.S. 677 (Rehnquist, C.J., plurality opinion).

[53] See *Youngstown*, 343 U.S. at 612–13 (Frankfurter, J., concurring). In particular, see the lengthy historical appendix, id. at 615.

[54] 518 U.S. 515 (1996).

[55] Id. at 566 (Scalia, J., dissenting).

[56] Id. at 567.

that this democratic liberty to alter existing practices on anti-Burkean grounds is itself time-honored: "So to counterbalance the Court's criticism of our ancestors, let me say a word in their praise: They left us free to change."[57] In short, Justice Scalia was writing as a kind of majoritarian Burkean—one whose Burkeanism provides a limitation on judges, but not on political participants.

But courts might also use Burkeanism as a sword. If government is dramatically altering the status quo, Burkeanism might be invoked as the basis for attacking the attempted alteration. We have seen that the due process clause has been so interpreted. This is Holmes's understanding of substantive due process as allowing courts to strike down government action on the ground that it violates traditions. In other domains, established traditions have helped to convince courts to impose limits on what government may do. In invalidating an unusual Colorado law that prohibited gays and lesbians from obtaining local antidiscrimination measures, the Court said, "It is not within our constitutional tradition to enact laws of this sort."[58]

It emerges that for purposes of constitutional law, Burkeanism comes in both antimajoritarian and majoritarian varieties. The antimajoritarian varieties emphasize the wisdom of traditions and regard innovations as modest versions of the French Revolution, reflecting hubris, passion, or folly. The majoritarian varieties are unwilling to allow any kind of theory-based revolution through the courts—but they are entirely hospitable to democratic efforts to rethink traditions.

Of course majoritarian Burkeanism might be seen as a contradiction in terms. To the committed Burkean, the decisions of representative institutions cannot easily claim legitimacy if they overthrow long-standing practices, and certainly not if those decisions are in the grip of a theory. Burke's own challenge to the French Revolution would apply whether or not that revolution had majority support. But more ambivalent and less committed Burkeans might contend that the argument for Burkeanism depends on who, exactly, is rejecting traditions—and that judges should accept Burkean principles to the extent of refusing to disrupt long-standing practices on their own.

---

[57] Id.
[58] Romer v. Evans, 517 U.S. 620, 633 (1996).

SHALLOW BUT WIDE?

In this light, we could identify a distinctly Burkean approach to the Constitution, one that endorses shallowness while also embracing width and sometimes even large steps in Burkean directions. This approach would be minimalist in its rejection of ambitious theories, but it would be nonminimalist in its enthusiasm for wide rulings, not limited to the facts of particular cases.

Suppose that tradition and experience are the best sources of constitutional meaning. Suppose we agree that under the due process clause in particular, traditionalism should discipline judicial judgment. Justice Scalia has so urged, largely in the interest of width.[59] Insofar as Chief Justice Rehnquist would invoke long-standing practices to permit public invocation of God, he would rule widely, not narrowly.[60]

Some Burkeans, insistent on rule-of-law virtues, share Burke's skepticism about abstract theories, and particularly about their deployment by judges, while also rejecting case-by-case particularism. Imagine, for example, a decision to return to a quite specific, historically rooted understanding of the scope of substantive due process—a decision that would have to count as a large step insofar as it would dramatically alter existing law (for example, by permitting restrictions on abortions and bans on sexual relations between people of the same sex). Or consider the view that public references to God raise no constitutional problem, simply because such references have been with us for a long time.[61] Of course a good Burkean would seek to know a great deal about context; perhaps some references to God are harder to defend, on traditionalist grounds, than others. But it is plausible that an investigation of actual practice would produce wide judgments, not narrow ones.

We might therefore distinguish between Burkean minimalists who prize narrowness as well as shallowness, and those ambivalently minimalist Burkeans who favor width but reject depth. Sensible Burkeans should reject a static approach to tradition, one that freezes existing practice, especially as circumstances change. But Burkeanism as such need not forbid width in constitutional law. Interestingly, however, Justices Frankfurter and

---

[59] See Michael H. v. Gerald D., 491 U.S. 110 (1989) (Scalia, J., plurality opinion).

[60] See, e.g., *Van Orden*, 545 U.S. 677 (Rehnquist, C.J., plurality opinion).

[61] See *Newdow*, 542 U.S. at 26–33 (Rehnquist, C.J., concurring in the judgment).

O'Connor—leading Burkean minimalists in the nation's history—favored narrowness no less than shallowness, on the ground that in the most controversial domains, wide rulings are too likely to produce error.[62] The only point is that Burkeans need not be committed to narrowness in principle.

We should now be able to see the central tendencies of Burkean approaches to constitutional law, and also to see the foundations of those approaches in the opposition between the "private stock of wisdom" and the judgments of many minds. But it remains to explore the grounds on which judges might reject Burkeanism.

[62] See, e.g., *Youngstown*, 343 U.S. at 594–95 ((Frankfurter, J., concurring); City of Chicago v. Morales, 527 U.S. 41, 64–69 (1999) (O'Connor, J., concurring).

CHAPTER 3

~

Rationalists vs. Burkeans

Rationalist minimalists seek narrowness and shallowness, but they are entirely willing to rethink traditions and established practices. Rationalists are interested in the reasons behind practices, not in practices themselves. An underlying idea is that traditions are often unjust or arbitrary and that society frequently progresses by subjecting them to serious challenge. On this view, the delegation of decision-making authority to long-standing traditions is perverse, and Burke was quite wrong to treat *prejudice* as a word of approval. The rationalist view can claim support in what might be called the Jeffersonian challenge to Burke. Jefferson emphasized that current generations are, in a sense, older than past ones, and that those who are now living are in that sense "the ancients" compared to their ancestors.

Consider, for example, the long series of judicial decisions striking down discrimination on the basis of sex.[1] In those decisions, the Court did not act abruptly. Instead it built up the doctrine by small, incompletely theorized steps. In that sense, the Court's decisions were minimalist. But the Court could not claim to rest its doctrine on traditions. On the contrary, the Court's sex discrimination decisions offer a narrative of progress and learning over time and thus squarely reject Burkeanism. They do so by repeatedly opposing "reasoned analysis" to "traditional, often inaccurate, assumptions about the proper roles of men and women."[2] They reject laws that are an "accidental byproduct of a traditional way of thinking

---

[1] See, e.g., Frontiero v. Richardson, 411 U.S. 677 (1973); Stanley v. Illinois, 405 U.S. 645 (1972); Reed v. Reed, 404 U.S. 71 (1971). Rebecca Brown, Tradition and Insight, 103 *Yale L.J.* 177 (1993), might well be understood as a general defense of rationalist minimalism.

[2] Heckler v. Mathews, 465 U.S. 728, 750 (1984) (citing Miss. Univ. for Women v. Hogan, 458 U.S. 718, 725 (1982)).

about females,"[3] with the suggestion that such laws are unconstitutional for that very reason.[4]

Tradition serves in these cases as a term of opprobrium, not praise. Indeed, the Court has struck down sex discrimination on the express ground that it is a product of habit and tradition, rather than reason. The Court has required government to defend any such discrimination in terms that many Burkeans would find puzzling.[5]

Nor can Burkeanism account for the Court's decisions establishing the right to vote, including the one-person, one-vote rule[6] and even *Bush v. Gore*.[7] The doctrine here developed by increments, but the Court hardly built on traditions. Indeed, the one-person, one-vote rule was originally criticized by Justice Frankfurter and many others on heavily Burkean grounds, with the suggestion that the Court was allowing a contentious theory to override long-standing practices.[8] The Court's decision in *Lawrence v. Texas*,[9] striking down the ban on same-sex sodomy, is a good illustration of rationalist minimalism. In *Lawrence*, the Court did not and could not claim that its decision was securely rooted in long-standing traditions. On the contrary, the Court emphasized an "*emerging awareness* that liberty gives substantial protection to adult persons in deciding how to conduct their private lives in matters pertaining to sex."[10] Hence the Court pointed to what has been learned, and looked forward to what was now emerging, not backward to what was long settled.

On this account, the present knows far better than the past. In the Court's view, what was emerging was a product of sense and hard-won wisdom rather than arrogance or hubris. This narrative of progress, seeing traditions as badly confused or even invidious, is foreign to Burkeanism.

---

[3] Miller v. Albright, 523 U.S. 420, 442 (1998) (Stevens, J., plurality opinion) (quoting Califano v. Goldfarb, 430 U.S. 199, 223 (1977) (Stevens, J., concurring in the judgment).

[4] *Heckler*, 465 U.S. at 750.

[5] See, e.g., United States v. Virginia, 518 U.S. 515 (1996); Miss. Univ. for Women, 458 U.S. 718 (1982). A noteworthy feature of *Virginia* is the suggestion that efforts to justify sex segregation in terms that involve educational diversity and opportunity might be plausible if those efforts had been made in the recent rather than distant past—with the corresponding suggestion that an old law, not plausibly rooted in those concerns, could not be so defended. *Virginia*, 518 U.S. at 540.

[6] Reynolds v. Sims, 377 U.S. 533 (1964).

[7] 531 U.S. 98 (2000).

[8] See Phil C. Neal, *Baker v. Carr*: Politics in Search of Law, 1962 *Sup. Ct. Rev.* 252 (1962).

[9] 539 U.S. 558 (2003).

[10] Id. at 572 (emphasis added).

Of course we could imagine a Burkean claim that at a certain point, an "emerging awareness" has become a tradition. We could also imagine a claim that over time, actual experience has produced the "emerging awareness," which is therefore a lived reality, not an abstract theory. This claim would be more plausible if the awareness were embodied not merely in judicial decisions, but also in social practices and norms. Perhaps the ban on sex discrimination can be so counted, as that ban has been understood in both law and practice after a period of several decades. Perhaps the same can be said for broad presidential power to protect national security—power that might seem a product of an "emerging awareness" of what is necessary for self-defense. But in *Lawrence*, the Court did not claim that, with respect to sexual privacy, the emerging awareness had become firmly entrenched. While the Court did point to current practices of nondiscrimination, it also offered an account of developing wisdom—an account that is embodied in a powerful challenge to Burkeanism by Jefferson and others, emphasizing that present generations have more information than past ones.

In many areas, the Supreme Court has acted in minimalist fashion, but in a way that is sharply critical of traditions and that looks toward to a constitutionally preferred future. Indeed, much of equal protection doctrine is forward-looking in this sense, rooted in a norm of equality that challenges long-standing practices. There is a large difference between the due process clause and the equal protection clause here. As we have seen, due process doctrine builds, if sometimes awkwardly and ambivalently, on traditions, and much of it can be seen as embodying Justice Frankfurter's approach to constitutional law. By contrast, equal protection doctrine is sharply critical of traditions, setting out a principle that challenges practices of racial subjugation, and that has been elaborated in a way that goes well beyond the defining case of race and that attacks, rather than incorporates, social traditions.[11] Much of the current debate involves the nature and extent of that attack, with Burkeans asking the Court to limit its reach.

Establishment clause doctrine has a similar feature, with history often creating problems for the Court's attempt to construct a theory of neutrality among religions and between believers and nonbelievers—a theory that is

[11] See id. at 1170–78.

in considerable tension with historical practices.[12] As I have noted, Chief Justice Rehnquist speaks in unmistakably Burkean terms in this domain. He would permit public invocations of God, justifying them almost solely by reference to traditional practices.[13] In sharp contrast, Justice Breyer insists that tradition is hardly enough; it is also necessary to show that any such invocations fit with the various purposes, properly conceived, of the establishment clause.[14]

Speaking as a committed minimalist, Justice Breyer emphasizes that "no single mechanical formula . . . can accurately draw the constitutional line in every case."[15] Speaking as a non-Burkean rationalist, Justice Breyer calls traditions to account, asking for assurance that a public display suggests "little or nothing of the sacred," and conveys "a predominantly secular message."[16] Justice Stevens, also a rationalist, writes in similar terms, insisting (against those who focus on "our heritage") that judges must apply "the broad principles that the Framers wrote . . . by expounding the meaning of constitutional provisions with one eye towards our Nation's history and the other fixed on its democratic aspirations."[17]

More generally, rationalist minimalists are willing to conclude that entrenched traditions might reflect power, confusion, accident, and injustice, rather than wisdom and sense. It should be no surprise that Justice O'Connor, with her Burkean inclinations, refused to join the Court's opinion in *Lawrence*,[18] partly because the Court was overruling its own fairly recent decision in *Bowers v. Hardwick*.[19] How might we evaluate this disagreement?

Is Burkeanism Coherent?

Rationalists might begin by challenging the coherence of Burkeanism. They might insist, against their Burkean adversaries, that traditions do not come in neat packages for judicial identification. Traditions are hardly self-

---

[12] See, e.g., County of Allegheny v. ACLU, 492 U.S. 573 (1989).
[13] Van Orden v. Perry, 545 U.S. 677 (2005) (Rehnquist, C.J., plurality opinion).
[14] Id. at 701–4 (Breyer, J., concurring in the judgment).
[15] Id. at 701.
[16] Id. at 702.
[17] Id. at 705 (Stevens, J., dissenting).
[18] *Lawrence*, 539 U.S. at 579–80 (O'Connor, J., concurring in the judgment).
[19] 478 U.S. 186 (1986).

defining, and this point severely complicates the Burkean enterprise. When a court attempts to follow a tradition, what, exactly, is it supposed to follow?

In short, rationalists are likely to press the following questions: Should traditions be characterized at a high level of generality (requiring, say, broad respect for intimate personal choices) or at a low level (allowing, say, government interference with such choices when public morality is being violated)? Or suppose that circumstances have changed—as a result, for example, of the rise of terrorism. If so, how should we characterize an apparent "tradition" of limited presidential prerogatives? Perhaps the tradition is limited to the particular circumstances that gave rise to it; if so, it is a hard question how to characterize it in a new situation. Might not any such characterization have an evaluative element—and might the task not be a simple matter of discovery? If so, the line between Burkeanism and rationalism makes no sense; traditionalists must reason, and they must do so by reference to something other than their own judgments.

Consider, for example, the question of whether tradition grants the president the authority to engage in foreign surveillance. Even if many presidents have exercised that authority, perhaps a modern surveillance program is relevantly different, because modern technologies, involving email and cell phones, permit far greater intrusions into the domain of personal privacy. If so, the existence of a long-standing practice need not count in favor of a contemporary assertion of power, for that power will be used in a way that goes well beyond traditions. Or perhaps a modern surveillance program is relevantly different from what happened in the past because the threat of international terrorism raises problems never before encountered. If so, the absence of a long-standing practice need not count against a contemporary assertion of power.

Indeed, Justice Thomas made an argument of exactly this sort in rejecting the conclusion that traditions forbid the use of military commissions to try conspiracy to violate the law of war. While also challenging that conclusion on its merits, Justice Thomas argued that the war against terror is genuinely new. In his view, old traditions, designed for old enemies, must be permitted to evolve in dealing with the kinds of war in which the United States is now engaged.[20] Justice Thomas argued that other justices erred in using traditions to forbid a practice that could not be said to be inconsistent

---

[20] See Hamdi v. Rumsfeld, 542 U.S. 507, 674 (2006) (Thomas, J., dissenting).

with the past, simply because the past did not reflect the current situation. We could easily broaden Justice Thomas's point. Even if a tradition does not protect the right to same-sex marriage, perhaps social circumstances are now quite different, in a way that ensures that the tradition does not speak to the problem at hand.

The general point here is that if Burkeans mean to emphasize that many minds have accepted or rejected some proposition, we need to ask what proposition, exactly, is involved. If things are different now from how they were before, then the many minds argument on behalf of accepting the tradition may well lose its force. Maybe many minds have not accepted any proposition that is relevant to the problem at hand.

Suppose, plausibly, that nearly every current dispute is, in one or another way, distinguishable from disputes that were settled in the past. If so, rationalists will object that Burkean minimalists must ultimately turn out to be rationalists too, in the sense that any particular account of tradition must ultimately be their own, and based on their "private stock of reason." Perhaps any Burkean account of the tradition will have an evaluative dimension. On this view, any characterization of a tradition will have to be interpretive, even perfectionist, in the sense that it will be a matter not simply of finding something, but of placing long-standing practices in what judges deem to be a reasonable or sensible light.

Some rationalists have argued that traditions should be read at a high level of generality, so as to contain certain abstractions that might then be used to test, and find wanting, particular practices, even long-standing ones.[21] If traditions are so used, changes might be sought not in spite of traditions but in their name. If so, the distinction between Burkean and rationalist minimalism starts to crumble. For this reason, rationalists will charge that any Burkean approach must have a crucial rationalist dimension, one that is obscured by talk of traditions and the judgments of many minds.

Traditions at low levels of abstraction. Burkeans have several responses. First, Burkeans might insist on reading traditions at a low level of abstraction, in a way that will minimize the theory-building and tradition-characterizing duties of the judiciary. Justice Scalia, calling for deference to tradi-

---

[21] E.g., Laurence H. Tribe and Michael L. Dorf, *On Reading the Constitution* (Cambridge: Harvard University Press, 1991).

tion, emphasizes the need to consider "the most specific level at which a relevant tradition protecting, or denying protection to, the asserted right can be identified."[22] This approach promotes width at the same time that it expressly denies judges the power "to consult, and (if possible) reason from, the traditions . . . in general."[23]

By rejecting that power, and by distrusting any effort to "reason from" tradition, Justice Scalia is squarely embracing a Burkean approach to the role of the Court in certain cases. He is reading the due process clause so as to delegate authority to tradition, rather than to authorize judges to use tradition as a foundation for judgments of their own. If traditions are being read at a low level of abstraction, then it is genuinely possible to follow them, rather than to characterize them.

Critics of Burkean minimalism might respond that Burkeanism cannot be really rescued, as a neutral method, through this route. What level of abstraction counts as "low"? The lowest level of abstraction would focus on what, very specifically, was done—in which case no tradition would resolve a current dispute, which, by hypothesis, involves a different time, different circumstances, and different people. If the government said that people may not have more than two children, it would be easy to say that such a prohibition violates long-standing American traditions, to which the prohibition is indeed foreign. But characterized at the lowest level of abstraction, the American tradition—of procreative liberty—may not really apply to the current dispute, which involves a new time and by hypothesis a new situation. The rationalist would insist that whether it does apply depends on an evaluative judgment about how to characterize it.

The best response, from the Burkean point of view, is that if there is indeed some kind of difference in circumstances, the tradition may not apply, and hence cannot be used. But the difference must be explained, not simply asserted. Sometimes there is no plausible difference between the past and the present. To know whether there is such a difference, it is true that the Burkean has to think about traditions rather than simply point to them. But much of the time, it is clear that no tradition supports a purported right, and it is also clear that the government is seeking to violate a

---

[22] Michael H. v. Gerald D., 491 U.S. 110, 127 n. 6 (1989).
[23] Id.

long-standing practice simply because it rejects it on principle. In such cases, the Burkean path is clear.

Here, then, is a sharp difference between Burkean and rationalist minimalists. While agreeing on the need for small steps, Burkean minimalists are reluctant to create new rights, such as the right to physician-assisted suicide. In contrast, rationalist minimalists are willing to do so. If the Burkean position is to be defended, it is on the ground that traditions, taken as they actually have been, are more reliable than individual judges using their private stocks of reason. I believe that rationalist minimalists have some strong objections here, but we should bracket that point for now.

Majoritarian Burkeanism redux. Alternatively, Burkeans might acknowledge the rationalist challenge and urge that their own kind of Burkeanism is fully consistent with it. Burke himself believed that traditions were far from static.[24] His claim was that social change should emerge from traditions, not in opposition to them. Rationalists will respond that in distinguishing between "emergence" and "opposition," we will have to do some work in characterizing traditions, and the characterization will have a rationalist feature. If this is the central point, the line between Burkean and rationalist minimalism does become thinner, if only because reason will have to be used in deciding what kind of change should occur—a major concession to rationalists.

But maybe we can thicken the relevant line. Maybe Burkeans will want to acknowledge the rationalist objection and adopt a presumption in favor of democratic outcomes—an inclination that divides Justice Frankfurter, who adopted such a presumption, from Justice O'Connor, who did not.[25] On this view, Burkean minimalism means that courts will rarely strike down legislation unless that legislation is palpably inconsistent with tradi-

---

[24] For example, Burke approved of the Glorious Revolution:

A state without the means of some change is without the means of its conservation. Without such means it might even risk the loss of that part of the Constitution which it wished the most religiously to preserve. The two principles of conservation and correction operated strongly at the two critical periods of the Restoration and Revolution, when England found itself without a king.

Burke, Reflections, at 424. Thus the revolution "was made to preserve our *ancient* indisputable laws and liberties, and that *ancient* constitution of government which is our only security for law and liberty." Id. at 428.

[25] See, e.g., New York v. United States, 505 U.S. 144 (1992).

tions that can be clearly understood as such, or defies the unmistakable lessons of long experience. Change may occur, and traditions may be revised, but through democratic rather than judicial judgments.

On this view, the difference between Burkeans and rationalist minimalists is that members of the latter group are far more willing to invoke their own moral and political arguments to invalidate legislation. Committed Burkeans will require a clear demonstration that a constitutional challenge is firmly and unmistakably rooted in tradition before invalidating a law—as in Justice Holmes's approach to the due process clause. If circumstances have changed, and if traditions do not clearly speak to the problem at hand, then judges must stand aside. The problem of characterizing traditions is resolved by refusing to strike down laws unless the characterization of tradition is uncontentious. And this position has a many minds dimension. The basic idea is that laws should be invalidated only if traditions, reflecting the judgments of many minds, squarely oppose them.

Recall that some people are majoritarian Burkeans. They will uphold government power unless it is inconsistent with tradition, but they are reluctant to invalidate official judgments even if those judgments depart from tradition. The absence of a clear tradition in favor of (say) foreign surveillance by the president need not decide the constitutional question, especially because the problem of international terrorism is novel.

This view cannot be supported by Burkeanism alone. It mixes Burkean claims with majoritarian ones, and in a way that Burke himself would have found quite puzzling. Because Burke was skeptical of majorities and their passions, he was no majoritarian. But the mixture is nonetheless attractive, especially to those who like many minds arguments. For majoritarian Burkeans, the central idea is that in a democratic society, judges should invalidate legislation only when it amounts to a clear violation of the Constitution, read with close reference to long-standing practices. At the same time, majoritarian Burkeans would also claim that citizens in the democratic process should usually feel free to invoke their convictions in order to challenge long-standing practices.

Majoritarian Burkeans accept two kinds of many minds arguments: those that honor traditions and those that honor the views of the public. If the public wants to reject traditions, it is entitled to do so. Citizens and their representatives are permitted to offer their own understandings of liberty and equality or even their own interpretations of the Constitution—

at least when they are expanding and not contracting rights as established by the Court. They are entitled to proceed in a non-Burkean way, even while judges are held to traditions. On this view, Burkeanism makes sense for federal courts whether or not it makes sense for the many minds that participate in the democratic process—who are certainly entitled to be rationalists, and to rethink past practices by reference to their own experiences and even their own theories.

If traditions are a mixed blessing, and if they reflect confusion and error (and if *prejudice* is properly taken as a word of opprobrium), then we would not want citizens to hew so closely to the past—even if judges should be constrained in that way. Using Burkeanism in pragmatic terms, a judge, or a critic of the judiciary, might well be drawn to this position.

Rationalists will be skeptical of this argument. They might well object that in many domains, citizens themselves are far too tradition-bound— too likely to follow old practices that are no longer legitimate, if they ever were, when legitimacy is assessed by reference to constitutional ideals. And this indeed is the view of rationalist minimalists and of perfectionists, who contend that the federal judiciary has a legitimate role in testing the grounds for such practices as restrictions on political dissent, favoritism toward certain religions, and discrimination on certain grounds.

We can now see how rationalists and Burkeans might differ on the possibility of following traditions without having to characterize them. The Burkean position emerges as bloodied but essentially intact. For the federal judiciary, it is possible to maintain the following position: *Where the Constitution is unclear, judges should uphold democratic initiatives unless they are palpably inconsistent with the views of many minds over long periods of time.* This position might be applied to many controversies, including those involving the power of the president, the separation of church and state, gun control, the creation of fundamental rights under the due process clause, and free speech problems involving obscenity, libel, and commercial advertising. While Burkeanism may not be appealing, it is coherent enough.

Is Burkeanism Good?

But is Burkeanism good? Should judges follow it? If we understand Burkean minimalism in pragmatic terms, we will be able to make progress toward specifying the conditions in which that approach is justified.

A great deal depends on an assessment of traditions and of the capacities of those who would reject them. The question must be whether Burkean approaches would produce good consequences. If Burkeanism is to be defended as a form of second-order perfectionism, it must be on that ground. But it should be clear that committed Burkeans will be skeptical about any such consequentialist assessment, which necessarily depends on evaluative judgments of the interpreter's own. Burkeans would be tempted to ask: Ought we not to trust our traditions as such, rather than trusting ourselves, or our judges, to decide whether and when traditions are trustworthy? We could read Burke himself to suggest that the conditions for Burkeanism are simple: When the tradition is long-standing, and has been accepted by many people, it should not be abandoned, especially when those who wish to abandon it have a great deal of power. It would even be possible to understand Burke in terms that see the past as having a kind of direct authority, the force of which has nothing to do with consequences.

But these understandings seem implausible for both politics and constitutional law. For politics, the problem is that traditions are often stupid or unjust. The experience of those who have lived under stupid or unjust traditions is enough to show that established practices need revision. That experience might even be enough to motivate the development and use of a theory,[26] certainly by citizens and their representatives and (more rarely) by judges. For constitutional law, the problem is that the process of adjudication, culminating in opinions by independent judges, properly holds traditions to account—at least under constitutional provisions that are best understood as critical, rather than celebratory, of entrenched practices.

The equal protection clause is the best example here. It is hardly enough to say, in response to racial discrimination, that racial discrimination has been part of American traditions. The free speech principle of the First Amendment is best understood in the same terms. Even if traditions have allowed public officials to bring libel actions against those who have published falsehoods about them, the free speech principle is properly read to call such traditions into question. The larger point is that with respect to constitutional provisions that challenge long-standing practices, Burkeanism verges on self-contradiction: the political and legal tradition, for such

---

[26] John Rawls, *A Theory of Justice* (Cambridge: Harvard University Press, 1971) and Rawls, *Political Liberalism*, might be understood in these terms, however "abstract" they are often taken to be.

provisions, is to engage in criticism of traditional practices, and the criticism operates by reference to at least some kind of theory.

While the equal protection clause is the simplest example, I do not mean to suggest that a rejection of Burkeanism is logically compulsory even with respect to that clause. Burkeans could insist on working from a tradition of opposition to racial discrimination—a tradition that has operated for a century and a half—and could see that opposition as exhausting the meaning of the clause. But rationalists will want to go much further. They will want to loosen judges from discriminatory traditions, so as to ask questions about (for example) discrimination on the basis of sex and sexual orientation. If judges who ask such questions are not unreliable or unmoored, and if the traditions themselves are badly suspect, Burkeanism loses much of its appeal. With these points, we seem to be starting toward specifying the contexts in which Burkeanism, with its emphasis on the judgments of many minds, deserves support.

At this point committed Burkeans have an additional set of arguments. They might object that any effort to specify the conditions for Burkeanism, in a way that allows judges to pick and choose, is simply too opportunistic—and that opportunistic Burkeanism is far worse than the real thing. This objection can be understood in two different ways. The first is pragmatic and very much in the spirit of my general argument here: perhaps a broad rule in favor of Burkeanism would be better than a more fine-grained approach, which asks whether Burkeanism makes sense in particular domains. In my view, this claim is wrong, but it cannot be defeated in the abstract; it must be evaluated by reference to the results that it would produce.

The second understanding of this objection is broader and less pragmatic. The claim would be that any approach to interpretation must be genuinely principled. It cannot be defended or rejected by reference to the results that it produces. Such a defense, or such a rejection, is indeed too opportunistic, too result-oriented.

So understood, the objection is unhelpful and confused. We have seen that an approach to interpretation has no appeal if it enables judges to do whatever they want in particular cases. Such an approach would produce bad consequences, including intolerable unpredictability. But as we have also seen, no approach can be defended on grounds that are indifferent to consequences; an approach is unacceptable if it leads to (many) unacceptable results. Many people favor rule-bound approaches, to be sure, and such approaches can produce many errors in individual cases; but even rule-bound approaches have to be defended on the ground that on balance, they produce fewer mistakes than the alternatives. In the end, Burkean minimalism must itself be defended on the ground that it will produce good consequences.

Let us now explore some details.

ORIGINALISTS AND BURKEANS

I have argued that there is no abstract argument against originalism. If originalism would produce the best results on balance, the argument for originalism would be very powerful. In our world, the strongest objection to originalism is that it would greatly unsettle existing rights and institutions, in a way that would make American constitutional law much worse rather than better.

Burkean minimalists reject originalism for exactly that reason. They believe that originalists are in the grip of an abstract theory, one that would do away with a kind of inheritance. That inheritance takes the form of numerous social judgments over long periods of time, in which public commitments, social learning, and desirable adaptation have produced constitutional rulings that diverged from the original understanding. Minimalists, Burkean and otherwise, typically contend that this process of evolution was itself anticipated by the founding generation, which did not attempt to freeze its particular views. If this view is correct, Burkeans and originalists can make common cause.

When Burkeans recoil at the suggestion that the founding document should be understood to mean what it originally meant, they are embracing a conception of the Constitution as evolving in the same way as traditions and the common law—not through the idiosyncratic judgments of individual judges, but through a process in which social norms and practices play the key role. It is in this vein that Justice Frankfurter contended, "It is an inadmissibly narrow conception of American constitutional law to confine it to the words of the Constitution and to disregard the gloss which life has written upon them."[27]

---

[27] Youngstown Sheet & Tube Co. v. Sawyer, 343 U.S. 579, 610 (1952) (Frankfurter, J., concurring).

Consider, for example, the question of whether a congressional declaration of war is a necessary precursor to the use of force by the president. On the basis of the constitutional text, read in light of its history, there is a strong argument to this effect.[28] The argument is controversial, but let us stipulate that on the original understanding, the president may not use force without a congressional declaration of war. On Burkean grounds, judicial insistence on this idea runs into a serious problem: since the founding, the United States has been involved in over two hundred armed conflicts, and Congress has declared war on only five occasions! Long-standing practices are inconsistent with the original understanding, and Burkeans insist that those practices must operate as a "gloss" on the document.

At a minimum, Burkeans will notice that a congressional authorization to use force has operated as the functional equivalent of a declaration of war, and they will contend that such an authorization gives the president the same power that is accorded by a literal declaration. When the tradition deems an authorization to be adequate, Burkeans will not insist on a declaration. But Burkeans will add that if the president has often gone to war with neither a declaration nor an authorization from Congress, constitutional law must give some attention to that fact—and at least consider the possibility that for some military actions, congressional authorization is not required at all. A sensible conclusion, fitting with long-standing practice, is that more minor or limited military actions by the president alone, not amounting to full-scale "war," are indeed permissible—but that either a declaration or an authorization from Congress is necessary for measures that cannot reasonably be counted as minor or limited. The example could easily be extended to many cases in which social practices and judicial decisions have outrun the original understanding.

To their Burkean adversaries, originalists have two possible responses. First, they might accept the claims of stare decisis and social traditions and acknowledge that much of the time, established doctrines and practices must be accepted, whatever the content of the original understanding. Justice Scalia has described himself as a "faint-hearted" originalist;[29] his faint-heartedness consists in his unwillingness to use the original understanding as a kind of all-purpose weapon against existing law and practices. On this

---

[28] See John Hart Ely, *War and Responsibility* (Princeton: Princeton University Press, 1995).
[29] Scalia, Originalism, 864.

count, Justice Scalia is very different from Justice Thomas, who is not so
faint of heart. Justice Scalia has said that Justice Thomas "doesn't believe
in *stare decisis*, period."[30] Justice Scalia remarks, "[I]f a constitutional line
of authority is wrong, [Justice Thomas] would say 'Let's get it right.' I
wouldn't do that."[31]

The line between Burkean minimalism and fainthearted originalism
might well turn out to be thin in practice. The question is under exactly
what conditions originalists will prove faint of heart. The answer turns on
the weight to be given to precedents and practices. If originalists are extremely fainthearted, they will usually agree with their Burkean counterparts. Indeed, they might even become Burkeans.

As an example, consider the question of whether originalists should
overturn *Brown v. Board of Education*[32] or *Reynolds v. Sims* if it turns out
that the ban on racial segregation or the one-person, one-vote rule is indefensible by reference to the original understanding. A fainthearted originalist might believe that a decision to overrule either of these decisions
would be a kind of revolution—one that would violate entrenched understandings, jeopardize the fabric of existing law, and have unanticipated bad
consequences. If those who are faint of heart emphasize these points, they
show strong Burkean impulses. The task for fainthearted originalists is to
specify exactly when, and why, they are willing to live with decisions that
were originally illegitimate under their preferred theory.

The second response, offered by originalists to Burkean minimalists, is
far more interesting. Originalists might well claim that the doctrines to
which they most strenuously object are not, in fact, a product of slowly
evolving judgments, firmly rooted in social practices and fitting the
Burkean model of constitutional change. On this view, presidential power
to make war and to engage in foreign surveillance may well be legitimate,
if these are actually rooted in decisions extending over time; but judicial
invention of baseless constitutional rights is not. Speaking in Burkean
terms, originalists might argue that the most objectionable doctrines are a
product of a kind of (French?) revolution, in which the Supreme Court,
above all under the leadership of Chief Justice Earl Warren, was captured
by a theory that was at once controversial and radical. Of course *Roe v. Wade*

[30] Stephen B. Presser, Touting Thomas, *Legal Aff.*, January–February 2005, at 68.
[31] Id. at 69.
[32] 347 U.S. 483 (1954).

is a particular target of originalist ire, but the right of privacy is generally controversial on originalist grounds, and the one-person, one-vote rule is vulnerable as well, as are judge-made doctrines requiring a rigid separation of church and state.

It may be that in its most objectionable decisions, the Court was paying insufficient attention to social practices, which it repeatedly rejected. Perhaps its own reasoning was, in the end, too theoretical and a priori, and not securely rooted in either precedent or practice. It is not at all clear that committed Burkeans must or should treat such a revolution as the established backdrop for constitutional law—just as it is not clear that after an illegitimate revolution, a Burkean polity should build on the revolution, rather than attempting a kind of restoration.

CONTEXTS

I have noted that both Justice Frankfurter and Justice O'Connor can be characterized as Burkean minimalists. But there are noteworthy differences between the two, stemming from the dramatically different contexts in which they sat on the Supreme Court.

Often a majoritarian Burkean, Justice Frankfurter typically invoked Burkean arguments as a shield for government's use in the face of constitutional challenge. Sitting at the beginning of the Warren Court, Justice Frankfurter insisted that social practices deserved respect. His form of Burkean minimalism raised a series of cautionary notes about the liberal initiatives of that Court, which he often rejected.[33] For Justice O'Connor, sitting long after the Warren Court, Burkean minimalism operated to insulate that Court's initiatives from significant or immediate revision.[34] This difference raises a number of questions about the appropriately Burkean response to a non-Burkean, or an anti-Burkean, period in constitutional history.

On one view, the essential fallacy of a Burkean understanding of contemporary constitutional law is that it creates a ratchet effect, in which

[33] See W. Va. State Bd. of Educ. v. Barnette, 319 U.S. 624, 646 (1943) (Frankfurter, J., dissenting); Baker v. Carr, 369 U.S. 186, 266 (1962) (Frankfurter, J., dissenting).

[34] See, e.g., Planned Parenthood of Southeastern Pa. v. Casey, 505 U.S. 833 (1992). *Casey* of course preserved *Roe v. Wade*, a decision of the Burger Court rather than the Warren Court; but *Roe* is appropriately placed within the general line of doctrine that the Warren Court inaugurated. See Griswold v. Connecticut, 381 U.S. 479 (1965).

Burkeans end up having to "conserve" the aggressive, illegitimate, and tradition-rejecting decisions of their liberal predecessors. Compare the question of whether the Supreme Court, in the late 1930s, should have taken
a Burkean approach to the aggressive and illegitimate body of doctrines
that emerged from the *Lochner* era, including invalidation of minimum
wage laws and rigid restrictions on national power under the commerce
clause. When the Court has built up a body of doctrine that is constitutionally unmoored, and has done so in a relatively short period, perhaps any
effort at conservation is not properly characterized as Burkean at all. Perhaps the Court's post–New Deal rejection of *Lochner*-era decisions, in
sweeping rulings not easily regarded as minimalist,[35] can be understood as
a plausibly Burkean effort to return to traditions after a period characterized by an indefensible judicial role (or rule).[36]

Of course those Burkeans who emphasize judicial judgments might well
wonder whether the Court was right to sweep away its *Lochner*-era decisions so abruptly. But if those decisions lack legitimacy, Burkean or otherwise, the decision to sweep might be right.

If this point is correct, Burkeans might well accept the Court's wholesale
rejection of much of its jurisprudence between 1905 and 1935. And if this is
so, it would be coherent for conservatives to think that on Burkean grounds,
Justice Frankfurter was right in his insistence on stability, but that Justice
O'Connor was wrong in hers. To be sure, the illegitimate decisions might
deserve respect if that respect is necessary to protect established expectations or to insure against a large-scale social upheaval. But on Burkean
grounds, there is no reason for a presumption on behalf of illegitimacy,
even if it has persisted for decades.

I believe that a dispute on these questions helps to illuminate the division between contemporary Burkean minimalists, most notably Justice
O'Connor, and the less fainthearted originalists, most notably Justice
Thomas. Burkean minimalists would be most unlikely to have joined all of
the controversial decisions of the Warren Court, but they are now willing
to accept some or even most of them in the interest of stability. The argu-

---

[35] See, e.g., West Coast Hotel Co. v. Parrish, 300 U.S. 379 (1937) (upholding minimum wage legislation against due process clause challenge); NLRB v. Jones & Laughlin Steel Corp., 301 U.S. 1 (1937)
(upholding National Labor Relations Act against commerce clause challenge).

[36] For a very different view, see Ackerman, *Foundations* (arguing that the New Deal period should be
regarded as a constitutional moment, not as a return to any tradition).

ment for doing so is strengthened if those controversial decisions can indeed be seen to have emerged from an acceptably Burkean process of case-by-case evolution, closely attentive to social norms and practices. On that count, originalists are skeptical.

In this dispute, there are powerful Burkean points against originalism. Some of those points involve the risks associated with wholesale disruption of contemporary constitutional law, containing understandings of rights and institutions on which many Americans have come to rely. In the domain of governmental institutions, the Court's validation of independent regulatory agencies is the simplest example. A dramatic departure, striking down the independence of such agencies, would unsettle much of American government, including such institutions as the National Labor Relations Board, the Federal Communications Commission, the Federal Trade Commission, and the Securities and Exchange Commission.

There are prominent examples in the domain of rights as well, including the rule of one person, one vote and the prohibition on school prayer. A decision to revisit these rulings would threaten deeply entrenched features of American constitutional doctrine. Many of the rights-protecting decisions of the Supreme Court of the 1950s, 1960s, and 1970s have become embedded in national life. Many such decisions are embedded not merely in national life but also in constitutional doctrine, in the sense that they cannot be rethought without making it necessary to rethink numerous other decisions as well.

True conservatives, skeptical about large-scale change, would reject originalism for that reason. But it must be acknowledged that the argument for large-scale change is weakened if the relevant changes are bad—if the rights-protecting decisions of the Warren Court have real value on the merits, and cannot be characterized as destructive or pernicious as a matter of principle. In my view, most of those decisions are far from destructive; consider the rejection of racial discrimination and the broad protection of political dissent.

Perfectionists and Burkeans

Recall that perfectionists think it appropriate for federal judges to cast constitutional ideals in the best constructive light. Of course they do not believe that judges can legitimately create the Constitution anew; their job involves interpretation, not rewriting. Hence judges owe a duty of fidelity to text, precedent, and all other relevant sources of law. But to the extent that fidelity permits, judges are entitled and even required to develop a principle that best justifies an area of law. If, for example, the most property-protective view of the takings clause puts that clause in its best constructive light, perfectionists believe that the Court should adopt that view. If a democracy-centered understanding of the First Amendment makes best sense of the free speech guarantee, giving less protection to commercial advertising, then the Court should adopt that understanding.

Burkeans should acknowledge that sometimes judges cannot decide cases without doing something like what perfectionists describe. But because Burkeans distrust abstract or ambitious reasoning, they will try to avoid perfectionism to the extent that they can. They emphasize that particular people—judges!—must decide what puts law in the best constructive light, and they doubt whether judges' decisions will be right. Indeed, Burkean minimalists might, and probably must, be willing to defend their own approach on the ground that Burkean minimalism both fits and justifies our practices, and hence defeats perfectionism under its own criteria. On this view, Burkean minimalism, calling for attention to tradition and for small steps, is itself a kind of second-order perfectionism—as we have seen, a form of perfectionism that is alert to the institutional weaknesses of the federal judiciary, and that therefore refuses to pursue perfectionism directly. That very refusal may help to perfect constitutional democracy, because it minimizes the theory-building demands on the federal judiciary. Second-order perfectionism is, in fact, the best understanding of Burkean minimalism as I am trying to understand it here.

Of course the argument for (first-order) perfectionism, and the attack on Burkeanism, would be strengthened if we were entitled to have real confidence in the theory-building capacities of federal judges. Such confidence might be spurred by the Jeffersonian observation that in an important sense, current generations are more experienced than past generations, with a greater stock of knowledge—and current judges are part of current generations. Perhaps current judges are deciding, much of the time, not on the basis of their own "private stock," but with close reference to social wisdom as it has accumulated over time. If so, the argument for first-order perfectionism is strengthened. (I shall return to this argument in later chapters.)

But even if current judges do qualify as able theorists, the argument on behalf of perfectionist judging is not airtight. We could identify two kinds of skeptics. Democratic skeptics might object that judicial perfection of constitutional ideals would threaten the right to self-government. Perhaps that concern could be eliminated through the right theory of interpretation—which would, by hypothesis, give self-government its due. Burkean skeptics might also worry that perfectionists would encounter serious pragmatic problems. By attempting to graft their preferred theories onto actual societies, judicial efforts might turn out to be futile or counterproductive, if only because societies would resist those efforts. But if a theory that fits our practices is indeed appealing in principle, and if courts can elaborate and implement it, perhaps they should do so.

It is here, of course, that Burkean minimalists break from perfectionists. Burkean minimalists notice that reasonable people will disagree about what principle casts constitutional provisions in the best constructive light. Is the free speech principle perfected, or instead ruined, by an account that gives broad protection to commercial advertising? Is the equal protection principle improved, or instead undermined, by an account that forbids discrimination on the basis of sexual orientation?

Burkean minimalists lack confidence in judges who have theoretical ambitions; in their view, such judges suffer from hubris. To the extent that judges are entrusted with power, Burkeans believe, it is because of their willingness and ability to elaborate the Constitution's text, read in light of society's traditions and practices. Whether the theorists are seeking to vindicate property rights, or a democratic conception of the free speech principle, or the abstract ideal of color blindness, or a particular conception of the separation of powers, the Burkean minimalist will oppose them. The opposition is based on the belief that perfectionism, unpromising even in the political domain, is a most unlikely foundation for judicial judgment.

To be sure, perfectionists will insist that traditionalism cannot work without a degree of independent thinking. They say that traditions do not come in packages, and the very act of characterizing them requires evaluative judgments. But as we have seen, Burkeans have some answers to this objection.

Are We the Ancients?

Suppose that we are trying to decide between the two forms of minimalism: Burkean and rationalist. On what assumptions should we choose the former?

Much of the answer depends on whether we agree with Burke. If established traditions reflect wisdom rather than accident and force, the argument for Burkean minimalism gains force. Suppose that a state wants to ban obscene material. Suppose that those who sell such material object that the Court's decisions should be understood to establish a principle of individual autonomy, one that does not allow government to ban adults from reading whatever they want. If we believe that the traditional practices that support the ban are likely to embody wisdom, we will want courts to uphold it, whatever the ideal of individual autonomy seems to require.

In the same vein, Burkeans would want the Court to permit "ceremonial deism,"[37] in the form of public recognition of God in official ceremonies (including the Pledge of Allegiance). When a constitutional challenge is raised against ceremonial deism, Burkeans reject the challenge largely by reference to American traditions, which have certainly permitted public acknowledgment of the existence of God.[38] The same analysis would suggest that when initially confronted with the issue, courts should have permitted state to deviate from the one-person, one-vote rule. Burkean minimalists want courts to try to avoid the "political thicket," not because they believe in judicial abstinence as such, but because they think that established practices of political representation deserve respect even if it is not easy to produce a theory to defend them.

Speaking of morality generally, ethicist Leon Kass contends that in some domains, "we intuit and feel, immediately and without argument, the violation of things that we rightfully hold dear."[39] For those who believe that judges ought not to challenge what "we intuit and feel, immediately and without argument," Burkean minimalism has considerable appeal. Recall Burke's enthusiasm for prejudice—an enthusiasm that fits well with Kass's suggestion that repugnance can be wise.

[37] See Steven B. Epstein, Rethinking the Constitutionality of Ceremonial Deism, 96 *Colum. L. Rev.* 2083, 2084–87 (1996).

[38] *County of Allegheny*, 492 U.S. at 595–96; Lynch v. Donnelly, 465 U.S. 668, 716 (1984).

[39] Leon R. Kass, The Wisdom of Repugnance, in Leon R. Kass and James Q. Wilson, *The Ethics of Human Cloning* 3, 19 (Washington, DC: AEI Press, 1998).

By contrast, rationalist minimalists are highly skeptical of prejudices. They are willing to listen to the claim that, in some domains, the Court ought to scrutinize traditions and should be willing to generalize, from emerging social commitments and judicial precedents, principles that operate as a sharp constraint on government. As we have seen, the ban on sex discrimination emerged from this process of generalization. In that context in particular, it is difficult to defend the view that long-standing practices, even though supported by many minds, reflected wisdom and sense rather than power and oppression.

Some theories of the establishment clause have produced sharp critiques of long-standing practices, based as they are on accounts of neutrality that jeopardize a number of traditions.[40] Rationalist minimalists are willing to impose fresh barriers in this way. They are also comfortable with permitting the government to develop new accounts of what it can legitimately do—accounts that might produce considerable novelty in the form, for example, of an expanded conception of when government may interfere with private property to protect endangered species and the environment under its "police power."

Justice Holmes originated a Burkean approach to the due process clause, but he was far more pragmatist than Burkean: "It is revolting to have no better reason for a rule of law than that so it was laid down in the time of Henry IV. It is still more revolting if the grounds upon which it was laid down have vanished long since, and the rule simply persists from blind imitation of the past."[41] In the greatest sentence of his great *Lochner* dissent, Holmes insisted that "the accident of our finding certain opinions natural and familiar or novel and even shocking ought not to conclude our judgment upon the question whether statutes embodying them conflict with the Constitution of the United States."[42] Holmes's key point, a deeply anti-Burkean one, is that whether we find opinions "natural and familiar" is itself an "accident" of our time and place. There could be no clearer rejection of Burke's suggestion that our "prejudices" are a reflection not of accident but of hard-won wisdom. Of course a rejoinder might be that on pragmatic grounds, there is much to be said on behalf of practices that have endured. But Holmes himself had little sympathy for this argument.

---

[40] E.g., Lynch, 465 U.S. at 698 (Brennan, J., dissenting). For a superb discussion, see Martha C. Nussbaum, *Liberty of Conscience* (Cambridge: Harvard University Press, 2008).

[41] Oliver Wendell Holmes, The Path of the Law, 10 *Harv. L. Rev.* 457, 469 (1897).

[42] Lochner v. New York, 198 U.S. 45, 76 (1905) (Holmes, J., dissenting).

The Federalist No. 1 offers a similar challenge to Burkeanism, with the suggestion, "It has been frequently remarked that it seems to have been reserved to the people of this country, by their conduct and example, to decide the important question, whether societies of men are really capable or not of establishing good government from reflection and choice, or whether they are forever destined to depend for their political constitutions on accident and force." The opposition between "reflection and choice" on the one hand, and "accident and force" on the other, suggests a sharp critique of those who value traditions as repositories of wisdom.

Consider too the words of James Madison, writing in a very young America:

> Is it not the glory of the people of America that, whilst they have paid a decent regard to the opinions of former times and other nations, they have not suffered a blind veneration for antiquity, for custom, or for names, to overrule the suggestions of their own good sense, the knowledge of their own situation, and the lessons of their own experience?[43]

In Madison's unmistakably anti-Burkean account, Americans "accomplished a revolution which has no parallel in the annals of human society. They reared the fabrics of governments which have no model on the face of the globe."[44]

These are largely rhetorical passages, but there is actually an argument in the background, one that turns Burkeanism on its head. Jefferson himself captured that argument with his objection that some people "ascribe to the men of the preceding age a wisdom more than human" and his response that the age of the founders "was very like the present, but without the experience of the present; and forty years of experience in government is worth a century of book-reading."[45] Burkeans cherish the wisdom of those long dead, but in Jefferson's view, their stock of wisdom was far more limited than ours; they were younger and knew less. In the same vein, Pascal

---

[43] The Federalist No. 14 (James Madison), at 72.

[44] Id.

[45] Letter from Thomas Jefferson to Samuel Kercheval (July 12, 1816), in *The Portable Thomas Jefferson* 552, 559 (Merrill D. Peterson ed.) (New York: Penguin, 1977). Note, however, that Jefferson is speaking of experience, not a priori reasoning (or "book-reading").

contended that we are the ancients: "Those whom we call ancient were really new in all things, and properly constituted the infancy of mankind; and as we have joined to their knowledge the experience of the centuries which have followed them, it is in ourselves that we should find this antiquity that we revere in others."[46]

Jeremy Bentham attacked ancient wisdom in identical terms, contending that those who were ancient were, in the relevant sense, very young.[47] Bentham acknowledged that old people have more experience than young people, but insisted that "as between generation and generation, the reverse of this is true."[48] In fact, "the wisdom of the times called old" is "the wisdom of the cradle."[49] Bentham deplored the "reigning prejudice in favor of the dead," and also the tendency to disparage the present generation, which has a greater stock of knowledge than "untaught, inexperienced generations."

These arguments turn chronology directly against Burke, not by attempting to vindicate abstract reason, but by suggesting that if experience is our guide, the present has large advantages over the past. This point helps support the idea that Burkeanism should not be used as a sword against government: if current generations would like to reject traditions, they should be permitted to do exactly that, because they have greater experience. A similar idea might be found in the Supreme Court's Pascal-like suggestion, in invalidating bans on relations between men, that what is crucial is not ancient practice, but an "emerging awareness."[50] This suggestion stresses the judgments of current generations, which are presented as more knowledgeable and reflective than those of the distant past.

But if their focus is on the Supreme Court, Burkean minimalists need not insist that respect for long-standing traditions always makes sense in the political domain. Burkean minimalists might plead agnosticism on the proper treatment of traditions in democratic processes, and contend more modestly that their approach is especially well adapted to the strengths and weaknesses of the federal judiciary. For judges, the question is an insistently

---

[46] Blaise Pascal, Preface to the Treatise on Vacuum, in *Thoughts, Letters, and Minor Works* 444, 449 (Charles W. Eliot ed., M. L. Booth et al. trans.) (1910).

[47] Jeremy Bentham, *Handbook of Political Fallacies* 43–53 (Harold Larabee ed.) (New York: Octagon Books, 1952).

[48] Id. at 44.

[49] Id. at 45.

[50] See *Lawrence*, 539 U.S. at 572.

comparative one. It is not whether traditions are good, or great, in the abstract. It is whether tradition-tethered judges are better than judges who think that they ought to subject traditions to critical scrutiny. Burkean minimalists believe that traditions are the best available guide, at least when judges are asked to invalidate legislation.

A committed Burkean might reject these qualifications, or any effort to think through the circumstances in which Burkeanism makes the most sense. To the committed Burkean, the analysis is simple: if a practice has persisted for a long period of time, it is entitled to respect, unless circumstances have changed or the proposed changes themselves build on experience. For the most consistent Burkeans, any effort to evaluate circumstances threatens to depend on abstract reason, which is unreliable.

But the more ambivalent Burkean, alert to Pascal's challenge and aware of Jefferson's words, would seek to identify the conditions under which Burkean minimalism is the best approach to constitutional law. Suppose, first, that originalism would produce intolerable results, in part because it would be too destabilizing. Suppose, second, that we have reason to distrust the theory-building capacities of judges, so that perfectionism is out of bounds. Suppose finally that, in general or in particular areas, traditions and established practices are pretty reliable. When these conditions are met, the argument for Burkean minimalism has considerable force.

Under some constitutional provisions, above all the equal protection clause, the Burkean approach is impossible to square with entrenched understandings in American constitutional law—and hence turns out to be self-contradictory. The reason is that some areas of doctrine have long operated on anti-Burkean premises. A form of rationalism, challenging certain forms of discrimination, has become part of the fabric of constitutional law. An even more serious problem is that for some forms of discrimination, it is exceedingly difficult to argue that long-standing traditions reflect wisdom, rather than power and injustice. Here the argument for a form of rationalism, subjecting traditions to critical scrutiny, is hard to resist, at least if we have a minimal degree of faith in our judges. In this context, Burke's celebration of "prejudice" makes no sense, and use of the word seems to be a cruel or stupid joke.

But in other domains, the Burkean approach can claim both to be consistent with existing law and to operate in a way that imposes appropriate discipline on judicial judgments. In the areas of separation of powers and national security, Burkean minimalism deserves to have a major role, as the Court has proceeded via small steps and with close attention to practices extending over time.[51] If Congress and presidents have settled on certain accommodations, there is reason to believe that those accommodations make sense. Justice Frankfurter offered the clearest statement of the Burkean position, with his suggestion that "a systematic, unbroken, executive practice, long pursued to the knowledge of the Congress and never before questioned, engaged in by Presidents who have also sworn to uphold the Constitution . . . may be treated as a gloss on 'executive Power' vested in the President."[52] In the particular context of national security, Pascal's challenge, emphasizing social learning over time, is least likely to support an aggressive judicial role against the elected branches, simply because this is a domain in which judicial expertise is unlikely.

THE BURKEAN DILEMMA

As I have suggested, Burkean minimalism is likely to run into serious problems whenever the legal system has operated for a long period on premises that Burkeans would reject. If an area of the law has been developed on perfectionist grounds, Burkeans might be tempted to abandon it, perhaps immediately; so too if rationalist minimalism has dominated a particular area of the law. But even more than most, Burkean minimalists respect the demands of stare decisis, believing as they do that entrenched decisions may well embody wisdom and that new departures are likely to have unanticipated adverse consequences, especially if existing law is embodied in social practices as well as judicial doctrines. As I have noted, Burkeanism risks self-contradiction insofar as it confronts an area of law that has long operated on non-Burkean grounds.

Burkean minimalists have no simple way out of this dilemma. It is certainly reasonable for Burkeans to conclude that their best option is to respect the existing decisions but to attempt to confine them, refusing to extend rulings that fall within the camp of perfectionism or rationalist min-

---

[51] See, e.g., Hamdi v. Rumsfeld, 542 U.S. 507 (2004); Dames & Moore v. Regan, 453 U.S. 654 (1981); Ex parte Quirin, 317 U.S. 1 (1942). For lower court decisions in the same vein from various stages in recent history, see, for example, Made in the USA Found. v. United States, 242 F.3d 1300 (11th Cir. 2001); Am. Int'l Group, Inc. v. Islamic Republic of Iran, 657 F.2d 430 (D.C. Cir. 1981); United States v. Allocco, 305 F.2d 704 (2d Cir. 1962).

[52] Youngstown, 343 U.S. at 610–11 (Frankfurter, J., concurring).

imalism. On this view, courts should not build on decisions lacking roots in long-standing traditions. They should narrow them without overruling them. It is easy to see how Burkeans might be drawn to this way of dealing with *Roe v. Wade*, refusing to reject the right to choose but allowing states to impose various limitations, at least if they are reasonably designed to protect legitimate public goals.

But it would not be out of bounds for Burkeans to conclude that the most indefensible departures from their preferred method must be sharply cabined or even overruled, at least if it is possible to do so without disrupting reasonable expectations or undoing a great deal of the fabric of existing law. Committed Burkeans might take this approach to *Roe*. On this count, rationalist minimalists are very different, tending to see *Roe* as established doctrine, even if they believe that it originally overreached.

These points help to illuminate the internal debate, among those with Burkean sympathies, about the proper approach to *Roe*. No Burkean is likely to believe that *Roe* was correct in the first instance; the best arguments for the Court's decision are rationalist or even perfectionist, emphasizing sex equality or personal autonomy. Skeptical of approaches of this kind, Burkeans reject those arguments. To the extent that they see *Roe* as an illegitimate departure from their approach, they might be willing to overrule it insofar as they could do so without undoing the fabric of current law or creating a kind of social upheaval. Majoritarian Burkeans would be especially comfortable with this route.

Other Burkeans believe, not implausibly, that *Roe* has become embedded not merely in constitutional doctrine but also in social practices, and that a decision to overrule it, especially in the name of some kind of theory, would be far too destabilizing. Consider here the Court's refusal to overrule *Miranda*—a refusal evidently based on Burkean grounds, seeing the Miranda warnings as ingrained in both law and society.[53] On Burkean premises, one can easily imagine reasonable disagreements on the question of whether to overrule *Roe*. Rationalist minimalists, ambivalent about both *Roe* as originally written and Burke, would be less likely to favor overruling the decision.

Many of the most vigorous disputes in contemporary constitutional law involve the proper resolution of this kind of dilemma. Recall that a similar

[53] See Dickerson v. United States, 530 U.S. 428, 443 (2000).

dilemma can be found in the aftermath of the *Lochner* era, in which the Court did not take a minimalist path, but on the contrary issued ambitious rulings that abruptly did away with decades of decisions. If these ambitious rulings were justified on Burkean grounds or otherwise, it was because of the absence of any legitimate basis for the decisions that preceded them— an especially severe problem in light of the fact that the decisions imposed serious obstacles to democratic initiatives.

If the decisions of the New Deal Court and the Warren Court deserve to be treated with more respect, it is because many of those decisions protect democratic prerogatives, and because many others have a strong claim to legitimacy, not least because they did not come as bolts from the blue. Perhaps the Court's rulings could claim a foundation in a legitimate but non-Burkean approach of one or another sort, calling for judicial deference to political judgments or for a democracy-reinforcing approach to judicial review. Perhaps the Court's rulings were sufficiently rooted in prevailing social commitments or in ordinary processes of case-by-case judgment; perhaps many or most of them were minimalist enough. In the end, a way out of the Burkean dilemma cannot avoid making some such assessment.

Unfinished Business

There are three more general issues in the background, and it is now time to bring them into the foreground. The first involves the foundations of Burkeanism; the second involves the grounds for specifying its domain; and the third involves the relationship between Burkeanism and shallowness.

Burkean foundations. As I have developed it here, Burkeanism does not rest on a belief that the past has any kind of inherent authority, or on a judgment that people owe some kind of duty to the past, or the notion that we are in some way constituted by our tradition (a claim at once true and vacuous). Burkeanism is best justified in pragmatic terms, on the ground that it is likely to lead to better results than the imaginable alternatives. But what can be said against pragmatism can be said here as well: it is necessary to offer some account by which to understand results as good or bad, and by itself, pragmatism cannot easily supply that account.

It is hard to see how pragmatists can be pragmatists all the way down, because they need some kind of account of the good or the right in order to decide what outcomes "work," or make pragmatic sense. So, too, it is hard to see how Burkeans can be Burkeans all the way down, in the sense that they need some evaluative standard, if only a very vague one, by which to know that traditions are good. Traditions cannot easily be said to be good simply because they are traditions. Would Burkeanism make sense for a nation that has experienced decades or centuries of injustice and oppression? Would Burkeanism, or Burkean minimalism, make sense for South Africa in 1950, or for contemporary Iraq, Iran, and Cuba?

Pragmatic Burkeans have several responses. They might believe that Burkeanism makes the most sense only for generally well-functioning democratic regimes, such as those in the United States and England. They might support this point with the suggestion that Burke's respect for traditions depends on a belief that many minds have participated in their construction. In an undemocratic regime, the many minds argument for Burkeanism is unavailable. Burkeans might add that the foundation for their own approach is (say) utilitarian, and that Burkeanism is the best way of promoting utilitarian goals. Alternatively, they might say that the foundation of their own view is more vague and less sectarian, in the sense that it attempts not to take a stand on the deepest philosophical questions. For example, they might be inclined to embrace a form of consequentialism that sees rights violations as part of what must be counted in the assessment of consequences.

In the end, Burkeans will have to generate some account to explain why traditions in general, or the traditions that they favor, deserve respect. We have seen that the best account, coming from Burke himself, emphasizes that many minds have contributed to long-standing practices, and thus give them a kind of epistemic credential. I will explore this account in more detail in the next chapter.

For purposes of evaluating Burkean minimalism in constitutional law, it is crucial to attend to the theory-building weaknesses of the federal judiciary. In light of those weaknesses, it might be possible to obtain an incompletely theorized agreement in favor of Burkeanism, at least in some areas—that is, an agreement in favor of Burkeanism amidst competing foundational views, or uncertainty about which of those views is correct. In some domains, Burkean minimalism might be acceptable to those with highly disparate foundational accounts.

Burkean domains. The second bit of unfinished business, directly follow-ing from the first, involves the specification of the domains in which Burkean minimalism makes sense. The analysis here has been inductive and impressionistic, with equal protection and separation of powers being taken as the polar cases. It would be much better to have a general account of when the grounds for Burkeanism are most likely to be satisfied, and to try to bring that account to bear on particular cases. The central point here is that Burkeanism is most appealing when traditions have been accepted by many independent minds. If so, we might be inclined to ask whether the relevant tradition does, in fact, reflect the independent judgments of many people, or whether it is likely to reflect instead a cascade, in which most people simply followed the initial practice. Or perhaps the tradition is a product of some kind of injustice and coercion—a kind of imposition from above, rather than a genuinely shared practice.

With an approach of this kind, we can offer a better explanation of why the equal protection clause, and perhaps the free speech principle as well, should not be understood in Burkean terms. For one thing, practices of discrimination on the basis of race and sex certainly do not reflect the inde-pendent judgments of those subject to discrimination. Often African-Americans and women rejected those very practices. To the extent that they were willing to accept them, their actions and even their beliefs were adap-tive to an unjust status quo.[54] The foundations for Burkeanism are absent.

Freedom of speech can be seen as a precondition for faith in traditions. If people are not allowed to say what they think, then the independent judgments that support traditions are much less likely to be found. At least with respect to political issues, it would be odd to say that a nation should allow suppression of speech if it has long allowed suppression of speech. An entrenched practice of censorship cannot provide its own foundations.

Return in this light to the cases with which this chapter began. The easiest involves the status of independent agencies. Such agencies have existed for many decades, and a judicial decision to forbid the independent agency form would wreak a kind of havoc—raising constitutional doubts

---

[54] On adaptive preferences, see Jon Elster, *Sour Grapes* (New York: Cambridge University Press, 1983); Cass R. Sunstein, *Free Markets and Social Justice* 256–58 (New York: Oxford University Press, 1997); Gary Blasi and John T. Jost, System Justification Theory and Research: Implications for Law, Legal Advocacy, and Social Justice, 94 *Cal. L. Rev.* 1119 (2006); and Christine Jolls and Cass R. Sunstein, The Law of Implicit Bias, 94 *Cal. L. Rev.* 969 (2006).

about the Federal Trade Commission, the Federal Communications Commission, the Federal Reserve Board, the National Labor Relations Board, and many other established institutions. There is no good reason to reject the Burkean suggestion that courts should not lightly unsettle existing arrangements, long accepted by Congress and the president alike.

The use of the words "under God" in the Pledge of Allegiance is harder. Of course the Burkean minimalist knows what to do, which is to uphold the Pledge in the current form in which it has existed for many decades. The problem, emphasized by rationalist minimalists and by perfectionists, is that millions of Americans do not believe in God—and their own convictions are rejected in the national pledge to the country that they love.

Some rationalists think that the establishment clause should be construed to require a principle of neutrality that would forbid government from referring to God in its national pledge. On balance, however, the better view seems to be that courts should permit the long-standing practice on the grounds that the Pledge is not a religious ceremony, that no one is required to speak the words, and that the mere use of the two words ("under God") is not so narrowly sectarian as to justify invalidation. With respect to a practice that has become so ingrained, it is probably best to say: *De minimis non curat lex.*

As I have suggested, the question of foreign surveillance cannot be resolved without carefully parsing the relevant statutes. It would be possible for Burkeans to say that if the president has long engaged in this practice, and if courts have long permitted him to do so, he can continue unless Congress has clearly said otherwise. If the Foreign Intelligence Surveillance Act clearly says otherwise, then the long-standing tradition should yield unless the Constitution is best read to give the president surveillance authority that is at once inherent and exclusive; and it is not easy to read the document, or the relevant traditions, to confer that authority.

The question of same-sex marriage raises different puzzles. There is a powerful argument that bans are a product of prejudice, in a bad sense, and hence that the judgments of many minds are not entitled to much deference. If courts should hesitate, it is largely for reasons of prudence. I shall explore this question in detail in chapter 5.

Burke and shallowness. Throughout I have treated Burkean minimalism as if it were committed to shallowness. In one sense this is obviously true:

Burkeans distrust theoretical ambition, and they hope for rulings that avoid abstract commitments or theoretical positions of any kind. But once we give an account of Burkeanism, it is not so clear that depth can be avoided. If Burkeanism is treated as a means of promoting some other goals—say, utilitarian ones—then it stands or falls with those goals. I have suggested the possibility of incompletely theorized agreements on behalf of Burkeanism, but it is not clear how incomplete the theorization will turn out to be.

For those who link Burkeanism and shallowness, there is an even more troublesome point. An understanding of Burkeanism might, in the end, require an account that is not so shallow after all. As I have presented it here, Burkeanism is most plausible if it is emphasized that traditions often reflect the independent judgments of many agents, and hence embody their dispersed wisdom or at least a good deal of sense. But once Burkeanism is understood and defended in these terms, it might appear at once deep and contentious—and thus prove unable to avoid disputes at the theoretical level. At that stage, the most that the Burkean might say is that if a practice embodies the judgments of diverse people, it is likely to be good, whatever our criteria for deciding what goodness entails. Perhaps that claim is enough to produce an agreement among those with competing theoretical accounts, or with a degree of confusion about the appropriate account.

BURKE AND MANY MINDS

My main goal here has been to offer a pragmatic understanding of Burkeanism, one that opposes each person's "private stock of wisdom" to the judgments embodied in long-standing practices. On this approach, Burkeanism is not best defended on the (unhelpfully platitudinous) ground that societies are constituted by their past, or on the (implausibly mystical) ground that the past has authority over the present. Burkeanism is best defended on the ground that those who follow entrenched practices, or who attempt humbly to build on them, will do much better than those who abandon traditions or evaluate them by reference to an abstract theory. And on this view, the apparent sentimentality of Burke's account, and his highly emotional writing, might themselves be understood in pragmatic terms. A sentimental or emotional attachment to traditions may be the best or per-haps the only way to prevent people from relying on their private stock of wisdom—especially in view of the risk that passions can be much stirred by those who attack traditions.

It is certainly possible to endorse a Burkean conception of the judicial role while rejecting a Burkean approach to politics in general. This position might be defended on the ground that while traditionalism is a helpful way of disciplining judges, citizens require no such discipline, and do not benefit from it. Jefferson, Pascal, and Bentham might be enlisted on behalf of this view; recall the suggestion that current generations are the ancients, because they have the most experience. Burkeans rely on a many minds argument; anti-Burkeans, emphasizing the experience of current generations, have a many minds argument of their own.

While the most committed Burkeans will favor their method in all domains, I have contended that the argument for Burkean minimalism is much stronger in some areas than in others. It has least force in cases involving official discrimination, where traditions are unreliable, and far more appeal in the area of separation of powers, where sensible practices are likely to have evolved over time. We can sharpen these claims by looking more closely at many minds arguments in a domain in which they have proved especially important: the definition of "liberty" under the due process clause.

CHAPTER 4

~

Due Process Traditionalism

We have seen that the Supreme Court and individual justices have often suggested that under the due process clause, rights qualify as such only if they can claim firm roots in long-standing traditions.[1] In denying the right to physician-assisted suicide,[2] for example, the Court appeared to settle on a kind of due process traditionalism, captured in the view that long-standing cultural understandings are both necessary and sufficient for the substantive protection of rights under the due process clause. On this view, no interest qualifies for protection under that clause if it lacks historical credentials; and interests that can claim such credentials deserve protection for that very reason.

Importantly, those who embrace due process traditionalism do not claim that *judicial* practices, as they develop over time, deserve support; they offer no plea for common-law constitutionalism[3] or for a strong rule of stare decisis. On the contrary, their focus is on the claims of the long-standing practices of "our people,"[4] not of our judges. It should come as no surprise to find that some due process traditionalists insist that judicial practices, constructing rights with reference to legal precedents, are illegitimate and should be overruled.[5]

---

[1] See, e.g., Washington v. Glucksberg, 521 U.S. 707 (1997); Michael H. v. Gerald D., 491 U.S. 110 (1989); Moore v. City of East Cleveland, 431 U.S. 494 (1977).

[2] *Washington*, 521 U.S. 707.

[3] See David A. Strauss, Common Law Constitutional Interpretation, 63 *U. Chi. L. Rev.* 877 (1996).

[4] Lawrence v. Texas, 539 U.S. 558, 593 (2003) (Scalia, J., dissenting) (quoting Reno v. Flores, 507 U.S. 292, 303 (1993). The full quotation—that a state regulation violates the due process clause only when it "offends some principle of justice so rooted in the traditions and conscience of our people as to be ranked as fundamental"—comes from Justice Cardozo's majority opinion in Snyder v. Massachusetts, 291 U.S. 97, 105 (1934).

[5] See *Lawrence*, 539 U.S. at 592–95 (Scalia, J., dissenting). Of course it is true that due process traditionalists must come to terms with the equal protection clause, which operates as a constraint on long-standing practices, such as discrimination on the basis of race. Due process traditionalists might

Although due process traditionalism has played a large role in the Court's decisions, it is highly controversial. Indeed, the major fault line within the Court itself has long been between those who seek to limit the reach of the due process clause to rights recognized by long-standing traditions, and those who believe that "evolving traditions" are what matter,[6] or that the Court legitimately brings its own moral judgments to bear on substantive due process questions. In striking down bans on sexual relations between people of the same sex, the Court explicitly relied on "evolving" judgments, rather than long-standing practices.[7] But the battle between traditionalist and more rationalist or critical approaches, requiring courts to scrutinize social practices, has yet to be resolved.

Due process traditionalists have not explained exactly why traditionalism might be an appealing approach to the due process clause. In this chapter, I attempt to deepen the understanding of Burkean approaches by exploring three families of explanations. The first and most ambitious points to the fact that traditions have been supported by many minds across long periods of time. The second sees traditionalism as a second-best substitute for more radical restrictions on substantive uses of the due process clause. The third justifies traditionalism on rule-consequentialist grounds, on the theory that traditionalism is likely to produce fewer errors, and less serious errors, than the likely alternatives.

What I shall call *many minds traditionalism* has intuitive appeal insofar as it attempts to anchor constitutional rights in practices that have wide and deep support. Many minds traditionalism has been defended in different ways by Burke[8] and Friedrich Hayek,[9] and under certain conditions, this defense is more than plausible. As we have seen, Burke's own account was largely *aggregative*, with the suggestion that numerous people have signed onto traditions and therefore given them epistemic credentials. Hayek's variety was *evolutionary*, with the suggestion that traditions have stood the test of time and are thus likely to serve valuable social functions. On both the aggregative and evolutionary accounts, the persistence of a

---

well acknowledge the tradition-rejecting nature of the equal protection guarantee while also insisting that long-standing practices are the best guide to understanding the scope of substantive due process.

[6] See *Lawrence*, 539 U.S. 558.

[7] Id.

[8] Burke, Reflections.

[9] See Friedrich Hayek, The Origins and Effects of Our Morals: A Problem for Science, in *The Essence of Hayek* 318 (Chiaki Nishiyama and Kurt Leube eds.) (Stanford, CA: Hoover Institution Press, 1984);

practice across many minds and many years makes it more likely to be correct, wise, or good. The two accounts might even be developed into a democratic defense of traditionalism, on the ground that participants in traditions are "voters," to whom judges ought to defer. In the end, however, I shall conclude that neither the aggregative nor the evolutionary account adequately justifies due process traditionalism.

If ambitious accounts of this kind fail, it might nonetheless be possible to defend due process traditionalism as a kind of second-best solution for those who would like to reject substantive due process altogether, but who accept the constraints of precedent. Some people think that the due process clause is best seen as purely procedural, that is, that the clause merely requires fair procedures before people are deprived of rights. On this view, restrictions on privacy or liberty are not objectionable merely because they intrude on important interests without adequate justification. The only constitutional requirement is that people get a hearing before the deprivation occurs. Many other people think that courts should approach legislation with a strong presumption of validity. (Recall the view of James Bradley Thayer, sketched in chapter 1.) If they are right, due process traditionalism can be understood as a precedent-preserving, indirect way of producing the results that would follow from either a procedural approach to the clause or a presumption of validity.

But there are two problems with this defense of due process traditionalism. The first is that it depends on a controversial judgment about what counts as a first-best approach. The second problem is that the purportedly second-best might turn out to be a wholly inadequate way of accomplishing the first-best goals.

A third justification for due process traditionalism is rule-consequentialist. The simple idea here is that whatever its faults, due process traditionalism produces better results than the likely alternatives. If judicial judgments about the substantive content of liberty were entirely unreliable, due process traditionalism might look plausible and even attractive by comparison. Perhaps traditions are not especially good, but perhaps they are not so bad, and perhaps it is better to tether judges to traditions than to ask them to think about the nature of "liberty" on their own. This argument

---

see also Michael Oakeshott, Rationalism in Politics, in *Rationalism in Politics and Other Essays* (Washington, DC: Liberty Press, 1998).

points to the most promising basis for due process traditionalism. In our world, however, it is not convincing.

My focus here is on traditionalist approaches to the due process clause, but if the analysis is correct, it should have implications for many other constitutional problems. We have seen that in numerous domains, traditionalism might be defended as reflecting the judgments of many minds. In those same domains, traditionalism might also be defended as a second-best substitute for an account that is preferable but forbidden by stare decisis, or on rule-consequentialist grounds. Whether such a defense could be made convincing cannot be resolved without an exploration of the particular domains. But the discussion of these justifications for due process traditionalism will bear on traditionalist approaches in numerous other areas.

The Test of Numbers

We have seen that Burke's central argument against the "private stock of reason," and on behalf of society's "general bank and capital," points to the many minds that are responsible for creating traditions. The "latent wisdom" of traditions lies in the fact that so many people have subscribed to them.

Suppose in this light that there is a long-standing tradition of allowing married people to decide how many children to have, and that there is no tradition of allowing people to commit suicide. If so, it seems clear that numerous people have believed that married people should be permitted to decide how many children to have, and that numerous people have also concluded that people should not be permitted to kill themselves. And if many people have reached these conclusions, perhaps the Court should pay careful attention to their judgments. Perhaps it would be foolish for the Court to use an abstract account, invoked by lawyers and theorists, as the basis for challenging practices long accepted by many. The aggregative view certainly so suggests.

We can readily see how the Condorcet Jury Theorem might support placing a great deal of faith in traditions. If the public has long rejected one alleged right, its judgments give a long-standing practice a kind of epistemic credential. Even if evolutionary pressures are put to one side, the support of large numbers of people suggests that traditions are likely to have solid foundations. On this view, the Court should be reluctant to reject rights that are deeply rooted in actual practice, or to create rights that are not so rooted, precisely because the Court's judges are few and the supporters of traditions are many. If the Constitution is unclear, the Court might do best to investigate long-standing social practices, instead of imposing a view of its own.

In many domains of social life, the aggregative view has considerable force. On television game shows, the most widely held view, within a studio audience, is usually correct. (If you ask many people about who has most recently played James Bond, the plurality view is highly likely to be right.) Sensible businesses often do best by surveying large groups of managers or employees, and taking the majority or average view. But as a defense of due process traditionalism, the aggregative view runs into three serious problems. Taken as a whole, these problems raise real doubts about the view that traditionalism can be supported by reference to the judgments of many minds.

WHAT PROPOSITION?

The Jury Theorem is concerned with the truth of certain propositions. If a majority of people believes that X is true, X is highly likely to be true (under the stated conditions). But what proposition does a tradition support? By participating in the creation of a tradition, have people really "voted" in favor of some proposition, and if so, which one?

Facts and values. It would be easiest to answer this question, and to speak in terms of truth, if the tradition reflected a judgment in favor of a proposition of fact. But is there a question of fact to which a tradition offers an implicit answer? Suppose that a society has long imposed capital punishment. It might be tempting to say that the tradition reflects a judgment that capital punishment has a deterrent effect. But such a tradition might persist not on deterrence grounds, but because most people believe that capital punishment is justified for reasons of retribution—in which case it would be hard to discern a factual proposition implicit in the tradition. Or suppose that a society has long permitted married couples to have as many children as they want, or that it has long forbidden people from committing suicide, smoking marijuana, or marrying people of the same sex. It would be difficult to say that the long-standing practice suggests support for some identifiable proposition of fact.

Much more plausibly, a long-standing tradition is best taken to suggest the truth not of some factual claim but of some normative proposition that the tradition endorses by definition, such as, "Married couples should be allowed to have as many children as they like," or "People should be prevented from committing suicide." Support for these propositions might stem from some judgment of value, or from a mixture of judgments of value and of fact. If many people have independently accepted or rejected such a proposition, their judgment might be entitled to weight. At first glance, the Jury Theorem so suggests.

But there are two objections to this view. The first is that the Jury Theorem is best taken to concern only matters of fact, on which it is easy to speak of truth or falsity. Many people might find it jarring to suggest that a judgment in favor of some tradition is "true." Is it sensible to say that if many people believe that married people should be allowed to choose the number of children that they will have, they are likely to be right? Skeptics will insist that words like *right* or *true* have no place in speaking about moral questions raised by same-sex marriage or suicide.

Of course it is sensible to speak in these terms if we are not skeptics about such questions, and if we believe that such questions have correct answers. But the simplest answer to skeptics is this: Those entrusted with the job of interpreting rights-protecting provisions of the Constitution had better avoid skepticism, because it is difficult or even impossible to construe the clause without thinking that it is possible to think well or badly about normative questions.[10] Courts cannot even decide what interpretive approach to follow without resolving such questions (see chapter 1). Suppose, for example, that courts are inclined to interpret rights-protecting provisions narrowly, on the ground that democratic self-government, and the will of the majority, should prevail unless the Constitution clearly requires otherwise. This is not a skeptical position; it depends on a position in favor of democratic self-government. Or suppose courts are inclined to accept

---

[10] An ambitious version of this view can be found in Ronald Dworkin, *Justice in Robes* (Cambridge: Harvard University Press, 2006). Contested moral or political arguments might be avoided if we could agree that the text of the clause forbids substantive due process, and if we believed that the word "liberty" should be given content by reference to the original understanding. But a controversial argument is needed on behalf of the view that the text should be controlling in light of many decades of decisions employing substantive due process, and also in defense of originalism.

originalism and to reject a claim for same-sex marriage or suicide on originalist grounds. As we have seen, originalists cannot be skeptics; they have to defend originalism.

I do not aim to sort out the philosophical issues here, though the grounds for moral or political skepticism are exceedingly weak.[11] The best approach might be to say that however we answer hard epistemological questions about the truth of normative claims, we should be able to agree that some normative positions are better than others, or more nearly right, or even right, and that this claim is enough to get many minds arguments off the ground. If large numbers of people have agreed that torture is generally wrong, or that human beings should not be permitted to enslave one another, the apparatus of the Jury Theorem can be brought to bear so long as all or most people are likely to be more nearly right than wrong. It follows that the Jury Theorem is indeed applicable to normative statements as well as to statements of fact.

The proposition in question. The second objection, briefly mentioned in chapter 2, is much more powerful. We might be able to agree that for a long time, many people have accepted the proposition that married couples should be allowed to have as many children as they like. But suppose that in 2050, the nation imposes a ceiling—say, of four—on the number of children that people may have. Does the tradition set itself in opposition to that ceiling? The answer may not be so clear. If the nation, or even a state, imposes such a ceiling, circumstances are likely to be very different from what they were when the tradition was in force. And if this is so, the proposition supported by the tradition is properly described in the following way: "Under the circumstances prevailing between (say) 1800 and 2049, married couples should be permitted to have as many children as they want." And if it is so described, it does not, in fact, bear on the problem at hand.

Perhaps circumstances have changed because of a significant problem of overpopulation; perhaps a new disease has prompted the new policy. Whatever the reason for that policy, the proposition supported by the tradition may not decide the question that arises if and when the government imposes the ceiling. Hence we may not be able to agree that many minds

---

[11] See, e.g., Bernard Williams, *Morality: An Introduction to Ethics* (Oxford: Oxford University Press, 1972).

have, in fact, committed themselves to the relevant proposition, which is whether a ceiling on the number of children is acceptable in 2050. And if the nation does impose that ceiling at that time, many minds are likely to have supported it under the current conditions.[12] Is it so clear that they do not deserve priority over the many minds who came before? By hypothesis, the current minds are speaking to the circumstances of the present, which no one has done in the past.

As I have suggested, the problem is that traditions apply only to the circumstances in which they governed, and when circumstances have changed, it is not clear that many minds have decided in favor of the particular tradition that is being invoked. This claim has general implications. Suppose that there is a tradition against physician-assisted suicide, extending from the founding until the day before yesterday. It remains possible that physician-assisted suicide under contemporary conditions is meaningfully different from physician-assisted suicide under previous conditions. Perhaps physician-assisted suicide is now acceptable because of technological changes that have made it possible for doctors to honor people's requests for death in a humane way. In that event, the proposition supported by the tradition does not speak to the current problem. Whenever a long-standing tradition is being violated, there is a good chance that the existing situation is indeed relevantly different.

It is true that due process traditionalists need not be entirely discomfited by this argument. Perhaps they must ultimately agree that traditions often will not speak, with any kind of clarity, to the current question, but perhaps that is no problem for them. They believe that a clear tradition is a *necessary* condition for a convincing substantive due process claim—and if no such tradition can be identified, the person who is claiming the right ends up losing. The real problem for due process traditionalism is the claim that a long-standing tradition is a *sufficient* condition for invalidation. If circumstances have changed, then the proposition for which the tradition speaks may not bear on the question at hand. To the extent that this is so, due process traditionalists will have to concede that even when a practice has endured for a long time, it may not justify invalidation of apparently tradition-rejecting enactments, because those enactments may not, on reflection, reject the proposition that the tradition actually supports.

---

[12] See Vermeule, Common Law Constitutionalism.

BIAS AND PREJUDICE

The Jury Theorem says that if group members are more than 50 percent likely to be right, the likelihood that the majority will be right approaches 100 percent as the size of the group expands. But suppose that all or most members are *less* than 50 percent likely to be right. If so, the likelihood that the majority will be wrong approaches 100 percent as the size of the group expands!

It follows that even if some proposition has passed the test of numbers, it will be incorrect if most people are more likely to be wrong than right. If most people have *wrongly* concluded that white people and African-Americans should not be allowed to marry, or that it is fine to include the words "under God" in the Pledge of Allegiance, then judges should pay no attention to them. This point raises exceedingly serious problems for many minds traditionalism.[13]

Condorcet himself emphasized that "prejudice" can introduce a distortion that makes aggregated judgments unlikely to produce good results: "In effect, when the probability of the truth of a voter's opinion falls below 1/2, there must be a reason why he decides less well than one would at random. The reason can only be found in the prejudices to which this voter is subject."[14] For due process traditionalists, the irony is that Burke himself wrote as if prejudices are reliable, contending that a "prejudice" is "wisdom without reflection, and above it." But if prejudices are systematic biases, then they are wisdom without reflection, and below it; and endorsement of a proposition by many minds is no protection against error.

Suppose that traditions reject a certain right—say, the right to same-sex marriage. If those who create the tradition are systematically biased, the tradition lacks epistemic credentials. For purposes of constitutional law, Condorcet's reference to "prejudice" suggests the possibility that the equal protection clause might be used to test the question whether the tradition embeds discrimination. Discriminatory traditions might violate the equality principle. Alternatively, judges who engage in substantive due process

---

[13] For an important qualification, see Krishna Ladha, The Condorcet Jury Theorem, Free Speech, and Correlated Votes, 36 *Am. J. of Poli. Sci.* 617 (1992). Ladha shows that the performance of a group can actually be improved if it includes worse-than-random guessers, at least if their biases are negatively correlated with the biases of the relevant experts. I am speaking in the text of correlated biases, that is, groups whose members are biased in the same direction.

[14] Condorcet, *Selected Writings* 62 (Keith Michael Baker ed.) (Indianapolis: Bobbs-Merrill, 1976).

might want not to entrench traditions but to ask whether there is, in principle, any distinction between a challenged practice and the practices that the tradition unambiguously supports. If no such distinction can be identified, a systematic bias might well be at work. At the very least, rationalist judges will insist on asking that question.

Consider in this regard Lord Devlin's influential discussion of the use of the criminal law to enforce public moral judgments, including the judgment that same-sex sexual relations are wrong. Lord Devlin asked: "How are the moral judgments of society to be ascertained?"[15] He answered, memorably: "It is the viewpoint of the man in the street—or to use an archaism familiar to all lawyers—the man in the Clapham omnibus. He might also be called the right-minded man. For my purpose I should like to call him the man in the jury box, for the moral judgment of society must be something about which any twelve men or women drawn at random might after discussion be expected to be unanimous."[16] The problem of course is that the views of "the man in the street," even after discussion with others in the same street, might be a product of a long-standing bias. The general point is that such a bias might mean that the proposition on which the tradition has converged is false or wrong. To the extent that this is so, the aggregative defense of many minds traditionalism, rooted in Burke, is in tatters.

Independent Judgments?

For the aggregative view to work, those who contribute to a tradition must be making independent judgments. This point raises distinctive difficulties.

Authoritarianism. It should be obvious that on the aggregative view, long-standing practices would have no epistemic force in an authoritarian society. In such a society, important traditions are an imposition; they are enforced by an oppressive government. If so, there is no reason to think that they reflect the judgments of large numbers of people. It follows that many minds arguments on behalf of long-standing practices are implausible in regimes that lack a high degree of freedom, at least if those practices are themselves an imposition by the few on the many.

---

[15] See Patrick Devlin, *The Enforcement of Morals* 14 (London: Oxford University Press, 1965).
[16] Id. at 15.

Burke's own claims have greatest weight in democratic societies whose citizens are able to assess and to refashion traditions. The force of those claims is greatly diminished in societies that have long lived under autocratic rule. We might therefore understand the conclusion that while many minds traditionalism makes sense for England and America, it is ill-suited to such nations as China, Iraq, and Saudi Arabia.

For purposes of substantive due process in the United States, the point about authoritarian societies might seem uninteresting. No one contends that judges in young democracies, such as South Africa, Hungary, and Poland, should decide on the content of rights by asking about the judgments of their authoritarian precursors. But even in free societies, there may be analogous problems. Perhaps a relevant tradition has been imposed by some on others through the force of law. The most obvious example is slavery. It is implausible to think that in (say) 1860, slavery could be defended by reference to the fact that many people lived with it. Or consider practices of discrimination on the basis of sex and disability. To the extent that these forms of discrimination have been imposed or encouraged by law, or otherwise imposed by some on others, it is odd to say that they should be perpetuated on the ground that many people have accepted them. The Jury Theorem is not easily invoked to suggest that the best way to evaluate social practices involving the treatment of those with mental illness, or the relationship between men and women, is to ask a large number of people and to accept the majority's answer.

As I have suggested, the equal protection clause is the natural source of judicial skepticism about long-standing practices. By requiring unequal treatment to be justified in principle, the equal protection guarantee explicitly rejects many minds traditionalism. But suppose that no serious equal protection issue is present, and that a tradition is challenged by those who contend that it has long been imposed rather than freely accepted. If the contention is correct, the force of the aggregative view is sharply diminished.

Cascades. An independent problem for the aggregative argument is that people's judgments may be the product of some kind of social cascade. When a cascade is at work, people are following one another; they are not making their own decisions in favor of the practice at issue. And when they are not making their own decisions, the practice may not, in fact, by supported by so many minds. Cascades come in two different forms: informational and reputational.

Cascades 1: the role of information. In an informational cascade, most people form their judgments on the basis of the actual or apparent judgments of others.[17] Consider a stylized example. Adams says that in her view, the death penalty deters crime. Barnes does not have a great deal of private information, but having heard Adams's belief, she accepts the proposition that the death penalty deters crime. Carlton might well believe that he must have reliable independent information in order to reject the shared views of Adams and Barnes—and he lacks that information. If he accepts the belief of Adams and Barnes on the ground that their belief is likely to be right, Carlton is in a cascade. David, Ellen, and Francis might well follow Adams, Barnes, and Carlton, at least if they do not have independent information that would outweigh the shared view of their predecessors.

This cascade involves a question of fact: whether the death penalty deters crime. But it is easy to imagine moral analogues,[18] in which Carlton follows Adams and Barnes, not because he independently agrees with them, but because he, like Barnes, does not have enough confidence in his own moral beliefs to reject the judgments of others who came before. People might believe that same-sex marriage should not be allowed, that mandatory school prayer is a good idea, that torture is sometimes acceptable, and that racial segregation is acceptable, not because they have thought these issues through independently, but because they are following their predecessors. On many issues of this kind, most of us lack a lot of independent information, and we pay careful attention to what we learn from others, which operates as a form of "social proof."

To Burkeans, the general objection is that many traditions persist only because of a cascade effect, depriving them of the epistemic credentials urged by the aggregative view. "Moral panics"[19] often reflect cascade effects. Perhaps some traditions are, to a greater or lesser extent, a product of moral

---

[17] See Sushil Bikhchandani et al., Learning from the Behavior of Others: Conformity, Fads, and Informational Cascades, 12 *J. Econ. Persp.* 151, 167 (1998).

[18] See Cristina Bicchieri, Informational Cascades and Unpopular Norms, in *The Grammar of Society* 176 (Cambridge: Cambridge University Press, 2005); Stanley Cohen, *Folk Devils and Moral Panics* (London: Routledge, rev. ed. 2003). Of course moral judgments might well be a product of relevant information, in which case moral cascades are informational cascades too.

[19] Id.

panics. And whether or not they are, it is easy to imagine traditions that continue through imitative behavior, ensuring the perpetuation of cascades, rather than independent support from many minds.[20]

For traditionalists, the best response is that an informational cascade is most unlikely to account for a tradition, simply because such cascades are often fragile. Suppose that people engage in certain behavior or accept certain beliefs solely on the ground that other people have engaged in that behavior or accepted those beliefs. Once private information begins to emerge, it should defeat the cascade. If people learn that a supposed cure for the common cold does not work, they will cease purchasing the supposed cure. If the emperor is really naked, someone will eventually say so, and he will be asked to put on some clothes. Informational cascades stop once people have sufficient information to disregard the signals given by the acts and statements of their predecessors.

Cascade effects can certainly account for fads and fashions. But traditionalists might urge that such effects cannot explain long-standing social practices, simply because those practices will be exposed if they are based on falsehoods or do not properly serve the people who participate in them. But for purposes of due process traditionalism, the problem of cascade effects cannot be dismissed so easily. A crucial problem is that in the key domains, people may not receive a sufficiently clear signal that the general practice is a bad one.[21] Slavery and segregation persisted for a long time, and millions of (white) people took them for granted. It would be truly astounding if we do not now live with practices that posterity will see as puzzling or even unconscionable. Outside of the constitutional domain, consider what has become a kind of tradition—a failure to intervene to protect people from genocide, even when the cost of providing such protection is not especially high.[22]

Cascades 2: the role of reputation. An additional problem is that peer pressure might ensure that people do not break the cascade, even if their private information suggests that they ought to do so. As a result, unpopular prac-

---

[20] See Bicchieri, Informational Cascades.

[21] See Gregory Moschetti, Individual Maintenance and Perpetuation of a Means-Ends Arbitrary Tradition, 40 *Sociometry* 78 (1977).

[22] See Samantha Power, *"A Problem from Hell": America and the Age of Genocide* (New York: Basic Books, 2002).

tices can persist for long periods of time. Many unjust practices—including discrimination on the basis of sex, sexual orientation, and disability—have persisted in large part because social pressures have led people to silence themselves.

Consider in this light the reputational cascade, in which people think that they know what is right, but nonetheless go along with the crowd in order to maintain the good opinion of others. Suppose that Allan suggests that female genital mutilation is a good idea, and that Barbara concurs with Allan, not because she actually thinks that Allan is right, but because she does not wish to seem, to Allan, to be ignorant or indifferent to entrenched social norms. If Allan and Barbara say that female genital mutilation is a good idea, Catharine might not contradict them publicly and might even appear to share their judgment—not because she believes that judgment to be correct, but because she does not want to face their hostility or lose their good opinion.

It should be easy to see how this process might generate a cascade. Once Allan, Barbara, and Catharine offer a united front on the issue, Deborah might be reluctant to contradict them even if she thinks that they are wrong. The apparently shared view of Allan, Barbara, and Catharine carries information; that view might be right. But even if Deborah has excellent reason to believe that they are wrong, she might not want to take them on publicly. As a result of reputational pressures, practices can persist, and even count as traditions, even though many or most people dislike or even abhor them. In the case of female genital mutilation, an account of this kind turns out to be quite plausible.[23]

Three Problems for the Aggregative Argument: A Brisk Summary

We should now be able to see that the aggregative defense of due process traditionalism runs into three problems. First: Even if a tradition has been accepted by many minds, it may not reflect approval of a proposition that is relevant to the question at hand. Second: Even if it does, those who created and perpetuated the tradition may suffer from a systematic bias.

---

[23] See Bicchieri, Informational Cascades.

Third: Even if no systematic bias is involved, many people may have simply followed the tradition, rather than independently agreeing to it.

It follows that even if a practice has been long-standing, it may lack the credentials that give many minds traditionalism its appeal. Many minds arguments, based on the wisdom of large groups, are often convincing not only on television game shows, but also in business and politics. But such arguments provide a fragile foundation for due process traditionalism.

THE TEST OF TIME

Perhaps due process traditionalists should emphasize not the test of numbers but instead the test of time. On one view, practices are likely to endure if and only if they are good. The central point is that an enduring tradition must be serving some valuable function. If it were not doing so, it would not be enduring. As we shall see, this point might ultimately form the foundation for a democratic conception of traditionalism, one that sees long-standing practices as a product of numerous "voters" extending over time.

The most elaborate version of this view comes from Hayek.[24] Like Burke, Hayek urges that existing moral commitments are not the product of any single mind; what Hayek adds is that our "undesigned moral tradition"[25] is a product of evolutionary pressures. That moral tradition covers the family and the rules of property, including "the rules of the stability of possessions, [the] transference [of property] by consent, and the keeping of promises."[26] Human beings were not clever enough to design the order "from which billions . . . now draw their sustenance." On the contrary, that sustenance comes from our "obedience to traditional customs which were selected by group evolution without [our] understanding them." The system of property rights developed "not because some liked or understood its effects, but because it made possible" faster growth for certain groups adopting that system.[27]

Hayek explicitly calls attention to evolution in this regard. What is crucial is the process of group selection, which "will select customs whose

---

[24] See Hayek, Origins and Effects.
[25] Id. at 321.
[26] Id.
[27] Id. at 322.

beneficial assistance to the survival of men are not perceived by the individuals."[28] Human beings are dependent for their survival on the observance of "practices which they cannot rationally justify, and which may conflict with both their innate instincts on the one hand, and their intellectual insight on the other." At least this is so for "the grown morals of tradition."[29]

In Hayek's hands, the villain of the piece is *rationalism*, which attempts to deduce moral principles from reason.[30] (The connection with constitutional debates should be plain.) In the end the "moral tradition remains a treasure which reason cannot replace, but can only endeavor to improve by immanent criticism, that is, by endeavoring to make a system which we cannot create as a whole, serve more consistently the same set of interests."[31] What rationalists ridicule as " 'the dead hand of tradition' may contain conditions for the existence of modern mankind."[32]

Mechanisms and criteria. Hayek's arguments grow out of his brilliant work on the price system. Hayek shows that prices do exceedingly well at aggregating dispersed information, and hence are more likely to be accurate than any committee or board.[33] His generalization of his argument extends his claims from prices to social traditions, which are also seen as an aggregation mechanism, but with a twist: traditions evolve, no less than species do, and those that survive are judged to be good. The extension and the twist have considerable intuitive appeal, but they face a central problem.[34]

In brief, those who defend traditions by reference to evolutionary accounts must undertake two independent tasks.[35] First, they must specify the mechanisms by which evolutionary pressures produce good outcomes. Second, they must offer some kind of account by which we can judge outcomes to be good. In biology, both the specification and the account are easy to produce. Natural selection ensures the survival of those who are most likely to be able to reproduce, and those who have survived are good

---

[28] Id.

[29] Id.

[30] See id; see also Oakeshott, Rationalism in Politics.

[31] Hayek, Origins and Effects, at 329.

[32] Id.

[33] See Friedrich Hayek, The Use of Knowledge in Society, 35 *Am. Econ. Rev.* 519 (1945).

[34] See Edna Ullmann-Margalit, The Invisible Hand and the Cunning of Reason, 64 *Social Research* 181 (1997).

[35] A superb discussion, from which I have learned a great deal, is Vermeule, Common Law Constitutionalism.

by reference to the criterion of reproductive fitness. In the domain of social practices, what is the analogue?

Hayek himself drew directly on natural selection, and if we are speaking literally of survival, his argument may be on firm ground. Perhaps some moral principles or commitments are necessary or at least extremely helpful for survival of the human species. In fact it is plausible to say that some such principles are hard-wired in human brains and have been specifically selected by their contribution to human survival.[36] Certain attitudes toward young children, and even respect for property rights, can be understood in these terms. But principles of this kind are most unlikely to be tested in modern substantive due process cases. If people are given a right to use contraceptives, to use marijuana or sexual devices, to seek physician-assisted suicide, or to ride motorcycles without wearing a helmet, the species will not be endangered. Human survival may well depend on some kind of system of property rights. But does it really depend on those aspects of traditional morality that are challenged in courts through a more critical or rationalist approach to the due process clause? Even if it did, many due process claims do not reject traditions; they simply cannot claim strong roots in traditions.

Perhaps survival is beside the point. Perhaps we should say that an enduring practice is likely, by definition, to promote economic efficiency (or some other conception of human welfare). If evolution itself is not at work, perhaps the mechanism is a form of market competition. The notion of "customary law," emphasized by Hayek himself, is helpful here.[37] Some people believe that the traditional rules of the common law were not really designed by judges. They are instead an effort to incorporate people's actual practices, as these have evolved over time. And if this is so, customary law is a product of a kind of spontaneous order, produced not by state officials, but by the individual decisions of the many minds that have contributed to that order.

To the extent that commercial practices are a product of a spontaneous order, reflecting market pressures, those practices might well operate to promote efficiency through the operation of an invisible hand. If commer-

[36] See *The Adapted Mind: Evolutionary Psychology and the Generation of Culture* (Leda Cosmides and John Tooby eds.) (New York: Oxford University Press, 1995).

[37] Friedrich Hayek, *Law, Legislation, and Liberty*, vol. 1, *Rules and Order* (Chicago: University of Chicago Press, 1973).

cial practices are not efficient, they will not survive; other practices will take their place. And if efficiency is desirable in the commercial arena, judges and legislatures might build on those practices, rather than displace them by reference to theories of their own. But this claim raises some immediate questions. What, exactly, is the market that produces traditional morality, and why is it so clear that this particular market functions well? Should invisible hands, or spontaneous orders, always be celebrated in the moral domain? And what does customary law have to do with substantive due process?

Recall the set of practices that have been or might be challenged in due process cases: bans on the use of contraceptives, on abortion, on certain living arrangements, on same-sex marriage, on physician-assisted suicide, on the use of sexual aids or certain drugs. To the extent that such bans are time-honored, it is clear that the political market, or the market for morality, has long favored them. But in a democracy, the political market and the market for morality hardly guarantee efficiency, and they need not promote welfare itself. In politics, interest-group pressures might well account for our practices. In markets, people face collective action problems, which may prevent them from achieving efficiency. In both politics and markets, people have incomplete information, and existing practices may be a product of that problem.

Even if the relevant "market" did promote efficiency, it remains necessary to defend the proposition that efficient traditions should be upheld because they are efficient.[38] In the commercial realm, it is plausible to say that courts should generally respect practices that have evolved in a way that ensures efficiency. But why should the due process clause be read to promote economic efficiency? Are bans on same-sex sexual relations defensible if they are efficient? What does the notion of "economic" efficiency even mean, in the context of claimed rights to end the use of life-saving equipment, to live with one's grandchildren, or to purchase and to use sexual aids?

The evolutionary defense of many minds traditionalism turns out to be no less fragile than the aggregative defense, at least in due process cases. To accept the evolutionary argument, we would need to identify mechanisms that ensure that long-standing practices are good by reference to

---

[38] See Vermeule, Common Law Constitutionalism.

some constitutionally relevant criterion. In the absence of such mechanisms, the most that might be said is that even if evolutionary practices offer no guarantees, the likelihood of judicial error is so high that judges do best if they attend to traditions. I will explore this (not unreasonable) claim below. But unless judges are wholly at sea, it might be best to explore whether the practice in question is, in fact, good, or good enough, by reference to a constitutionally relevant criterion. Evolutionary pressures are not enough.

DEMOCRATIC TRADITIONALISM

Perhaps it would be possible to understand many minds traditionalism in general, and the tests of numbers and time in particular, in a different way. On one view, the judgments of many people, extending over long periods, deserve respect on essentially democratic grounds. The claim is not that people's judgments are necessarily right or true. It is instead that they are, in a sense, votes. If the same votes have been made by numerous people across multiple generations, then they deserve respect.

We might describe this approach as a kind of democratic traditionalism. It supports traditionalist approaches to the due process clause not on the epistemic grounds suggested by the aggregative and evolutionary accounts, but on the theory that if so many citizens have committed themselves to a practice, their judgments deserve judicial deference for that very reason. Justice Scalia, speaking for a plurality of the Court, has argued in just these terms, suggesting that consultation of specific traditions ensures that judges will remain faithful to "the society's views."[39]

To be sure, it is difficult to see either Burke or Hayek themselves as thoroughgoing democrats. Both had serious reservations about self-government as an organizing ideal.[40] But if traditions have been created and repeatedly affirmed by free citizens, they might well be defended on democratic grounds. Courts might be asked to consult those traditions, and to uphold them, on the ground that the judges' "private stock of wisdom" has far less legitimacy than do practices that so many people have voluntarily accepted.

[39] See *Michael H..*, 491 U.S. at 115.

[40] On Burke's skepticism about democracy, see Herzog, *Poisoning the Minds*; for Hayek's complex and ambivalent view, see his own Whither Democracy? in *The Essence of Hayek*, at 352.

The initial problem for this defense of due process traditionalism is that democratic processes might and often do reject long-standing practices. Suppose that a democratic public challenges practices of discrimination on the basis of sex or sexual orientation, or that a democratic public concludes that the occupancy of buildings should be narrowly limited to "a few categories of related individuals."[41] On democratic grounds, why should the old tradition prevail over the current judgment, which includes the views of many minds as well? Democratic traditionalists will want to reply that long-standing practices have survived the test of time, but we have seen many problems with that particular test. For this reason, democratic traditionalists might have to agree that long-standing practices must yield before an explicit democratic repudiation. Perhaps they will ask for a clear democratic judgment in opposition to the tradition; but if such a judgment has been made, traditions will have to bow before democracy.

What remains, for such traditionalists, is the narrower but nonetheless important claim that courts should not lightly reject long-standing practices on their own. If a plaintiff's claim cannot find support in such practices, judges should reject it. This approach is undoubtedly attractive, for it might be seen as doubly democratic. First, it refuses to permit plaintiffs to attack long-standing practices. Second, the refusal operates to support existing legislation against judicial attack. The problem with this position is that for reasons explored above, traditions may lack anything like a good democratic pedigree. They might be an imposition. They might reflect a systematic bias. People might have supported traditions not because they like them, but because they are following their predecessors. The problems with the aggregative and evolutionary accounts turn out to beset democratic traditionalism as well.

To be sure, those problems need not be taken as decisive. We could imagine domains in which practices are not an imposition, are unlikely to reflect a bias, and have been perpetuated by a large number of independent judgments. All that can be said in the abstract is that in many cases in which long-standing practices are challenged, democratic traditionalism will not have much force.

---

[41] See *Moore*, 431 U.S. at 494.

TRADITIONALISM AS A SECOND-BEST SOLUTION

There are other grounds for due process traditionalism. Most obviously, the effort to root substantive due process in long-standing practices might operate as a second-best substitute for another, preferable approach.

First-Best, Second-Best

Many people believe that the due process clause is purely procedural and that the whole idea of substantive due process is unrooted in the text of the Constitution.[42] The simple idea here is that the text says that governments may not deprive people of "life, liberty, or property, without due process of law." These words seem to suggest that if governments are to deprive people of life, liberty, or property, they must provide a fair hearing ("due process of law"). It follows that if government is going to lock you up or take your property, or for that matter execute you ("life"), it cannot do so without some kind of procedure.

To say the least, this is an extremely important safeguard. But it is a limited one. So long as the government has provided you with a fair procedure, it can do as it wishes. On this reading, the government is permitted to ban contraceptives, to forbid people to have abortions, to stop grandparents from living with their grandchildren, to require people to become sterilized. Nothing in the due process clause suggests "substantive," as opposed to procedural, protection of liberty.

On this understanding of the text, the best approach would be to abandon substantive due process altogether. But for those who care about precedent, it would seem too late in the day to take that approach, which would challenge not merely the Court's most controversial exercises in substantive due process,[43] but also a range of decisions that are firmly entrenched in constitutional law.[44] If those decisions are taken as given, due process traditionalism might be seen to be a second-best substitute for the complete abandonment of substantive due process. Here is the crucial point: With

[42] See, e.g., John Hart Ely, *Democracy and Distrust: A Theory of Judicial Review* (Cambridge: Harvard University Press, 1981).

[43] See Roe v. Wade, 410 U.S. 113 (1973).

[44] See Meyer v. Nebraska, 262 U.S. 390 (1923); Pierce v. Society of Sisters, 268 U.S. 510 (1925); Griswold v. Connecticut, 381 U.S. 479 (1965).

due process traditionalism, it should be possible to prevent other ventures in substantive due process while also preserving a great deal of existing law.

There is a second view for which due process traditionalism might be a second-best substitute. Recall the position associated with James Bradley Thayer, which asks judges to defer to any plausible understanding of the Constitution.[45] Whether or not Thayerism makes sense in general, perhaps it makes sense in the domain of substantive due process in particular, above all because of the difficulty in giving principled content to the idea of "liberty." It should be easy to see how due process traditionalism might be a second-best substitute for a Thayerian approach to the Constitution.

Suppose that judges believe that very few legislative decisions will actually violate long-standing understandings of rights, and that most people, invoking the due process clause, will be attempting not to vindicate traditions but to create new rights grounded in their own theory of what people should be able to do—as, for example, in *Washington v. Glucksberg* (physician-assisted suicide), *Roe v. Wade* (abortion), and *Lawrence v. Texas* (same-sex sexual relations). If this is so, then due process traditionalism is likely to operate as a kind of shield for government, one that produces results identical to those that would be achieved by a Thayerian approach. It is for this reason that committed Thayerians, aware that their general approach is both inconsistent with current law and unlikely to receive widespread assent, might be drawn to due process traditionalism. In fact it is easy to imagine an incompletely theorized agreement between proceduralists and Thayerians, both taking traditionalism as an acceptable second-best.

Here is a different way to understand the basic point. To decide difficult cases, judges must identify their preferred approach to constitutional provisions; they must also ask how that approach can be squared with existing law. If judges are committed to respecting precedent, they might have to depart from the reasoning and the results suggested by their preferred approach. From one perspective, the departure is actually the first-best, because it incorporates the (principled) commitment to respecting past rulings. When I describe traditionalism as a second-best, it is with the understanding that if the slate were clean, a procedural approach, or a Thayerian one, would be preferable.

---

[45] For the best treatment, see Vermeule, *Judging under Uncertainty*.

Three Problems

For both camps, however, there are serious problems.

Traditions can be swords. Traditionalism can operate as a sword against government, not merely as a shield in government's favor. To that extent, it disserves the goals of those who seek to cabin the role of substantive due process.

I have noted that in striking down President Bush's effort to use military commissions to try suspected terrorists, a plurality of the Court relied heavily on its judgment that conspiracy allegations had not, by tradition, been subject to trial in military courts.[46] The Court's decision was not based on the due process clause, but it would not exactly be stunning to find that traditionalism could lead to invalidations no less than validations. Indeed, two of the most prominent due process cases are examples. Justice John Marshall Harlan defended the outcome in *Griswold*, striking down bans on the use of contraceptives within marriage, by reference to what he described as the long-standing tradition of respect for sexual privacy within marriage,[47] and Justice Harlan's view is now taken to provide the most sensible understanding of *Griswold*.[48] And Justice Powell's plurality opinion in *Moore v. City of Cleveland* struck down a ban on family living arrangements on the ground that the ban was inconsistent with long-standing traditions.

Perhaps second-best defenses of due process traditionalism might recognize that on some occasions, the approach will require invalidation. But perhaps the fear of invalidation should not be taken as devastating to the second-best project, because new practices will frequently be distinguishable from those that came before, and hence will rarely be struck down under a traditionalist approach. On this view, *Griswold* and *Moore* are outliers and unlikely to have many successors. It is true that traditions may turn out to be swords, but traditionalists will insist that their approach will rarely require invalidation of democratically approved legislation.

Traditions unleashed. Even if this is so, there is an additional problem. We have seen that traditions can be read at many different levels of general-

---

[46] Hamdan v. Rumsfeld, 126 S. Ct. 2749 (2006).

[47] *Griswold*, 381 U.S. at 501 (Harlan, J., concurring).

[48] See, e.g., Planned Parenthood v. Casey, 505 U.S. 833 (1992) (citing Justice Harlan's approach); *Moore*, 431 U.S. 494 (citing Justice Harlan's approach).

ity, ranging from the highly particularistic to the very abstract. Because traditions can be read abstractly, due process traditionalism might not constrain discretion at all. On the contrary, it might turn out to be an invitation for judges to invalidate practices however they see fit. If judges read American traditions to create a right to sexual autonomy, bans on prostitution and incest would run into serious constitutional doubts. If judges read American traditions to suggest a right of free choice in the domain of marriage, bans on same-sex marriage would be in constitutional jeopardy. Judges often disagree about the appropriate characterization of traditions; and perhaps these disagreements will defeat the goals of those who favor proceduralism or Thayerism.

To avoid these problems, and to ensure that due process traditionalism will actually operate as a second-best, proceduralists and Thayerians have to urge that traditions, to count as such, must be read at a low level of specificity.[49] Specific readings are necessary both to cabin judicial discretion and to ensure that judges behave (roughly) in a way that proceduralists and Thayerians approve.[50] Thus Justice Scalia has urged that the problem with general readings is that they provide "such imprecise guidance" and "permit judges to dictate rather than discern the society's views." If judges are not bound "by any particular, identifiable tradition," they are not bound by the "rule of law at all."[51] If these cautionary notes are kept in mind, perhaps due process traditionalism can operate as a second-best, and in any case succeed in disciplining judicial discretion, if past practices are read at a level of great specificity.

Attentive to the arguments made thus far, a skeptic might respond that if past practices are so read, they will not offer guidance at all. We have seen that when read specifically, traditions govern only the periods and persons to whom they actually applied. There does appear to be a tradition in favor of allowing parents to have as many children as they like. But as we have also seen, traditions, read at a level of great specificity, may not "apply" in any context in which democratic processes have repudiated them. A traditionalist must acknowledge that specific readings of past practices

---

[49] See *Michael H.*, 491 U.S. 110.

[50] At the same time, specific readings will appeal to many minds traditionalists, who believe that the specific traditions have epistemic credentials, because those are the traditions of which many minds have approved.

[51] *Michael H.*, 491 U.S. at 115.

will have an irreducible evaluative dimension—at a minimum, requiring the judge to explain whether current circumstances are relevantly different, so as to render the tradition inapplicable. If a due process traditionalist will not allow states to restrict couples to two children, or to ban married people from using contraceptives, it must be because any difference between the past and the present should be deemed irrelevant.

But perhaps traditionalists need not be disturbed by this concession. Of course judges must characterize traditions, and of course characterization cannot be discretion-free. In insisting that traditions must be read at a level of great specificity, traditionalists are saying only that judges must avoid general characterizations that turn their an approach into a license for open-ended judgments about the substantive content of liberty. If this is their claim, the real problem is empirical, not conceptual: If specific readings are unlikely, then due process traditionalism will fail to serve as a second-best.

Optimistic proceduralists and Thayerians will think that failure is avoidable, and they will work hard to vindicate their optimism. They will devote every effort to reading traditions in such a way as to reduce the risks of open-ended judicial judgments. But as a matter of actual practice, they cannot exclude the possibility that their efforts will fail. Traditionalist approaches to individual rights might well turn out to be unstable.

First-best? The second-best defense of due process traditionalism will lack much appeal for those who count neither proceduralism nor Thayerism as a first-best. It is true that the text of the due process clause is naturally read to be purely procedural, but there are countervailing indications in the history of the Fourteenth Amendment,[52] and in any event the existence of a substantive component is well settled in current law. It would be a radical step to say that there is no such component—and to conclude, for example, that government could ban the use of contraceptives within marriage or forbid family members from living together. Within American culture, there seems to be broad and deep convergence on some form of substantive due process, captured in the view that certain intimate choices deserve protection against democratic intrusions, at least if those

---

[52] See Laurence Tribe, The Puzzling Persistence of Process-Based Theories of Constitutional Law, 89 *Yale L.J.* 1063, 1066 n. 9 (1980).

intrusions cannot be convincingly justified. To the extent that a purely pro-cedural reading of the due process clause is unappealing, second-best justi-fications of due process traditionalism will seem weak.

Thayerism has been defended quite powerfully,[53] but it has no supporters on the Supreme Court, and it will hardly seem a first-best to those who believe, as I do, that in some domains, relatively aggressive forms of sub-stantive due process are both legitimate (in view of the precedents) and desirable. To defend due process traditionalism as a second-best for Thayerism, it is necessary to convince skeptics both that they should sup-port a Thayerian approach to the due process clause and that traditionalism is a reasonable way of adopting the basic goals of that approach. Skeptics will not be easily persuaded.

RULE-CONSEQUENTIALISM

There is a final possibility. Perhaps due process traditionalism can be justi-fied on rule-consequentialist grounds. The basic idea is that if judges are unleashed from traditions, they will produce many bad results, and that if judges are tethered to traditions, they will do fairly well—simply because our particular traditions, with respect to substantive rights, outperform any catalogue likely to be produced by judges. At least this might be so if we consider the fact that democratic majorities, at the state or federal level, can create substantive rights, including rights of privacy, if they choose to do so. On this view, due process traditionalism is likely to produce fewer mistakes, and less damaging mistakes, than the alternatives.

A basic concern here is that the idea of "liberty," taken in the abstract, can be read in diverse ways, and there is no particular reason to trust judicial readings, even or perhaps especially if they are morally infused. It is true that the aggregative and evolutionary accounts do not provide adequate reason to accept many minds traditionalism in its most ambitious forms. But the real question is comparative, and perhaps we can agree that at least in the United States, traditional conceptions of individual rights are a good place to start. When such conceptions prove inadequate, political processes can and often do pick up the slack, as for example through statutory protec-

---

[53] See Vermeule, *Judging under Uncertainty.*

tions accorded to rights of privacy and personal autonomy.[54] And when traditions are palpably unjust, the equal protection clause is the natural route by which they might be challenged. If judicial judgments about the substantive content of "liberty" are highly unreliable, due process traditionalism might turn out to be the best imaginable approach.

The underlying questions cannot be answered in the abstract. Due process traditionalists fear that judicial judgments will reflect moral and political commitments that do not deserve special respect and that in any case ought not to be imposed on the nation's citizens. *Lochner v. New York*,[55] striking down maximum hour legislation and prompting Holmes's traditionalism, is the obvious example for most, whereas *Roe v. Wade* is the salient example for many. By contrast, those who reject due process traditionalism insist that judicial elaboration of the content of "liberty" is far more likely to produce better outcomes than an approach that is tied to long-standing practices. They favor a more rationalist or critical approach to the due process clause, in which judges question traditions by the light of reason, ensuring that they can survive the appropriate standard of review. They are likely to insist that the more rationalist or critical approach is not untethered, but builds carefully and incrementally on existing law. They might well contend that a minimalist form of due process rationalism, rejecting some traditions as baseless, is superior to traditionalism.

These are powerful arguments, and in the end I believe that they are persuasive. To those who fear judicial discretion, it might be responded that the appointments process, together with internal restraints on judicial judgments, creates real protection against the most serious risks. Judges do not create due process doctrine out of whole cloth; they rely on their previous decisions, and they rarely depart radically from them. If judges have the capacity to think well about our practices, and if the external and internal constraints on judicial discretion are real, the rule-consequentialist defense of due process traditionalism is unlikely to seem unconvincing. We are better off if traditions are a place to start but not to end, and if courts occasionally deploy a more rationalist approach, testing whether the tradition is sensible in principle.

[54] See, e.g., 5 U.S.C. 552A (Privacy Act of 1974); 35 U.S.C. 3501 et seq. (Right to Financial Privacy Act of 1978).
[55] 198 U.S. 45 (1905).

For judicial interpretation of the due process clause, it is not clear that the underlying disagreement between rationalists and traditionalists can be resolved in the abstract. Any resolution must depend on both evaluative judgments and predictions about judicial performance. To the extent that judicial rationalism is likely to produce confused and unappealing understandings of liberty, the argument for traditionalism gains force. To the extent that traditional understandings suffer from a systematic bias, as they frequently do, the argument for a dose of rationalism is strengthened. In the end I believe that traditionalism should be rejected in favor of rationalism. But at the very least, we should now be in a position to identify the questions on which reasonable people might disagree.

Traditionalism Chastened

The most ambitious defenses of due process traditionalism, drawing on Burke and Hayek, emphasize that many minds are necessary to constitute a tradition, and that many minds are far more likely to be right than those who deploy their private stock of reason. But the aggregative version of this view runs into three problems. First, numerous people may not have accepted a proposition that is relevant to the legal issue at hand. Second, many minds might suffer from a systematic bias. Third, many minds may have participated in a cascade, depriving the tradition of the degree of support that the aggregative view demands.

The problem with the evolutionary account is that it is hard to identify a mechanism to ensure that traditional practices are good, or even good enough, in any relevant sense. Democratic traditionalists insist that long-standing practices are supported by numerous "votes." But at least for the questions typically raised in due process cases, the same difficulties that undermine the aggregative and evolutionary accounts beset efforts to defend traditions on democratic grounds.

Alternative defenses see due process traditionalism as a kind of second-best substitute for a procedural account of the due process clause or for a form of Thayerism. Unfortunately, the substitute is likely to be quite crude, and it is not clear that a procedural account or Thayerism can be convincingly described as first-best.

It is also possible to defend due process traditionalism in rule-consequentialist terms. The central idea would be that our own traditions are generally good, and judicial judgments about the content of "liberty" are systematically unreliable. The rule-consequentialist argument, favoring traditionalism over rationalism, cannot easily be rejected in the abstract. On the one hand, it is easy to imagine a world in which the rule-consequentialist argument might be persuasively defended. On the other hand, it is most doubtful that this world is our own.

A Brief Note on Aspirations

Some people think that the Constitution should be taken to set out broad aspirations, and to serve as the basis of a challenge to long-standing practices. Such people think that ideal judges should not worry so much about their own potential errors; they should also grab opportunities to set things right. To those who have an aspirational conception of constitutional law, traditionalism seems to be a form of cowardice. Judges are attempting not to rock boats—to ensure that other minds have thought what they now think. But what about constitutional bravery? Is it not best for judges to generate a sense of constitutional commitments that embarks on a new course, or that seizes on emerging understandings to frame and concretize that course? These are the questions posed by constitutional visionaries.

Any answer must acknowledge that in some of the glorious moments in constitutional democracies, judges are hardly Burkean. They are willing to evaluate past practices in critical terms; they do not entrench them. Of course we would not favor these moments if traditions were generally excellent and if judges were generally stupid or evil. But in a democracy in which judges are capable of critical thinking, and responsive to the force of arguments, the relevant moments should be celebrated, not lamented. These are challenges to Burkeanism in any form.

It is now time to explore a different kind of many minds argument— one that points not to past judgments, but to contemporary ones. Should constitutional understandings reflect what people now think? It seems jarring to say so. But if many minds deserve respect, widespread public judgments may, in fact, have constitutional relevance. We should start with the problem of backlash.

PART III

Populism

CHAPTER 5

‿

Backlash's Travels

Let us define "public backlash," in the context of constitutional law, in the following way: Intense and sustained public disapproval of a judicial ruling, accompanied by aggressive steps to resist that ruling and to remove its legal force. In cases of backlash, many minds have rejected the Court's decision, and they have done so with conviction.

It is easy to imagine cases in which a controversial judicial ruling is likely to produce public backlash. Perhaps the ruling involves property rights, presidential power in connection with the war on terror, the use of the words "under God" in the Pledge of Allegiance, the placement of the Ten Commandments on public property, or same-sex marriage.

Let us simply stipulate that if the Court rules in a certain way in such cases, public outrage, embodied in the objection of many minds, could significantly affect national politics and undermine the very cause that the advocates of the ruling are attempting to promote. Perhaps the Court's ruling would prove futile or counterproductive, or produce overall social harm. Perhaps the ruling would set in motion forces that would ultimately lead to its own demise. How should the nation, or a social planner, want courts to respond to the risk of backlash?

My principal claim in this chapter is very much in keeping with my general claims about the judicial role: No sensible answer to this question can be given in the abstract. Any judgment must depend on certain assumptions about the capacities and characteristics of courts, democratic institutions, and the citizenry as a whole. Under easily imaginable assumptions, courts should ignore the risk of backlash and rule as they see fit. Under different assumptions that are also easily imaginable, the restraining effect of backlash is highly desirable, and it is very good when courts are affected by it. The risk of backlash has sometimes proved a deterrent to desirable rulings from the Court; it has also helped to deter rulings that are not at all desirable.

If these conclusions are right, they raise serious questions about a tempting and popular view, to the effect that courts should decide as they see fit and let the chips fall as they may. That view might ultimately be right, but it depends on controversial judgments about the fact-finding and theory-building abilities of both courts and the public.

As we shall see, those who believe in popular constitutionalism might well be led to the conclusion that judges should pay careful attention to the risk of backlash. For example, Stanford Law School dean Larry Kramer writes that under the original understanding of the document, "[f]inal interpretive authority rested with 'the people themselves,' and courts no less than elected representatives were subordinate to their judgments."[1] On this view, backlash deserves careful attention when it occurs, simply because backlash is a reflection of the judgments of the people themselves. And if judges anticipate backlash, they would do well to limit themselves accordingly, perhaps by invoking doctrines that allow them to avoid the merits, perhaps by ruling narrowly, perhaps by deferring to the elected branches. These forms of self-restraint reflect respect for the interpretive authority of We the People.

If the argument here is correct, the claim that judges should attend to the reality and prospect of backlash stands or falls on particular judgments about constitutional method and the capacities of courts and legislatures. If we believe that the meaning of the Constitution is settled by the original understanding of the ratifiers, then the people themselves are probably ill-equipped to uncover that meaning, and judges should pay little or no attention to the public's desires. But if we believe that the meaning of the Constitution is legitimately settled by reference to moral and political judgments, and if courts are not especially good at making those judgments, then popular constitutionalism—and attention to backlash—have far more appeal.

I shall defer until the next chapters a detailed treatment of the appropriate response to the risk and occurrence of backlash. My goal here is to begin to explore the grounds on which any such response must be defended.

[1] Id. at 8.

I attempt that exploration through an admittedly fanciful route. I specify a diverse array of nations, or lands, in which the analysis of backlash must take a distinctive form. Unlike Gulliver, backlash is not a person; but we can learn a great deal by investigating backlash's travels.

OLYMPUS

Let us imagine a nation—call it Olympus—in which judicial judgments are reliably right, from the relevant point of view, and in which public opposition to those judgments, when it exists, is reliably wrong. To make the example simple and intuitive, let us begin by stipulating that judicial decisions about constitutional meaning require moral judgments of one or another sort. On this assumption, the constitutionality of racial segregation, restrictions on the right to choose abortion, or bans on same-sex marriage turns, in significant part, on moral judgments. Perhaps the relevant practices are valid if and only if they can be supported by reference to justifications that are at once legitimate and weighty.

In Olympus, we are supposing that judges can assess that question reliably, and that any public backlash is based on grounds that are either illegitimate or weightless. For this reason, the argument for taking account of backlash seems very weak. At first glance, the duty of Olympian judges is to rule on the Constitution's meaning by reference to the relevant sources; if backlash occurs, it is by hypothesis irrelevant to the judges' job.

The first glance is essentially right. For those who believe that our world is Olympus, it is usually inappropriate for judges to attend to backlash. But things are not quite so clear, even in Olympus. To see why, consider the old debate between Alexander Bickel and Gerald Gunther about judicial exercise of the "passive virtues," captured in the Supreme Court's refusal to decide certain controversial questions.[2] Bickel seemed to think that the United States is, in an important sense, Olympus. He insisted that the Court's role was to announce certain enduring values—to discern principles that would properly organize constitutional life. Bickel believed that courts were in a unique position to carry out that role. In his view, "[C]ourts have certain capacities for dealing with matters of principle that legislatures and

[2] See Alexander Bickel, *The Least Dangerous Branch: The Supreme Court at the Bar of Politics* (New Haven: Yale University Press, 2d ed. 1986; originally published 1962); Gerald Gunther, The Subtle

executives do not possess."[3] Indeed, "Judges have, or should have, the leisure, the training, and the insulation to follow the ways of the scholar" in thinking about those enduring values.[4]

To this extent, Bickel showed great faith in the capacities of judges to think about what political morality requires. "Their insulation and the marvelous mystery of time give courts the capacity to appeal to men's better natures, to call forth their aspirations, which may have been forgotten in the moment's hue and cry."[5] Thus, "No other branch of government is nearly so well equipped to conduct" a kind of "vital national seminar," through which the most basic principles are discovered and announced.[6] Pressed by expediency and by short-term pressures, other institutions are poorly equipped to understand what principles are required, at least by comparison with the judiciary.

Nor was Bickel especially enthusiastic about "the people themselves." On the contrary, he wrote that "the people themselves, by direct action at the ballot box, are surely incapable of sustaining a working system of general values specifically applied."[7] In his view, "matters of principles" require "intensive deliberation" and should not be submitted to a direct referendum.[8] It should be clear that this is an emphatically Olympian conception of the role of the Supreme Court. What is perhaps most remarkable about that conception is how many people have shared it in the decades since Bickel wrote.[9]

At the same time, Bickel believed that a large and diverse society could not possibly be principle-ridden. Too much of the time, citizens of such a society would resist the imposition of principles, even if they were entirely sound. In this respect Bickel invoked the example of Abraham Lincoln, whose effort to accommodate principle and necessity seemed to him a model for the Supreme Court itself.[10] Bickel read Lincoln to be unambivalent in his condemnation of the institution of slavery, but also to believe

---

Vices of the "Passive Virtues"—a Comment on Principle and Expediency in Judicial Review, 64 *Colum. L. Rev.* 1 (1964) (criticizing use of justiciability doctrines to avoid principled decision-making).

[3] Bickel, *The Least Dangerous Branch*, at 25.

[4] Id.

[5] Id. at 26.

[6] Id.

[7] Id. at 27.

[8] Id.

[9] See, e.g., Dworkin, *Justice in Robes*.

[10] Bickel, *The Least Dangerous Branch*, at 66–70.

that immediate abolition was impractical, simply because it would meet with such widespread opposition. In Lincoln's view, the feeling of "the great mass of white people" would not permit abolition.[11] In his most striking formulation, Lincoln declared: "Whether this feeling accords with justice and sound judgment, is not the sole question, if indeed, it is any part of it. A universal feeling, whether well or ill-founded, can not be safely disregarded."[12] It is worth lingering over Lincoln's words. His claim here is that even if a moral commitment is right, and wrongly rejected, it cannot be "safely" imposed on a nation that rejects it.

Bickel argued that the Supreme Court has maintained a kind of Lincolnian tension, and that it has done so through the use of the "passive virtues," by which it refuses to decide cases, staying its own hand in deference to anticipated public resistance. In Bickel's view, a court that invalidates legislative policy "must act rigorously on principle, else it undermines the justification for its power."[13] The same is true when the Court validates a legislative action. But the Court has an alternative to invalidation or validation: It might simply refuse to decide. It might give the political processes relatively free play, because it has neither upheld nor struck down their decisions. In the contemporary context, the Court might refuse to decide how much gun control is too much gun control, or it might decline to say whether states can forbid same-sex marriage.

In Bickel's view, "No good society can be unprincipled; and no viable society can be principle-ridden."[14] The task of judicial review is to maintain both "guiding principle and expedient compromise"—and to do so by staying its hand in the face of strong popular opposition, however indefensible the opposition might be.

In response, Gunther was mostly aghast.[15] In his famous phrase, Gunther complained that Bickel seemed to believe that the Supreme Court should maintain "the 100 percent insistence on principle, 20 percent of the time."[16] By contrast, Gunther thought that the Court should be 100 percent

[11] Id. at 66 (quoting Abraham Lincoln, Speech at Peoria, Illinois [October 16, 1854], in 2 *The Collected Works of Abraham Lincoln* 256 [Roy P. Basler ed.] [New Brunswick, NJ: Rutgers University Press, 1953]).

[12] Id.

[13] Id. at 69.

[14] Id. at 64.

[15] Gunther, Subtle Vices.

[16] Id. at 3.

principled, 100 percent of the time. Accepting Bickel's basic conception of the Court's role as the elaborator of sound principles, Gunther insisted that the Court should not invoke the passive virtues as a basis for refusing to invalidate unconstitutional action. If government has acted unconstitutionally, courts should say so.

We should be able to see that both Bickel and Gunther write as if our world is Olympus—as if the Supreme Court has special access to constitutional meaning, understanding that concept in terms that acknowledge the Court's creative role in discerning the governing principles. Bickel and Gunther believed, moreover, that public backlash is not well founded—that it is essentially unprincipled, a refusal to act in accordance with constitutional commands. Undoubtedly they were influenced in this regard by their distinctive time, when the Warren Court was engaged in a series of projects, involving liberty and equality, that seemed (to many) required from the moral point of view. Recall here that Bickel's model frames the conflict between the Court and the public with the analogy of Lincoln's moral commitments opposing the intransigence of those who defended slavery. Recall too that the ban on racial intermarriage is the problem in which Bickel praised, and Gunther condemned, the Court for exercising the passive virtues by initially refusing to resolve the constitutional controversy.[17] In Bickel's view, the Court was prudent to stay its hand in a time when the nation was sharply divided on the issue of desegregation; an early invalidation of bans on interracial marriage could intensify social conflicts at a time when the Court was attempting to desegregate the schools. But in Gunther's view, the ban on interracial marriage was clearly unconstitutional, and the Court had no excuse for ducking the issue.

However we resolve this disagreement, the simple conclusion is that to the extent that our world is Olympus, it is not easy to defend the proposition that courts should care about public backlash. The most that can be said is that even in Olympus, courts might plausibly use the passive virtues so as to preserve the Lincolnian tension between principle and expediency. This is not a trivial point, but it is merely a qualification of the main conclusion, which is that because judges are right and an outraged public is wrong, backlash deserves consideration only rarely and only for prudential reasons.

[17] See Naim v. Naim, 350 U.S. 985 (1956).

THE LAND OF THE ANCIENTS

Now let us adopt different assumptions. Let us imagine that we have arrived at the Land of the Ancients, in which constitutional meaning is best understood in originalist terms. In this land, the meaning of the document is captured by the intentions of the ratifiers, or perhaps by its original public meaning. In the Land of the Ancients, all judges are self-conscious and unambivalent originalists.

Let us assume as well that the Supreme Court is especially good at discerning constitutional meaning, thus understood, and that the public is very bad at that task. Perhaps the public is essentially uninterested in the outcomes dictated by originalism. Perhaps the public is incompetent in thinking about what originalism requires. When backlash occurs in the Land of the Ancients, it is because the public's (legally irrelevant) judgments of policy and principle have been rejected by the Court's (legally sound) judgments about the original understanding. In this particular land, some members of the public are skeptical of originalism as such. Some people reject the outcomes that originalism produces. Many people reject originalism *because* it produces outcomes that they abhor.

In the Land of the Ancients, judges are entirely comfortable with democratic efforts to create new rights, going well beyond those in the Constitution itself. Suppose, for example, that if we refer to the original understanding, the Constitution is best taken not to create a right to choose abortion, and not to ban discrimination on the basis of sex. If political majorities seek to use political processes to protect the right to choose abortion, and to ban sex discrimination, judges in the Land of the Ancients will have no complaint.

Of course such judges will not permit democratic majorities to defy the original understanding—by, for example, denying African-Americans the right to vote or allowing legislation to have the force of law when it has not been presented to the president for his signature. But originalists emphasize that political majorities can supplement the Constitution's catalogue of rights. Of course they agree that citizens can produce constitutional change through using the ordinary channels for amendment.

If judges are right to commit themselves to originalism, it seems clear, at first glance, that judges would be wrong to take account of backlash. By hypothesis, the Court is correct on the key questions and the public is not.

Indeed, the situation here is exceedingly close to the situation in Olympus. Even or perhaps especially if the favored interpretive method is originalist, the public's views about the meaning of the Constitution are irrelevant. The Court should rule as it sees fit, whatever the public's response. With respect to backlash, we could easily imagine a working alliance between Olympians, who read the Constitution in moral terms, and originalists, whose lodestar is history. The alliance includes people with different interpretive methods who nonetheless agree that the Court ought not to attend to the risk and reality of backlash.

But there is a counterargument. Perhaps the passive virtues, and a Bickelian approach, make sense in the Land of the Ancients. Perhaps those who use the passive virtues, by refusing to decide cases, could be convinced that originalism is the correct approach and that the original understanding exhausts constitutional meaning—while also acknowledging that *no society can be 100 percent originalist 100 percent of the time.*

One reason might be Burkean—the existence of long-standing departures from the original understanding, some of which were permitted, and others engineered, by the Supreme Court itself. Perhaps a theory of stare decisis, or of respect for settled social practices, is necessary or appropriate in the Land of the Ancients. Perhaps some originalists have Burkean sympathies. If the nation has long allowed independent regulatory agencies, or if the Court has long banned sex discrimination, judges in the Land of the Ancients might not try to change the status quo, even if originalism condemns independent regulatory agencies and permits sex discrimination. Even in the Land of the Ancients, judges might not want to disturb long-standing social practices, notwithstanding the tension between those practices and the method of interpretation that they endorse. If so, judges might decide not to decide, simply to avoid undue intrusiveness on their part.

One version of this view is Lincolnian. Perhaps there are quasi-Bickelians even in the Land of the Ancients, who believe that adherence to the original meaning is what principle requires, while also insisting that prudence—understood as caution in implementing understandings rejected by the public—has an important place. Even if in principle nothing can be said to support the public's resistance to judicial adherence to the original understanding, the social consequences of judicial insistence on that understanding might well be unacceptable. Those consequences are especially likely to be unacceptable if the public is genuinely outraged. It follows that originalist judges might stay their hand, at least if they can do so without greatly compromising the rule of law.

Notwithstanding the large differences in interpretive methods, it emerges that the Land of the Ancients is pretty close to Olympus. There is a strong presumption that backlash is immaterial. But in extreme cases, there is a prudential argument for anticipating backlash, and for refusing to cause it, at least if the consequences would be very bad. An Olympian judge might hesitate before declaring that the Constitution requires states to recognize same-sex marriages. A judge in the Land of the Ancients might hesitate before ruling that the Endangered Species Act is beyond congressional power under the commerce clause, or that racial segregation, if required by the national government, offends no provision of the Constitution—even if such a judge believes that the original Constitution does not allow the Endangered Species Act and fails to forbid racial segregation at the national level.

It is true that in the Land of the Ancients, the views of the public have no interpretive authority; they tell us nothing about what the Constitution means. But a judge who works there might be willing to try to avoid controversial decisions, or rule in minimalist fashion, in order to avoid especially bad consequences. Crucially, such a judge will want to see that the use of such strategies can itself be justified by reference to the original understanding. Perhaps the relevant strategies can be so justified, and perhaps they will allow courts some room to maneuver. At the very least, an originalist judge might dare to hope so.

LOCHNERLAND

Now let us alter our assumptions in a more significant way. In the land that I now propose to investigate, things are closer to Olympus than to the Land of the Ancients in the following respect: Constitutional meaning is properly, or even inevitably, a product of the political or moral judgments of the interpreter. Let us assume further that interpreters, to qualify as such, cannot be freestanding moral or political arbiters; they owe a duty of fidelity to the relevant legal materials. Nonetheless, these materials contain significant ambiguities or gaps, so that ultimate judgments often depend on contestable views about policy and principle. Let us assume finally—and this is the key step, the departure from Olympus—that judicial views about policy and principle are systematically unreliable and that public backlash, when it occurs, is founded on good grounds, in the sense that the public's judgments are simply better than that of the Supreme Court.

In short, we are now speaking of Lochnerland, so named after the Court's decision in *Lochner v. New York*, invalidating maximum hour legislation.[18] In Lochnerland, judicial errors are inevitable. How, if at all, should the analysis of backlash be affected?

Judicial Error

It should be clear that under the stated assumptions, we should very much want the Court to take account of the risk of backlash. By hypothesis, consideration of backlash will move the Court in better directions. At a minimum, we might hope that the judges of Lochnerland will pay attention to public judgments as they are reflected in genuine backlash—perhaps by staying their hand, or by ruling narrowly and shallowly, if the risk of significant backlash is high. But we might well go much further. Indeed, the assumption that we are in Lochnerland would help to explain the influential views of James Bradley Thayer, suggesting that the Court should give the democratic process the benefit of every reasonable doubt. (See chapter 1.) We can think of Thayerism as a generalization of the idea that courts should anticipate backlash and be cautious if it is likely to occur.

To be sure, those who accept Thayer's views are far more ambitious than that. They believe, much more broadly, that the Court should generally defer to the public's judgments, and to its judgments about constitutional commands, unless those judgments are palpably wrong. (Thayer himself was speaking of Congress, not the public generally, but his argument is often understood in broad terms.) To say that courts should hesitate in the face of backlash is to offer a modest version of Thayer's general view.

Thayer's approach does leave a large gap, one that Thayer himself did not fill: By what theory can we tell whether there is a constitutional violation? Thayerism cannot possibly be a *complete* account of the judicial role, because the question whether there is a clear violation depends on the method by which the Constitution is read. We could imagine originalist Thayerians, who believe that legislation must be upheld unless the

[18] 198 U.S. 45 (1905).

violation of the original understanding is palpable. On this view, the legislature would receive the benefit of all reasonable doubts in the face of originalist challenges. We could also imagine Olympian Thayerians, who believe that legislation must be upheld unless the violation of relevant moral
principles is plain.

But the core point is that Thayerian approaches emphasize the likelihood of judicial error. In Lochnerland, attention to the risk of backlash
seems obligatory, simply because it produces better results by stipulation.
In Lochnerland, it is highly desirable for judges to anticipate public backlash and to attempt to avoid it. The reason is that judges will do better, in
principle, if they defer to an excited citizenry.

It is sad but true that the judges of Lochnerland might not willingly
adopt Thayerism or even attend to the risk of backlash. After all, these are
the judges of Lochnerland, and their judgments are systematically unreliable. Such judges are likely to err while also being confident that they are
unerring. Perhaps the judges of Lochnerland think they live in Olympus;
it would not be the first time. But perhaps a norm or practice of judicial
self-discipline might be developed, even in Lochnerland, so that fallible
judges, made alert to their own fallibility, adopt measures to limit their own
mistakes. Such measures might involve use of the passive virtues, designed
to reduce judicial intervention in American life; or minimalism, designed
to ensure a degree of narrowness and shallowness; or generalized deference,
designed to impose a heavy burden of proof and persuasion on those who
challenge legislatures.

Popular Constitutionalism, Jefferson's Revenge, and Condorcet

Let us now explore the idea of "popular constitutionalism" by considering
what it is actually like to live in Lochnerland. Many of those who embrace
popular constitutionalism believe that constitutional interpretation requires
judgments of basic principle, and they insist that those judgments are more
reliably made by the public than by the judiciary. And in this light, we can
see the close links among popular constitutionalism, judicial responses to
backlash, and Jefferson's plea for frequent constitutional amendment by an
engaged citizenry. If constitutional intepretation turns on judgments of
morality and fact, and if those judgments change over time, a "living constitution" might turn out to have a powerful Jeffersonian element—at least if

the public, and not the judges, breathes life into the document. Perhaps judicial anticipation of backlash can be justified in Jeffersonian terms, as a way of allowing public participation in ultimate conclusions about the meaning of the founding document.

In Lochnerland, the argument for judicial attention to popular judgments in general, and to backlash in particular, might be fortified by reference to the Condorcet Jury Theorem. We can certainly imagine a situation in Lochnerland in which (*a*) large populations have a constitutionally relevant judgment (about, say, free speech or privacy) and (*b*) most individuals are more than 50 percent likely to be right. If so, the majority is overwhelmingly likely to be right. If the population assents to a proposition that is constitutionally relevant, judges would do well to pay attention, perhaps especially if people's convictions are firm.

These claims raise many questions and serious doubts, not least from the Olympian point of view. I will return to those questions in the following chapters. The simplest point is that in Lochnerland, the argument for attention to popular backlash is very strong. When judges make constitutional judgments on their own, there is a serious risk of error. Anticipation of backlash, and humility on the part of judges, reduce that risk. And we can identify a sharp difference, in this light, between Lochnerland on the one hand and Olympus and the Land of the Ancients on the other. In the latter jurisdictions, there is no reason to think that most members of the public are more likely than not to be right on a constitutionally relevant proposition. Judges lack an epistemological reason to care about what the public thinks. In Lochnerland, things are altogether different.

ATHENS

Now suppose that there is no particular reason to believe that judges are especially good or especially bad at giving meaning to ambiguous constitutional phrases. Let us imagine that we are agnostic on that question, at least over long periods of time. We do not know whether we are in Olympus or Lochnerland. No global assessment is possible. But let us suppose that the Supreme Court operates in an essentially well-functioning democracy, in which relevant judgments are made through a system that combines reflection and reason-giving with accountability. Let us give this happy democracy a familiar name: Athens.

In Athens, we might well want judges to pay careful attention to the risk or existence of backlash. The reason is that backlash reflects the public's judgments about basic social questions—the best conception of equality and liberty, the proper understanding of religious freedom, the role of property rights, the power of the president. For democratic reasons, such judgments deserve respect whether or not they are likely to be right. A self-governing people deserves to be ruled by its own judgments, at least if those judgments cannot be shown to be wrong, in the sense of plainly inconsistent with the founding document.

It is here, in fact, that we might find another reason for Thayerism—a reason founded not on the risk of judicial error, but on the commitment to democratic self-government. In Athens, that commitment might well be taken to justify a high degree of judicial modesty. But even in Athens, there is a serious flaw in the use of this commitment to justify Thayerism. The flaw is that it is rooted in a misleading view of what self-government requires. The ideal of self-government comes with its own internal morality; it does not require respect for whatever majorities choose to do. Self-government has preconditions, including freedom of speech and the right to vote; judicial review might help to ensure those preconditions.[19] Self-government, properly understood, requires respect for a wide range of individual rights, which make that ideal possible. Judicial protection of those rights may be indispensable.

These are powerful responses to Thayerism in any form. But if judges do not have the capacity to make superior judgments on the relevant questions, Thayerism looks much more appealing. At the very least, we might be able to say that on democratic grounds, the Supreme Court should, in Athens, be reluctant to rule in a way that produces significant backlash—and it should attend closely to the existence of backlash when it does occur.

It should be clear that popular constitutionalism is alive and well in Athens. The commitment to popular constitutionalism is not founded on the view, held in Lochnerland, that the underlying questions are likely to be resolved correctly by the public and erroneously by courts. Instead the commitment rests on a judgment in favor of (one account of) self-government as such. A full account of judicial deference, in Athens, will require a great deal of elaboration. But we should now to be able to glimpse the

[19] See generally Ely, *Democracy and Distrust*.

possibility that on democratic grounds, judges might want to hesitate in multiple domains, at least if the preconditions for self-government are not themselves at stake.

Amendiana (Briefly)

In the United States, the Constitution is especially hard to amend, because changes must be ratified by three-quarters of the states. As a practical matter, the Supreme Court is generally the only institution that can revisit and reject its own decisions. But in many nations, constitutional rulings are much easier to override. In Canada, for example, the legislature is usually permitted to reject constitutional rulings by a simple majority vote. In South Africa, Hungary, Columbia, and India, constitutional amendments face far fewer obstacles than in the United States. Let us imagine, then, that we have come to Amendiana—a small nation whose constitution allows popular majorities to reject judicial rulings or to make constitutional amendments essentially as they wish.

The key point about Amendiana is that in that nation, judges need not much worry about public backlash, simply because the stakes are so much lower. If judges err, or if the public is greatly disturbed, a simple corrective is available. We could easily imagine that in Amendiana, courts will be much readier to ignore the risk of public disapproval. They can do so because they are secure in the knowledge that if public disapproval is intense, it can be channeled into law.

Of course the underlying concerns are not entirely absent from Amendiana. Constitutional change always requires significant effort, as does a legislative override, and judges might not want to force citizens and officials to make that effort if they are unsure that they are right. Anticipating intense public opposition, and humble about their own judgments, courts might hesitate to invalidate legislation even in Amendiana. But it is clear that they need not hesitate nearly so much if the public has a simple mechanism for response.

Our World and Welcome to It

We have now seen how public backlash might be analyzed as it travels through a set of imaginable worlds. For us, however, no clear conclusion has yet emerged. It is tempting but far too simple to contend that judges should simply ignore the risk of backlash and refuse to attend to it when it occurs. This was essentially Gunther's view, and it depends on the controversial assumption that we live in Olympus (or perhaps the Land of the Ancients). Undoubtedly Gunther was influenced by the context in which he wrote, involving judicial efforts to vindicate palpably sound principles of racial justice in the face of indefensible public opposition. But it should be unnecessary to say that that context is hardly the inevitable one in American political life.

We should also be able to see that Bickel neglected the risk of judicial error in the announcement and elaboration of moral principles. He assumed, wrongly, that the only reason for "prudence" was to maintain a Lincolnian tension. The assumption is wrong because judges might stay their hand not only for the sake of expediency, but also out of an awareness of their own limitations and their capacity for error.

Which world is our own? That question cannot be answered without making some controversial judgments. One person's Olympus will be another's Lochnerland. In any case our world does not fit any of the ideal types. My goal here has not been to reach a final judgment on the place of actual and anticipated backlash; it has been to suggest the kinds of assumptions on which any such judgment must be based. An understanding of backlash's travels provides the place to start. Let us now see how further progress might be possible.

CHAPTER 6

⌒

Public Opinion and Social Consequences

Judicial rulings can, and sometimes do, offend public opinion. They might even provoke outrage. If the Supreme Court ruled, today or tomorrow, that states must recognize same-sex marriages, national politics would undoubtedly be affected, and a movement for a constitutional amendment would be highly likely. If the Court said that the establishment clause forbids the use of the words "under God" in the Pledge of Allegiance, the Court would face a great deal of public outrage. If the Court struck down measures designed to protect against the risk of terrorism, especially in a period in which that risk is acutely felt, significant parts of the public would be outraged as well.

Many judges are drawn, on occasion, to interpretations of the Constitution that would disturb large segments of the public. How, if at all, should courts think about, or deal with, the prospect of public opprobrium?

A detailed literature attempts to show that the Supreme Court's decisions are generally in line with public opinion and that, in light of the Court's actual practices, the "countermajoritarian difficulty" is far less difficult than it might seem.[1] To this extent, a degree of popular constitutionalism, captured in a measure of public control of constitutional meaning, seems to be alive and well. The Court rarely embarks on courses of action that are wildly out of step with the strongly held views of citizens as a whole. But there can be no question that the Court sometimes works hard to reduce the likelihood and intensity of that outrage.

---

[1] For an early treatment, see Robert Dahl, Decisionmaking in a Democracy: The Supreme Court as National Policymaker, 6 *J. Pub. Law* 279 (1957). For a recent and broadly compatible discussion, see Klarman, *Jim Crow.*

The most famous example is *Naim v. Naim*,[2] in which the Court refused to rule on the constitutionality of a ban on racial intermarriage, largely because it feared that its ruling would provoke outrage, in a way that might diminish the Court's own authority. It is reasonable to speculate that the Court's refusal to decide the constitutionality of the use of the words "under God," in the Pledge of Allegiance, had similar motivations.[3] We have seen that the invocation of the "passive virtues" is often understood as an effort to ensure that the Court's timing is "prudent," in the sense of reducing the danger that judicial decisions will produce public reactions that will compromise the Court's goals.

The close connection between legal outcomes and community senti- ments was famously pressed by Edward Levi in his illuminating book on legal reasoning, published in 1949.[4] Levi contended that judges engage in "reasoning by example"—a process that strongly suggests a form of judicial minimalism. In Levi's account, reasoning by example has a powerful demo- cratic element, because the community's wishes are crucial in producing judicial judgments about appropriate analogies. Is discrimination on the basis of sex analogous to discrimination on the basis of race? What about discrimination on the basis of age, disability, and sexual orientation? Legal rules are often unclear in advance, and Levi insists that analogical thinking "provides for the participation of the community in resolving the ambiguity by providing a forum for the discussion of policy in the gap of ambiguity."[5] The legal process is highly sensitive to the fact that "people's wants change," and constitutional provisions themselves "come to have new meanings" in virtue of those changing wants.[6] If we understand how reasoning by exam- ple actually works, we will see "the decisive role which the common ideas of the society . . . can have in shaping the law."[7]

Unfortunately, Levi did not specify the mechanisms by which "people's wants" produce changes in constitutional law. Levi did emphasize the fact that people are able to participate, through the arguments of their lawyers, in the legal process itself. Competing examples, and arguments of policy and principle, are offered to the court, and those examples and arguments

---

[2] 350 U.S. 891 (1955).
[3] See Elk Grove Unified Sch. Dist. v. Newdow, 542 U.S. 1 (2004).
[4] See Edward Levi, *An Introduction to Legal Reasoning* (Chicago: University of Chicago Press, 1949).
[5] Id. at 1.
[6] Id. at 4.
[7] Id. at 5.

reflect existing social beliefs. In that sense, the legal process has a democratic element. Perhaps the judicial obligation to listen, and to offer reasons
in response to what has been said, ensures a connection between what
judges do and what the public wants. Indeed, Levi portrayed the legal
process as a kind of town meeting, involving an exchange of arguments
from diverse perspectives.

In this respect, Levi's argument is greatly overstated; the legal process,
dominated as it is by judges and legal conventions, is no town meeting. But
we might buttress his basic claim by noting that the appointments process
provides an element of democratic control as well. If the Supreme Court
interprets the Constitution in a way that sharply and regularly diverges
from the public's will, presidents will attempt to bring the Court into line.
In any case the Court itself tries to conserve its own "political capital," and
hence it is unlikely to reject a widely held view on many occasions in a
short period of time. Perhaps most important, the members of the Court
are part of the society whose constitution they interpret. They are unlikely
to interpret that constitution in a way that society as a whole finds abhorrent or incomprehensible. Here again, we can find a Jeffersonian element
in the American constitutional system, captured in a measure of continuing
popular control over constitutional meaning.

I do not mean to deny that constitutional law has a countermajoritarian
feature, and I have said that on prominent occasions, the Court has construed the document in a way that produces widespread disapproval. But
the Court is much more tightly connected to public consensus than we
often acknowledge. Those who like popular constitutionalism, or who believe that most people are likely to be right, should be comforted to find
that when the Court innovates, it almost always does so in a way that is
responsive to a widely held social judgment, or one that is clearly emerging.
For all its aggressiveness, the Warren Court can itself be seen, most of the
time, as reflecting rather than spurring social change.

My goal here is to investigate whether and why public opinion should
matter to judicial decisions. At first glance, it might seem clear that public
opinion is irrelevant. On a conventional view, the central goal of constitutional law, or at least judicial review, is to impose a check on public judgments, and sometimes to override those judgments even if they are intensely held. It would be odd to say that the Supreme Court should not
protect free speech or should allow racial discrimination if and because it

anticipates that the public would be outraged by protection of free speech or by bans on racial discrimination. The idea that the Court should anticipate and consider public opinion and its effects seems inconsistent with the role of an independent judiciary in the constitutional system.

Questioning the conventional view, I shall suggest two reasons why intensely held public convictions might matter—and in the process attempt to explain the Court's occasional reluctance to trigger public outrage, as embodied in use of justiciability doctrines, narrow rulings, and deference to elected officials. The first reason, explored in this chapter, is consequentialist; the second, explored in chapter 7, is epistemic. The consequentialist claim is that if a ruling would turn out to have terrible effects, judges should take those effects into account. It is tempting to think that judges should rule as they see fit even if the heavens would fall. But if the heavens really would fall, perhaps judges should not rule as they see fit.

The epistemic reason, which should now be familiar, involves humility. Judges cannot always know whether they are right, even about the meaning of the Constitution, and intense public convictions may provide relevant information about the correctness of their conclusions. Whether public convictions are pertinent depends in part on their foundations and in part on the prevailing method of constitutional interpretation. If the prevailing method makes constitutional adjudication turn on disputable judgments of fact or morality, the beliefs of the public may indeed be relevant. It is important, however, to know whether these public beliefs are subject to a systematic bias or to cascade effects. If so, there is much less reason to consider them, because they lack epistemic credentials. Here I shall be returning to some of the objections to constitutional traditionalism. As we shall see, the same problems faced by traditionalism beset populism as well.

To assess the consequentialist and epistemic reasons for considering public outrage, we need to distinguish between invalidations and validations of decisions of the elected branches. Courts have far less reason to consider public opinion before validating democratic decisions; if the public greatly objects to a law, it can respond by changing that law through democratic means. There is, however, a plausible rule-consequentialist argument for asking judges not to consider public opinion and its effects even in the context of invalidations: Judicial projections of public reactions may be unreliable, and judicial attention to those reactions may produce excessive timidity in the protection of either rights or institutions.

While plausible in the abstract, this argument depends on contestable empirical assumptions and may turn out to be wrong. Suppose that it is clear that a decision would outrage the public and that such outrage would be both intense and very harmful. If so, courts have reason to hesitate before invalidating the decisions of the elected branches. The Court's seemingly opportunistic use of justiciability doctrines, and puzzlingly narrow and shallow rulings, are often best defended in this light. I shall ultimately conclude that while the epistemic arguments for considering the effects of intensely held public convictions are fragile, the consequentialist arguments do justify judicial hesitation in some unusual but important domains.

While my focus is on intensely held public opinion and its consequences, the discussion will bear on several other questions. Nearly every public institution is barred from taking account of certain considerations that plainly ought to matter from a consequentialist perspective. The ban on consideration of certain factors often operates as a legal or moral taboo; but why? The most plausible answer is that in some settings, the overall consequences are much better if institutions refuse to take account of certain consequences. A larger implication of this answer is that in both the private and the public spheres, "role morality"—the particular moral principles associated with particular social roles—may be best justified on rule-consequentialist grounds.

Invalidations, Public Outrage, and Consequences

Let us focus on cases posing the question of whether intensely held public convictions should play a role in a judge's decision to vote to invalidate a decision of the elected branches, whether state or federal, on constitutional grounds. Outrage is the extreme case of a conflict between the Court and the nation, and for those concerned with consequences, it makes sense to focus on the extreme case.

To clarify the problem, consider the thinking of a member of the Supreme Court, Justice Bentham, who is a committed consequentialist (taking his name, of course, from Jeremy Bentham, founder of utilitarianism). Bentham is convinced after due deliberation of the following propositions:

1A. The ban on same-sex marriages is a violation of the equal protection clause.

1B. The ban on polygamous marriages is a violation of the due process clause.

1C. The use of the words "under God," in the Pledge of Allegiance, is a violation of the establishment clause.

1D. Capital punishment is inconsistent with the Eighth Amendment.

1E. The president may not commit troops to a military conflict without either a formal declaration of war or an authorization to use force from Congress.

1F. Racial segregation in a high-security prison is a violation of the equal protection clause.

Suppose that all six of these propositions are at issue in cases before the Court (it is an exciting term). In all six cases, the Court is deadlocked four to four; Justice Bentham has the deciding vote. Suppose finally that Bentham believes that if he votes as his convictions suggest, there will be extremely serious public opposition, going well beyond disagreement to outrage. In all six cases, he believes that the Court's decision will become highly relevant to national politics, and that those who side with the Court, and even those who do not vigorously oppose it, will suffer badly. In cases 1A–1D, he thinks that it is quite possible that many officials will refuse to accept the Court's decision, and the Constitution will be amended to overturn the Court's decision. In case 1E, troops have already been committed, and Bentham thinks that from the standpoint of national security, and protection of lives of American soldiers, the Court's decision is very bad. In case 1F, Bentham believes that if he votes in accordance with his commitments, so as to require immediate desegregation, officials will refuse to obey, and segregation will continue. What should Bentham do?

To orient the discussion, let us begin with two simplifying assumptions (eventually to be relaxed). First, Bentham has no doubt at all about the correctness of his views in the six cases. He is certain that he is right about the meaning of the Constitution. Second, Bentham has no doubt about his predictions about the consequences of the Court's decision. He happens to have an entirely accurate crystal ball, and he knows what will happen if the Court does as he thinks best, as a matter of principle.

For Bentham, the ultimate conclusion is straightforward. In cases that are rare but important, he will attend to outrage and its effects. His own theory of interpretation is consequentialist, and he is entirely willing to consider the consequences of his rulings. He is aware that some judges adopt theories of interpretation on nonconsequentialist grounds, but he thinks that if the consequences of a judicial ruling would be especially bad, all judges should be prepared to take them into account. Bentham takes very seriously the view that on rule-consequentalist grounds, he should not consider the effects of intensely held public convictions, because such consideration might lead to undue judicial timidity, encourage strategic behavior, or otherwise distort the judicial process. In the end, however, Bentham rejects the rule-consequentialist argument, concluding that in unusual cases, consideration of outrage is appropriate and will support use of the passive virtues, narrow rulings, and deference to elected officials. These are Bentham's conclusions; let us see how he arrives at them.

Kantian Adjudication

Most judges do not attend to public convictions at all. Perhaps Bentham (notwithstanding his name) will be willing to consider a practice of Kantian adjudication: Even if the heavens will fall, the Constitution must be interpreted properly. Indeed, Kantian adjudication appears to be the informal working theory of judges and lawyers, so much so as to make it plausibly outrageous for judges to defer to outrage. Though actual judicial practices suggest a far more complicated picture, the idea of Kantian adjudication seems to capture the conventional view about how courts should approach public opinion and its potentially harmful effects.

According to those who endorse Kantian adjudication, the proper interpretation of the Constitution has nothing to do with what the public believes or wants. The role of the Court is to say what the law is (under the appropriate interpretive method), and its conclusions on that point should be unaffected by the public's will. Indeed, a sharp separation between law and politics might be thought to depend, crucially, on a commitment to Kantian adjudication. Compare the domain of statutory interpretation. Suppose that Bentham believes that the Endangered Species Act compels the termination of a popular and nearly completed project,[8] or that the Civil Rights Act of 1964 permits affirmative action;[9] suppose too that both of these rulings will provoke public outrage. At least at first glance, it would seem implausible to say that Bentham should alter his votes about statutory meaning to avoid such outrage. Bentham should consult the standard sources of statutory meaning, above all the enacted text, and public convictions are neither here nor there.

In the context of potential invalidations, the argument for Kantian adjudication might seem even more forceful. Why should judges uphold unconstitutional measures—for example, racial discrimination or detention without due process of law or restrictions on free speech—merely because the public would be outraged if they refused to do so? Deference to public outrage seems hopelessly inconsistent with the role of judges in a constitutional system.

But for two reasons, there is a serious question whether judges should be unconditionally committed to Kantian adjudication. The first reason is that even Kantians typically believe that moral rules can be subject to consequentialist override if the consequences are sufficiently serious.[10] If total catastrophe really would ensue, judges should not rule as they believe that principle requires. Suppose that the consequence of a ruling consistent with 1E would be to endanger national security; perhaps judges should refuse to issue that ruling. Consider in this regard Justice Jackson's suggestion that his conclusion that courts should not enforce the military order to detain Japanese-Americans on the West Coast need not be taken to "suggest that courts should have attempted to interfere with the Army in carrying out its task."[11] In so suggesting, Justice Jackson is suggesting that if the consequences might be really bad, judges should hesitate.

Or suppose that the consequence of a ruling consistent with 1A would be merely to hasten a result that would have taken place without the Court's invalidation—while also heightening political polarization, promoting the electoral prospects of those who reject same-sex marriage, increasing hostility to gays and lesbians, and eventually leading to a constitutional ban on

---

[8] Cf. TVA v. Hill, 437 U.S. 153 (1978) (enjoining such a project under the Endangered Species Act).

[9] Cf. Steelworkers v. Weber, 443 U.S. 193 (1979) (upholding affirmative action plan).

[10] For an overview, see Larry Alexander, Deontology at the Threshold, 37 *San Diego L. Rev.* 893, 898–901 (2000).

[11] See Korematsu v. United States, 323 U.S. 214, 248 (1944) (Jackson, J., dissenting).

same-sex marriage. In this way, a ruling consistent with 1A would prove self-defeating in the particular sense that it would greatly decrease the likelihood that same-sex marriages would ultimately be recognized. Even a committed Kantian adjudicator might well hesitate to rule in the way indicated by 1A.

The second and more fundamental reason is that it is not clear whether the principle of Kantian adjudication makes much sense, at least not if it is defended on strictly Kantian grounds. The core Kantian claim is that people should be treated as ends, not as means.[12] One person should not lie to another, or trick another into doing his bidding, because lies and tricks treat people as mere instruments, and do not give them the respect that they deserve. Is Kantian adjudication necessary to ensure that people are treated as ends rather than as means?

Perhaps the answer is affirmative. Suppose that Justice Bentham hesitates to invalidate a law banning same-sex marriage because he believes that the public will be outraged, in a way that will produce overall harm. The plaintiffs might ask: If Justice Bentham fails to invalidate the law, not on the ground that he believes it to be constitutional, but to avoid other adverse consequences, is he not treating us as means to other ends? Why should our rights be sacrificed because their vindication would produce bad consequences?

Justice Bentham might respond that in taking account of the effects of his ruling, he is not treating anyone as a means. He is concerned with the protection of rights, and he fears that rights, properly conceived, might ultimately be undermined if he rules in the plaintiffs' favor. To assess that concern, we would have to understand exactly what sorts of adverse consequences he fears. I will take up that question shortly. For now, the simple point is that whether Justice Bentham is violating Kantian strictures is likely to depend on why he hesitates to protect the rights in question.

A natural defense of Kantian adjudication lies in the thought that the judiciary must remain faithful to the law; whatever judges might think of Kant, their duty is to say what the law is (and hence to disregard public disapproval however intense). In the end, this conclusion may be right, but as stated, it is a conclusion in search of an argument. I shall ultimately

[12] For a good discussion, see Christine Korsgaard, The Right to Lie: Kant on Dealing with Evil, 15 *Phil. & Pub. Aff.* 325 (1986).

suggest that Kantian adjudication might well be best understood as a kind of moral rule-of-thumb, or heuristic,[13] justified on rule-consequentialist or systemic grounds. The claim must be that certain people in certain roles ought not to consider certain consequences, because consideration of such consequences would likely lead to bad consequences. If, for example, the Supreme Court decided voting rights cases by asking whether one or another decision would have good consequences by helping the best political candidates, the social consequences would not be good. In short, the intuitive judgment that certain consequences, or all consequences, are off-limits to certain officials might itself be justified on consequentialist grounds. But to say this is to get ahead of the story.

INTERPRETIVE THEORIES AND CONSEQUENCES

If Bentham is inclined to consider the effects of intensely held public convictions, there is an immediate puzzle: What is the theory of constitutional interpretation that gives rise to Bentham's judgments in cases 1A–1F? Is it a consequentialist theory? Does Bentham hold it because of its consequences? A consequentialist had better give an affirmative answer. At first glance, any judgment about whether judges should consider public convictions and their effects turns on the underlying theory of interpretation.

To come to terms with this point, we should distinguish between Bentham's theory of interpretation and Bentham's theory of adjudication. We could imagine a judge who has a consequentialist theory of both interpretation and adjudication, that is, whose view about constitutional interpretation depends on the consequences, and who is alert to consequences in deciding how, exactly, to rule. Justice Stephen Breyer and Judge Richard A. Posner fall in this category.[14] Their accounts of interpretation are based on consequences, and they also think that judges should attend to consequences in particular cases. By contrast, we could imagine a judge who has a nonconsequentialist theory of interpretation, believing (for example) that originalism is the only plausible approach, but also agreeing that consequences matter when a judge is deciding whether and how broadly to rule. We could imagine a judge who believes that consequences are irrelevant

---

[13] See Cass R. Sunstein, Moral Heuristics, 28 *Behav. & Brain Sci.* 531 (2005).

[14] See Breyer, *Active Liberty* (invoking consequences to assess theory of interpretation); Posner, *Law, Pragmatism, and Democracy* (same).

both to interpretation and to adjudication. We could even imagine a judge who adopts a theory of interpretation on consequentialist grounds, but who believes that consequences are irrelevant to judicial rulings, once the appropriate method is applied.

It should be clear that Bentham is not an originalist; but why not? Suppose that Bentham rejects originalism because in his view, it would produce unacceptable consequences. Suppose that Bentham also believes that the Court should usually be reluctant to strike down acts of the elected branches, because a presumption of validity will lead to good consequences. Suppose finally that the other ingredients of Bentham's own approach to interpretation are somewhat eclectic. Perhaps he is inclined to require the president to be able to show clear legislative authorization for intruding on liberty, even if national security is at risk. Perhaps he believes that the Court properly takes an aggressive role in protecting traditionally disadvantaged groups and in protecting the most intimate of choices. Suppose that Bentham is ultimately prepared to justify his approach, however eclectic it may be, in terms of its consequences. If so, consideration of public outrage seems at first glance reasonable and perhaps even obligatory, at least if that outrage would lead to bad consequences.

Passivity, Minimalism, and Deference

If Bentham is inclined to consider public outrage and its effects in cases 1A–1F, he is likely to ask: What are my options here? Perhaps Bentham can refuse to address the merits at all, postponing them for another day. In case 1C, for example, Bentham might look for some ground, such as standing or ripeness, that would allow him not to express a view on the underlying issues. To see why, recall Alexander Bickel's influential discussion of the "passive virtues," outlined in chapter 5. Notably, Bickel did not specify the precise grounds on which courts should stay their hands. Was the ultimate concern the preservation of the Court's own authority, the risk of rebellion and violence, or something else? In any event, a judgment about the consequences of excessive intervention would undoubtedly motivate their hesitation.

Perhaps Bentham is unwilling or unable to exercise the passive virtues so as to avoid addressing the merits. Even if so, Bentham might be able to decide the case in a way that reduces the magnitude and effects of public outrage. He might ensure that the Court rules modestly or in a way that avoids theoretical ambition. In case 1A, for example, Bentham might say: "States must provide the incidents of marriage to same-sex couples; we need not decide whether states must make marriage itself available." In case 1B, Bentham might say: "States may not forbid religious institutions from performing and respecting polygamous marriages; we need not decide whether states must perform and respect such marriages." In either case, Bentham might attempt to avoid theoretically ambitious claims about the nature of "liberty" under the due process clause, or the ideal of equality under the equal protection clause. In short, a minimalist strategy, reducing or eliminating public outrage, might be tempting to Bentham.

Bentham is most unlikely to want to join the view of those justices with whom he disagrees on the merits; he will not be inclined to commit himself to an interpretation of the Constitution that he rejects as a matter of principle. Nor will Bentham want to misstate the actual grounds for his conclusion. But suppose that he cannot invoke any basis for avoiding the constitutional question, and that he is certain that if public outrage and its effects are considered, the Court should greatly hesitate before ruling in favor of propositions 1A–1F. Perhaps he could write a concurring opinion that starts with these two sentences: "I am not convinced that the prevailing view is correct in its interpretation of the Constitution. But in view of the appropriately modest role of the judiciary in a democratic society, I concur in the judgment."

To make this opinion plausible, Bentham would have to spell out, in some detail, exactly what is entailed by the second sentence. He might gesture toward his own propensity to error, pointing to the need to pay respectful attention to the considered judgments of other branches and his fellow citizens. He might add an explicit reference to consequentialist considerations, pointing to sharp social divisions and the potentially unfortunate effects of judicial intervention into a sensitive area. To see how an opinion of this kind might be elaborated, we need to investigate some details.

CONSEQUENTIALISM

Suppose that Bentham believes that actions must be evaluated by asking whether they produce good consequences, all things considered. Let us stipulate that Bentham's theory of constitutional interpretation is itself based on consequentialist considerations. If Justice Bentham is a consequentialist, of course, he will not be much interested in public convictions as such. The question is whether those convictions, or outrage, will produce bad effects. But if so, it would seem especially odd for him to refuse to consider public convictions to the extent that they bear on the consequences of one or another ruling.

Futility, perversity, and overall harm. We might imagine three reasons that outrage might lead to bad consequences. First, it might render a judicial decision futile. Suppose, for example, that in 1954, a ruling in favor of immediate desegregation would simply be ignored. An argument in favor of the controversial "all deliberate speed" formulation in *Brown v. Board of Education* was that it was necessary to ensure that desegregation would actually occur and that the Court's ruling would ultimately be obeyed.[15] (In the early 1980s, I clerked for Justice Thurgood Marshall, who argued *Brown*, and once he said to me, "After all the years I finally figured out what 'all deliberate speed' means: Slow.")

Second, outrage might make a judicial decision perverse, in the sense that it might produce consequences that are the opposite of those intended by the Court. In the political domain, it is easy to think of illustrations, such as when an environmental regulation imposed on new polluting sources turns out to increase pollution by increasing the life and use of old polluting sources. In the constitutional arena, we can imagine how a decision in (say) 1958, requiring states to recognize racial intermarriage, might have fueled resistance to racial desegregation and thus disserved the goal of ensuring compliance with the Court's desegregation decisions and the equal protection clause in general. Third, outrage may render a judicial decision neither futile nor perverse, but might produce overall harm, as when the Court vindicates a constitutional principle in such a way as to endanger national security. Some people insist that judges rightly interpret the Constitution with an eye toward consequences, above all to ensure that national security is not threatened by their rulings.[16]

---

[15] Paul Gewirtz, Remedies and Resistance, 92 *Yale L.J.* 585 (1983), is a valuable discussion of the role of public resistance, and outrage, in the selection of remedies.

[16] See Richard A. Posner, *Not a Suicide Pact: The Constitution in a Time of National Emergency* (New York: Oxford University Press, 2006) (arguing for pragmatic approach to the Constitution in the context of national security, in a way that allows the executive wide room to maneuver).

Judicial self-preservation. If Bentham is concerned with the risk of futility, he will immediately focus on a distinctive consideration, involving the Court's own political "capital." On one view, judges should attend to public outrage because of the particular risks to the judiciary itself. Lacking either electoral legitimacy or a police force, judges are highly dependent on public acceptance of their authority. If the public is outraged, that authority might well be jeopardized. And indeed, most academic and public discussion of the "passive virtues," and of judges' caution in imposing their will on the public, has been focused on this consideration.[17]

Perhaps a controversial ruling, involving the words "under God" in the Pledge of Allegiance or same-sex marriage, will increase public attacks on the Court, making the judiciary a salient target in elections and spurring jurisdiction-stripping bills and other legislative efforts to reduce the Court's authority and independence. If the Court is concerned about its own place in the constitutional order, and wants to maintain its legitimacy and power, it might take account of outrage as a method of self-preservation.

Judicial self-preservation should be only a small part of the picture, because the Court's authority has proved remarkably robust over time, and because harmful effects on the Court's legitimacy are only a subset of the consequences that count. The Court might well be unduly sensitive to the risk to its own authority, in a way that will distort its rulings on the merits. But there can be little doubt that this risk has, on occasion, led to a degree of judicial hesitation. And if a judicial ruling really would compromise the Court's own role in the constitutional structure, it may well make sense to exercise the passive virtues or to proceed in minimalist fashion.

Assessing consequences. Bentham will be interested in the full set of adverse consequences, not simply the effects of public opinion on the Court itself. If very bad things will happen as a result of a ruling consistent with 1A–1F, Bentham will be inclined to exercise the passive virtues, to proceed in minimalist fashion, and perhaps even to defer to the political process on the merits. But if Bentham attempts to investigate consequences more broadly, he will encounter an immediate problem: By itself, the idea of consequentialism is insufficiently informative. It does not tell him how to

---

[17] See, e.g., Bickel, *The Least Dangerous Branch.*

characterize the potential consequences, how much weight to assign to them, or even whether certain outcomes count as good or bad.

Suppose, as seems plausible, that *Roe v. Wade* led to a great deal of political polarization, which would not have occurred if the Court had refused to recognize a right to choose abortion or if the Court had proceeded more cautiously.[18] If so, did *Roe* have bad consequences on balance? That question cannot be answered without assigning weights to its various effects, including immediate legalization of most abortions in the United States. It is also possible that Bentham will conclude that for good consequentialist reasons, some consequences should not be considered at all. Bentham might ultimately adopt a form of second-order or rule-consequentialism, through which he blinds himself to certain effects of his decisions.

To see the difficulties here, suppose that Bentham has three options: (1) vote to strike down bans on same-sex marriage, (2) refuse to rule on the merits, or (3) vote to uphold such bans. Maybe Bentham thinks that if he takes the first course, same-sex marriage will be outlawed by constitutional amendment, raising risks of both futility and perversity. Maybe Bentham knows that if he refuses to rule on the merits, same-sex marriage will be widely permitted in the United States, and sooner rather than later. Maybe Bentham believes that if he votes to allow bans on same-sex marriage, legislation permitting same-sex marriages will actually be passed relatively quickly; the Court's unfortunate ruling will actually promote the achievement of a situation that (in Bentham's view) the Constitution now requires.

How should Bentham assess this possibility? Maybe Bentham believes that as a matter of principle, same-sex marriages ought to be recognized in a free society. But perhaps Bentham believes only that the existing Constitution is best interpreted to require states to recognize such marriages— and that it is also perfectly legitimate, and entirely appropriate, for a constitutional amendment to disallow same-sex marriages if We the People ratify that amendment. Whether the prospect of such an amendment counts as a bad consequence cannot be resolved unless Bentham makes supplemental judgments of various sorts. Bentham might believe that an amendment is not a relevant consequence, because his own personal views about same-

---

[18] See Rosenberg, *The Hollow Hope*.

sex marriage are immaterial; his legal judgments matter, not his personal views. If this is his belief, then there is no risk of either perversity or futility.

To be sure, Bentham might be willing to consider public outrage in deciding on the appropriate remedy for a constitutional violation, if outrage is relevant to the effectiveness of any such remedy; hence outrage bears on judicial selection of remedies. But if outrage will culminate in an amendment, perhaps Bentham need not and should not pay attention. If this is so, it is because the ultimate fate of same-sex marriage is none of his concern. This is a plausible view, but it ultimately requires some kind of consequentialist defense—as, for example, in the view that judges will do best, and things will be best on balance, if judges do not take account of the risk that their decisions will be rejected through amendment.

Even if Bentham's preferred ruling—to invalidate bans on same-sex marriage—does not produce an amendment, perhaps that ruling will mobilize opponents of the rights or interests in question, and demobilize those who endorse those rights or interests, in a way that will disserve some of Bentham's deepest convictions. Perhaps the ruling will alter the nation's political dynamics, promoting the interests of one party and undermining the interests of another. Perhaps the ruling will have no such effects, but perhaps it will sharply increase political polarization, leading to a great deal of hostility between those who approve and those who disapprove of the Court's decision. Bentham must decide whether these consequences matter and, if so, how much weight to assign to them.

Or suppose more particularly that Bentham's crystal ball tells him that if he votes to strike down bans on same-sex marriages, such marriages will occur, and be respected, in all states; that the nation will have an intense and hostile debate about the question; that the Republican Party will greatly benefit from the debate; and that a proposed constitutional amendment to ban same-sex marriages will ultimately fail. How is Bentham to assess these consequences? Perhaps he does not consider these consequences especially bad. Perhaps he does not much like consequences of this kind, but perhaps his commitment to the underlying principle is sufficiently strong that he is prepared to vindicate it so long as same-sex marriages will occur and be respected and so long as the proposed amendment will fail. Perhaps the increase in polarization, and the political consequences, are not sufficient to outweigh the desirable consequences that would follow from the ruling he favors. The simple point is that even if outrage leads to unintended or harmful consequences, Bentham cannot know that he should avoid outrage, because the good consequences might nonetheless outweigh the bad ones.

Or suppose Bentham's crystal ball shows that if he votes to strike down capital punishment, that form of punishment will cease in the United States for a long time; that the nation will have an intense and hostile debate about the question; that the Republican Party will greatly benefit from that debate; that a proposed constitutional amendment to allow the death penalty will ultimately fail; and that the Court itself will be subject to extremely harsh attacks for at least a decade. How should these consequences be assessed? Perhaps Bentham's commitment to the abolition of capital punishment, on grounds of constitutional principle, is very strong, and perhaps nothing in this catalogue of consequences outweighs that commitment. Why should human beings be executed, in violation of constitutional commands, merely because the nation will be more polarized, some politicians will win and others will lose, and the Court itself will come under assault?

As I have suggested, Bentham might believe that certain consequences— such as the prospect of a constitutional amendment or the favorable effects on one or another party—ought not to be counted at all. This conclusion would itself have to be explained on consequentialist grounds. If one party would produce better consequences than another party, is it so clear that consequentialist judges should ignore that fact? (What if a particular outcome would ensure the defeat of the Nazi Party?) Under ordinary circumstances, consequentialists should be prepared to accept a second-order constraint on judicial consideration of political effects, on the ground that the overall consequences would be bad if judges asked whether their rulings would favor one or another political party.

Compare the debate over *Bush v. Gore*,[19] by which the Supreme Court effectively ended the 2000 election in President Bush's favor. In that debate, no one contended that a member of the Court could legitimately take account of whether George Bush or Al Gore would be a better president. In fact some people criticized the Court's opinion on the ground that the Court was doing exactly that. It is interesting that even pragmatic observers, insistent on taking account of consequences, implicitly ruled that con-

[19] 531 U.S. 98 (2000).

sideration entirely out of bounds. Consider, for example, the views of Judge Richard Posner, who defends the Court's ruling on pragmatic grounds—as a way of ending a potentially chaotic situation—but without so much as hinting that the Court could ask which candidate would be a better president.[20] The puzzle for the committed consequentialist is: Why? The best answer is that the consequences would be very bad if, in resolving cases, judges asked themselves whether one or another candidate is better. We could generalize from this answer. Perhaps judges ought not to ask whether a constitutional amendment would ensue, on the ground that the overall consequences would be better if judges did not consider that question.

The most general point is that the consequentialist needs an account of value to know whether the various consequences are good or bad, and to assess the magnitudes of the various effects. The difficulty and contentiousness of the assessment might well lead courts to adopt a general presumption or even a firm rule against considering the effects of public outrage. But notwithstanding this point, it seems clear that in some cases, of which 1A–1F are plausible examples, bad consequences are inevitable, and consideration of those consequences will tip the balance against deciding the case in accordance with the principles to which Bentham otherwise subscribes. Thus far, then, use of the passive virtues, or of minimalism, will sometimes be the right response to the prospect of public outrage. And in some cases, Bentham might even be willing to defer to the political process so as to avoid especially bad consequences.

Judicial fallibility in assessing consequences: of rule-consequentialism and system design. If Bentham sits on the Supreme Court, however, he might well be nervous about certain forms of consequentialism. Let us relax a central assumption and assume that Bentham has no crystal ball. He likes to think that he is not at sea in deciding whether the public will be outraged, and he has a degree of confidence in his judgments about the likely consequence of that outrage in particular cases. But Bentham knows that he may be wrong. He is entirely alert to human fallibility, including his own, and he is aware that even if his own judgments are fairly good, others are not so lucky.

[20] See Richard A. Posner, *Bush v. Gore* (Cambridge: Harvard University Press, 2000).

There are three independent problems here. The first is a simple lack of information. A projection of intensely negative public reactions may be a shot in the dark. A projection of the effects of such reactions may be more speculative still, not least because judges may rely on sources of information that are themselves unrepresentative and therefore biased. The second problem is motivational. Desires can influence judgments, and judges who favor certain results, or who are generally self-protective, may make inaccurate judgments about the likelihood and effects of outrage. The third problem involves strategic behavior. If judges are willing to consider public reactions, and are known to be so willing, people will have an incentive to exaggerate their outrage and their likely response, producing a kind of "heckler's veto" against judicial efforts to interpret the Constitution.

Suppose that because judges lack crystal balls, Bentham thinks that consideration of the risk of public outrage will seriously complicate judicial judgments, without at the same time improving them from the consequentialist standpoint. Bentham would be inclined to consider the following view: Even if accurate judgments about public outrage would be, at least in extreme cases, a legitimate part of judicial thinking, the risk of error means that courts should not consider public outrage at all. Consideration of outrage makes judicial decisions more difficult and unruly. And in the end, consideration of outrage might make decisions worse, not better, on consequentialist grounds. Suppose that judges will see outrage when it does not exist. Suppose that judges will exaggerate the effects of outrage even when it does exist. Perhaps the natural human tendency toward self-protection will make judges risk-averse with respect to outrage. Perhaps they will give undue weight to the possibility that the Court will be sharply criticized in public (not itself an especially bad consequence) or face some kind of political reprisal.

Suppose too that because public attacks on the judiciary will be especially salient to judges, consideration of outrage would produce undue timidity, in a way that will make judges less likely to do what they ought to do. Perhaps the role of an independent judiciary would be seriously undermined by consideration of outrage. On rule-consequentialist grounds, Bentham would be willing to consider a prohibition on such consideration. History suggests that Bentham might well be right to do exactly that; in the domain of free speech, judges have tended to overestimate the adverse consequences of allowing the airing of dissenting views, especially in wartime.[21] If judges consider outrage and its effects, they might be inclined to overstate the problem, thus adding to the excessive caution that judges might already feel when the stakes and the heat are high.

There is another possibility. Bentham might ultimately reject the rule-consequentialist argument on the ground that he is only one person and hence powerless to ban consideration of outrage on his own. Even if this is so, a social planner, engaged in system-wide design, might support that ban. Such a planner might attempt to inculcate a strong norm, or even a taboo, against judicial consideration of public opinion, including outrage. Return to the question whether judges should ask if one or another political party would be benefited by a judicial decision. As we have seen, we should not want judges to ask that question; consideration of the political consequences would make the legal system much worse. Perhaps a similar argument justifies a general ban on consideration of public outrage, especially if judges cannot reliably assess the question of consequences. If they cannot do so, consideration of outrage may increase the burdens of decisions while also leading, on balance, to worse results.

The rule-consequentialist argument certainly cannot be ruled out of bounds a priori. But it is not at all clear that this argument can be made convincing, at least not in the abstract. Even if judges have fallible tools for considering public outrage, they are not wholly at sea. If the Court invalidated the use of the words "under God" in the Pledge of Allegiance, public outrage would be entirely predictable; so too if the Court required states to recognize same-sex marriage; so too if the Court dramatically restricted Congress's powers under the commerce clause. At least in cases in which outrage and its consequences are easily foreseen, it is hard to rule its consideration off-limits on rule-consequentialist or systemic grounds. Cases 1A through 1F are plausible examples.

The conclusion is that for consequentialist reasons, widespread public outrage is a legitimate consideration where it would produce serious harm. It is appropriate for judges to decline to resolve certain issues, or to rule narrowly and shallowly, if steps of this kind would make such harm less likely to occur. If this conclusion is not especially surprising in light of actual practice, all the better. We are now in a position to understand the grounds for that practice.

[21] See Geoffrey R. Stone, *Perilous Times* (New York: Norton, 2005).

Kantian adjudication revisited and some speculations about institutional morality. Let us return in this light to Kantian adjudication, captured in the view that judges should pay no attention to the risks of futility, perversity, or overall harm. Compare those who exercise the social role of doctors. In deciding what treatments to prescribe, doctors do not and should not ask whether extending the life of a particular patient will produce good consequences. Doctors are not permitted to prescribe ineffective treatments or to hasten death on the ground that the world would be better if certain patients died. Nor is it appropriate for lawyers, representing especially bad people, to collude with the prosecution to ensure a conviction and a stiff sentence. Defense lawyers are obliged to provide the best possible defense, and are not supposed to ask whether the consequences might be better if their clients were convicted.

Perhaps judges are analogous. Perhaps their social role requires them to rule consideration of certain consequences off-limits. Perhaps judges should think in the following way: My job is to decide as the law requires. In the most extreme cases, I might consider resigning from the bench, or I might consider engaging in a form of civil disobedience. But while exercising judicial power, my sole responsibility is to the law.

As we shall see in the next chapter, a central problem with this view is epistemic: Judges might be unsure what the law requires, and public outrage might be relevant to that question. But the deeper problem is that a consequentialist justification is required for most judgments about what is appropriately considered by either private or public actors. Institutional morality, and role morality more generally, might have to be defended in terms of its effects. The reason that lawyers should not ask themselves about the consequences of helping a particular client is that the legal system, taken as a whole, is far better if lawyers do not so inquire.

To be sure, the question is not identical for doctors. Human beings should be treated as ends rather than means, and there is a legitimate Kantian objection to a medical decision to hasten a patient's death on consequentialist grounds. But consequentialists, as such, might be able to agree that people should be treated as ends; treating people as means is a part of the set of (bad) consequences that count. We should also be able to agree that if doctors thought themselves entitled to ask, in particular cases, whether the world would be better if a certain patient lived or died, the consequences would be very bad. In any event, judges are more analogous to lawyers than to doctors. If their decisions really would be futile or perverse, or produce overall harm, they might well take those possibilities into account—unless rule-consequentialist arguments convincingly suggest otherwise. Kantian adjudication, and the distinction between following the law and civil disobedience, are best understood as products of an intuitive form of rule-consequentialism.

There is a broader point here about the moral obligations of those who find themselves in certain social roles. Nearly every public institution is barred from taking account of certain considerations that ought to matter from a consequentialist perspective. Jurors are not supposed to ask whether a particular verdict would contribute to an increase in Gross National Product or find a favorable reception among most of their fellow citizens. Panels for the National Academy of Sciences are asked to say what is true, whatever the consequences. It would be outrageous to ask such a panel to distort scientific findings about climate change, nuclear power, or tobacco in order to avoid public outrage (or to obtain public favor). Members of public institutions—including juries, National Academy of Sciences panels, and regulatory agencies—are not supposed to ask whether one or another conclusion would help their preferred political party, even if members of such institutions believe that the consequences would be much better if their preferred party were helped.

The ban on consideration of certain factors often operates as a moral taboo; but why? One answer is that in most settings, the overall consequences are much better if institutions refuse to take account of certain consequences. A virtue of assessing institutional morality in this way is that it permits us to explore whether, in fact, any particular taboo can be justified in consequentialist terms.[22]

Judicial hedometers and consequentialism writ (very) large. I have emphasized that outrage is an extreme reaction to a judicial ruling, and it is dis-

---

[22] Compare Bernard Williams's well-known suggestion that in certain domains those who make consequentialist assessments have "one thought too many." If someone makes such an assessment before deciding to save his wife rather than a stranger from a burning building, we might well conclude that he is having an excessive thought. See Bernard Williams, Persons, Character, and Morality, in *Moral Luck* 18 (Oxford: Oxford University Press, 1981). So too, it might be thought, for those in certain institutional roles. If a doctor asks whether a patient is benefiting society before undertaking a diagnosis, or if a judge thinks about the consequences for the unemployment rate of a certain ruling, excessive thinking is taking place. It is worth considering the possibility that Williams's claim is correct, but only for reasons of system design: The consequences are best if spouses do not think that way, and so too for doctors and

tinctly associated with a risk of bad consequences. But the more general issue is the nature of public opinion, and it is easy to imagine other reactions. Perhaps people would not be outraged. Perhaps they would be disgusted, dismayed, frustrated, or disappointed. Alternatively, they might have a range of positive reactions to a ruling. They might be happy, gratified, relieved, thrilled, delighted, or exhilarated. Perhaps those positive reactions will produce an array of valuable consequences. If the Court invalidated certain restrictions on the rights of property owners, surely many property owners would be pleased, and their positive reactions might have desirable economic effects. (Perhaps the consequences would be good for economic growth.) When the Court struck down the ban on same-sex sexual relations in 2003,[23] many people were undoubtedly elated.

Let us be fanciful for a moment. Suppose that all judges had in their chambers a well-functioning "hedometer"—a device that could produce accurate measures of people's affective reactions to judicial decisions. Should judges consider the hedonic consequences of their rulings, either in themselves or because of their eventual effects? Or suppose that judges could consult contingent valuation studies, in which people state their willingness to pay for certain judicial decisions.[24] People are willing to pay significant amounts to ensure the existence of pristine areas and animals; "existence value" is an established part of the practice of contingent valuation.[25] Surely people would also be willing to pay significant amounts to ensure the existence of certain legal outcomes; these too have an existence value, and sometimes that value is extremely high. Ought judges to pay attention to any relevant evidence? Such questions are admittedly peculiar, but we should try to figure out why.

For the committed consequentialist, it is tempting to answer that judges should consider all relevant consequences, not merely those associated with outrage. Negative feelings are themselves a social loss, and positive feelings are a social gain. And if negative feelings would result in adverse effects,

---

judges. For a critique of Williams's position, see Elinor Mason, Do Consequentialists Have One Thought Too Many? 2 *Ethical Theory and Moral Practice* 243 (1999).

[23] See Lawrence v. Texas, 539 U.S. 558, 578 (2003).

[24] See Stephen Breyer et al., *Administrative Law and Regulatory Policy* 335–36 (Boston: Aspen, 6th ed. 2006).

[25] See *Valuing Environmental Preferences: Theory and Practice of the Contingent Valuation Method in the US, EU, and Developing Countries* (Ian Bateman and Kenneth G. Willis eds.) (New York: Oxford University Press, 1999).

or if positive feelings would produce desirable effects, they should certainly count. A political leader, deciding whether to support a proposed bill, might well be influenced by negative reactions of this kind, not only because her reelection prospects might be affected, but also because she is a considered consequentialist. If judges have hedometers and crystal balls, and are therefore able to make perfect forecasts, the consequentialist judgment would seem to be that they should reach the same conclusion, considering not merely outrage, but the full array of effects of their decisions.

But for rule-consequentialist reasons, and from the standpoint of system design for real-world judges, that conclusion would be hard to defend. It is an understatement to say that judges lack reliable methods for measuring the hedonic effects of their rulings. Any attempt to try would undoubtedly be subject to distortions, including those that come from the judges' own beliefs and commitments. There are also questions about whether all hedonic effects should count in the social welfare calculus, independently of whether they should count in the judicial calculus: If people would be pleased at the continuation of torture or discrimination, does their pleasure count? If judges attempted the relevant measurement, and made its outcome relevant in hard cases, the consequences would be worse, not better. If judges should care at all about public reactions, the argument for doing so is strongest in the case of intensely held beliefs, above all outrage, because outrage is likely to produce the most damaging consequences. The effects associated with other hedonic states are exceedingly difficult to predict.

Bentham's Conclusion

With respect to public outrage and its effects, Bentham is left with two possible conclusions. Perhaps Kantian adjudication is ultimately best, because blindness to consequences is likely to produce the best consequences. This conclusion might be defended on several grounds. First, courts lack reliable tools for deciding whether outrage and adverse effects would be present; they might well produce false negatives and false positives. Second, consideration of outrage might produce undue timidity, especially in areas in which the Court's role is most important. If widespread outrage is taken as a legitimate reason for the Court to fail to act, then the Court will uphold government decisions that, by hypothesis, violate the Constitution, simply because people are going to be outraged at what the Constitution commands. If the document is taken as a kind of precommitment strategy, designed to check certain actions however intensely those actions are supported at any moment in time, then consideration of outrage will produce bad consequences, once those consequences are properly understood and weighted. Third, consideration of intensely held public convictions would undoubtedly lead to strategic behavior, making public outrage partly a product of the Court's very willingness to take it into account. If people are aware that their outrage will affect the Court, then they will have every reason to produce outrage, creating a kind of heckler's veto.

But another conclusion is possible, and to Justice Bentham it will seem more reasonable still: In unusual but important cases, judges are likely to have enough information to know whether outrage will exist and have significant effects, and in such cases they should hesitate before imposing their view on the nation. This claim helps to explain the view that the Court was right not to invalidate the ban on racial intermarriage in the 1950s[26] and wrong to rule so broadly on the abortion question in the early 1970s.[27]

It is easy to imagine analogues today, including invalidation of bans on same-sex marriage and a constitutional attack on references to God in currency or in the Pledge of Allegiance. In these cases, consequentialist considerations do seem to justify a degree of judicial hesitation. To the extent that judges proceed cautiously in cases of this kind, we are now in a good position to see why.

[26] See Naim v. Naim, 350 U.S. 985 (1956).
[27] See Roe v. Wade, 410 U.S. 113 (1973); see also Ginsburg, Some Thoughts on Autonomy.

CHAPTER 7

⌒

Public Opinion and
Judicial Humility

Justice Bentham cares about the views of many minds, because those views bear on the effects of his rulings. But Justice Bentham has no doubt about whether he is right. Let us now imagine a different judge, one who is not entirely confident of his views; he knows that he might be wrong. To clarify the problem, let us imagine that we are dealing not with Justice Bentham but with someone else, who happens to be named Justice Condorcet—so named, of course, because of his interest in the Condorcet Jury Theorem.

To clarify the problem, recall propositions 1A–1F, sketched at the outset of the previous chapter, and capturing a range of controversial positions on important questions. Let us suppose that Condorcet accepts those propositions, but he is not entirely certain that he is correct to do so. Let us stipulate that in these cases, Condorcet is aware that most officials and most citizens disagree with him about the right understanding of the Constitution. If so, Condorcet might find public opinion relevant not on the consequentialist grounds discussed thus far, but for an epistemic reason: *Intense public opposition is a clue that his interpretation of the Constitution is incorrect.* During World War II, court of appeals judge Learned Hand said that the "spirit of liberty is that spirit which is not too sure that it is right."[1] Justice Condorcet wants to respect the spirit of liberty as Hand understood it.

To make the argument most plausible, let us suppose that Condorcet's acceptance of propositions 1A–1F is inconsistent with the shared judgments of the president, almost all members of Congress, and the over-

[1] See Learned Hand, *The Spirit of Liberty and Other Essays* (Irving Dilliard ed.) (New York: Knopf, 1953).

whelming majority of state and local officials and ordinary citizens. Condorcet is inclined to hesitate on grounds of humility.

The Basic Argument

To understand his hesitation, return to the Jury Theorem and consider a mundane application from the constitutional domain. Suppose that there is a dispute about the original understanding of some constitutional provision—say, about whether the equal protection clause, as originally understood, forbids racial segregation. Suppose that Condorcet is interested in the original understanding and that he believes that the equal protection clause was, in fact, originally understood to ban racial segregation. If it turns out that Condorcet's view is an outlier, and is accepted by almost none of those who have studied the relevant period, the Jury Theorem suggests that Condorcet is probably wrong. And if most specialists are stunned by Condorcet's conclusion, Condorcet has particular reason to hesitate on epistemic grounds.

Alert to the Jury Theorem, Condorcet might think the following: I accept propositions 1A–1F. But most of the public disagrees with me. If crowds are wise, I may well be wrong, at least if the public's disagreement bears on an issue that is relevant to the legal conclusion. As in the context of traditionalism, it is useful to distinguish between judgments of fact and judgments of political morality. Suppose that Condorcet is not an originalist and that he believes that the constitutionality of capital punishment turns, in part, on whether that form of punishment has a deterrent effect. Suppose that the death penalty is constitutional only if it produces significant deterrence. On the basis of his own view of the evidence, Condorcet may doubt that there is any such effect. But if most people believe that capital punishment does, in fact, have a deterrent effect, then Condorcet might want to pay careful attention to their beliefs. Perhaps Condorcet is more interested in the views of specialists than in the views of the public at large; but if members of the public have access to relevant information, the view of a strong majority might bear on the factual question.

By contrast, suppose that the constitutionality of the ban on same-sex marriage does not turn on disputed facts, but instead on a judgment of political morality. Suppose that the question is whether the grounds for discriminating against gays and lesbians, in the particular domain of marriage, are legitimate. Is the Jury Theorem relevant? Suppose we agree that such judgments are in fact subject to evaluation, in the sense that the arguments that support them can be good or bad; if Condorcet's moral views are relevant to his legal conclusions, he had better share that belief. If a moral judgment is crucial, the views of the public might provide some clues about what morality requires. Condorcet is most unlikely to think that on moral questions, the public is always right. But if most people reject Condorcet's moral conclusions, he might worry that he is missing something or that his conclusions are wrong.

To come to terms with these possibilities, much will depend on the prevailing theory of constitutional interpretation. If Condorcet's theory is originalist, the views of the public should not matter; as should be evident, those views are not likely to tell Condorcet much about the nature of the original understanding. (As we have seen, the Jury Theorem suggests that he should be interested in the views of specialists.) But suppose that Condorcet's conclusions about the meaning of the Constitution do in fact depend on some judgment of political morality. If so, then the views of others might well be pertinent. And indeed, the Court's decision to strike down criminal bans on same-sex sexual relationships had a great deal to do with its perceptions of contemporary social values, in a way that suggested a hint of an implicit Condorcetian logic.[2]

Or consider the Warren Court's decisions to strike down racial segregation and to vindicate a right to privacy within marriage. Those decisions are reasonably taken to have responded to, rather to have rejected, widespread public convictions. It would be too much to say that the Warren Court was generally Condorcetian. But it would not be too much to say that many of the Court's most controversial rulings were actually in line with public opinion.

Suppose that Justice Condorcet is a perfectionist in the particular sense discussed in chapter 1. He believes that in cases 1A–1F, he is obliged to try to bring forward the best justification, in principle, for the fabric of existing law. The public's views might provide valuable information about which justification is best. Of course Condorcet will not be much interested in those views if they are irrelevant to what matters under his theory of interpretation (a point to which I will return). A strong division

[2] See Lawrence v. Texas, 539 U.S. 558, 572, 576 (2003).

between the domain of law and the domain of politics and morality would weaken and possibly eliminate the many minds argument for attending to public outrage.

WHAT PROPOSITION?

To sharpen the question, we need to know what proposition, exactly, the public's reaction can be taken to affirm. The initial objection to the many minds argument, here as in the case of traditions, is that public reactions may not be related to any proposition in which Justice Condorcet should be interested.

If the public strongly disagrees with 1A–1F, it is most unlikely to be motivated by its independent interpretation of the Constitution. Its reaction is more likely to reflect a judgment about the actual social risks, speaking empirically, that would be created by (for example) same-sex or polygamous marriages or abolition of the death penalty—or about the social values, speaking in purely moral terms, that the existing practices promote. If the public's reaction is to matter to Justice Condorcet, it must be because the public's judgments on these points bear on, or overlap with, or are, the judgments that give rise to constitutional interpretation. This is hardly unimaginable. Perhaps the public believes that there is a legitimate and weighty reason to ban polygamy, and perhaps that belief bears on the constitutional issue. Perhaps the public believes that under contemporary conditions, the president needs the authority to commit troops without congressional authorization, and perhaps that judgment of necessity is relevant to the meaning of the Constitution.

Suppose that propositions 1A–1F are supported by a "moral reading" of the Constitution, which asks judges to treat the founding document as establishing moral aspirations, which they should attempt to place in the best possible light, consistent with respect for the past. For judges who are committed to moral readings, should intensely held public convictions receive consideration? At first glance, Justice Condorcet is unlikely to think so. The point of the moral reading is to say (for example) how liberty and equality are best conceived in light of our practices; often the moral reading will run in the face of the public will, and sometimes the moral reading will produce outrage (if only because the existing practice is outrageous). For moral readers, the problems of school segregation, censorship, and sex discrimination are likely to loom large; and in all of those domains, the Court was willing to risk public opprobrium. If Justice Condorcet attends to what the public thinks, perhaps he will not be giving moral readings at all.

But this conclusion is premature. Suppose that judges who aspire to be moral readers are humble; they believe that the Constitution's broad phrases should be read in the best constructive light, but they also agree that their own answers are fallible. Humble readers, moral or otherwise, might pay attention to the public's judgments, perhaps especially if those judgments are intensely held. If the public's conception of liberty and equality is consistent with some practice, and if judicial validation of that practice would produce outrage, judges might pay attention to those facts. But for two reasons that should also be evident from the treatment of traditions, Condorcet will want to ask certain questions about whether widely held public convictions can, in fact, be trusted.

BIASES AND PREJUDICES

We have seen that if a systematic bias is present, the majority will not be right. If most people think that free trade is bad, even though it is (usually) good, governments will do badly if they follow the view of most people. If most people think that it is good to double the minimum wage, even though doubling the minimum wage would produce a significant increase in unemployment, then there is no point in following the supposed wisdom of crowds. Democracies that rely on public opinion can get into a lot of trouble for that reason.[3]

Now turn to the constitutional domain and consider the constitutional validity of legal bans on racial intermarriage. It should hardly be controversial to suggest that public disapproval of racial intermarriage was a product of a systematic bias. Insofar as that disapproval bears on the constitutional issue, it is easily understood as a product of "prejudice" in light of the relevant equal protection principles, in which Condorcet deserves to have confidence. Public disapproval of racial intermarriage stemmed from systematic biases with respect to facts as well as values. Why should Condorcet

---

[3] See Bryan Caplan, *The Myth of the Rational Voter: Why Democracies Choose Bad Policies* (Princeton: Princeton University Press 2007).

pay attention to people's error-prone judgments? Recall here the problems in Lord Devlin's suggestion that "the moral judgements of society" should be ascertained by asking for the view of "the man in the street."

Alert to the presence of systematic biases, many theorists of democracy emphasize that it does not make much sense simply to aggregate the views of the men, or the people, in the street. Jürgen Habermas, for example, stresses norms and practices designed to allow victory by "the better argument":

> Rational discourse is supposed to be public and inclusive, to grant equal communication rights for participants, to require sincerity and to diffuse any kind of force other than the forceless force of the better argument. This communicative structure is expected to create a deliberative space for the mobilization of the best available contributions for the most relevant topics.[4]

In Habermas's famous "ideal speech situation," all participants attempt to seek the truth; they do not behave strategically; they accept a norm of equality.[5] Other advocates of deliberative democracy have spoken similarly about what appropriate deliberation entails.[6] On this view, democratic judgments, properly understood, are not obtained simply by conducting surveys. Deliberation imposes its own requirements and preconditions. Indeed, deliberation, like self-government, has its own internal morality, one that should overcome some of the harmful effects of systematic biases in the real world.

It may be doubted, however, whether deliberation will actually have that consequence, even under ideal conditions.[7] Often deliberation amplifies individual biases, rather than correcting them. The process is not merely one of "garbage in, garbage out"; it is often "some garbage in, more garbage out." If members of a deliberating group are subject to a systematic bias, there is a danger that deliberation will magnify the original error.

---

[4] Jürgen Habermas, Between Facts and Norms: An Author's Reflections, 76 *Denv. U. L. Rev.* 937, 940–41 (1999).

[5] See Jürgen Habermas, What Is Universal Pragmatics? in *Communication and the Evolution of Society* 1, 2–4, 32 (Thomas McCarthy trans.) (Boston: Beacon Press, 1979) (discussing preconditions for communication).

[6] See Amy Gutmann and Dennis Thompson, *Democracy and Disagreement* 7–8 (Cambridge: Harvard University Press, 1998) (outlining foundations of deliberative democracy).

[7] See Cass R. Sunstein, *Infotopia* (New York: Oxford University Press, 2006).

The problem, then, is that if Condorcet has good reason to believe that most people suffer from a prejudice that infects their judgments, he ought not to pay attention to what they think, even if they have deliberated. The more particular question is whether a bias might distort people's judgments with respect to 1A–1F, in which case those judgments have no epistemic value. It would be entirely reasonable for Justice Condorcet to worry about the risk of such a bias; propositions 1A and 1E are especially good candidates.

Cascades

Cascades again. An additional problem is that people's judgments may be a product of an informational, moral, or strictly legal cascade, in which case they lack the independence that the Jury Theorem requires. Informational and reputational cascades might well be responsible for public outrage in response to a judicial ruling. Suppose, for example, that people believe that same-sex marriage is morally unacceptable, not because of any private information or even judgment, but because they are reacting to the informational signals given by others.

In the particular domain of same-sex marriage, there is nothing fanciful about this suggestion. People's beliefs about same-sex marriage are frequently a product of the perceived beliefs of others. Most people have not thought long and hard about that topic. A moral judgment, even a degree of outrage, may be a result of a cascade, in which most participants have not reflected on the issue on their own. The information provided by the (actual or apparent) views of others may be the source of most people's judgments. And when people do not actually rely on that information, they might go along with the crowd, simply so as not to incur the disapproval of others.

We could readily imagine constitutional cascades as well, in which the public's constitutional judgments develop not on the basis of independent assessments of the merits, but in response to the constitutional judgments of others. Even within the lower courts, legal cascades do seem to develop, as judges are heavily influenced by the rulings of other judges.[8] If preceden-

---

[8] See Andrew F. Daughety and Jennifer F. Reinganum, Stampede to Judgment, 1 *Am. Law & Econ. Rev.* 158 (1999).

tial cascades can be found within the court system, there is every reason to believe that law-related cascades occur within the public culture in general, as the constitutional judgments of a few help to produce an apparently widespread view in favor of one or another position. If such cascades are pervasive or enduring, they might even become self-confirming, as the widespread judgment becomes entrenched within the public and eventually within the law. The contrary judgment may move from being unpopular to being unthinkable, in the sense of wholly abhorrent, and finally to being unthought, in the literal sense that no one thinks it.[9] Consider the view that the Constitution permits racial segregation. Widely accepted in 1950, that view was unpopular by 1970, unthinkable by 1980, and it is nearly unthought today.

Cascades might be spontaneous or deliberately induced. Spontaneous cascades arise after a few early movers, not really seeking to steer the public, express their view about a judicial decision in a prominent way; the early movers increase the salience of the decision, and might eventually produce widespread outrage. More often, political actors in the public or private sectors work very hard to generate a cascade effect, using the popular media to generate a great deal of public opprobrium. With respect to the Constitution, it is easy to imagine "meaning entrepreneurs," who take it as their task to inculcate a certain view of constitutional mean-ing, and to spread that view far and wide. Meaning entrepreneurs often produce constitutional cascades; prominent media voices are the most obvious examples.

Consider the view that the Second Amendment confers an individual right to own guns. This view is respectable, but it may also be wrong, and prominent specialists reject it on various grounds.[10] As late as 1980, it would have been preposterous to argue that the Second Amendment creates an individual right to own guns, and no federal court invalidated a gun control restriction on Second Amendment grounds until 2007. Yet countless American politicians, in recent years, have acknowledged that they respect the individual right to bear arms, at least in general terms. Their views are a product of the energetic efforts of meaning entrepreneurs—some from the National Rifle Association, who have pressed a particular view of the

[9] See Timur Kuran, *Public Lies, Private Truths* (Cambridge: Harvard University Press, 1998).
[10] For a fair-minded overview, see Mark Tushnet, *Out of Range* (New York: Oxford University Press, 2007).

Second Amendment. A constitutional cascade produced a dramatic shift in public understandings, and eventually the Court's own understanding, in a relatively short period.

If the public comes to abhor a Supreme Court decision, or to press a certain view about constitutional meaning, relatively few people may have made an independent judgment on the matter at hand. The key point is that when cascades are at work, there is no particular reason to trust the apparent judgments of large groups on Condorcetian grounds. By hypothesis, such groups are responding to the beliefs of only a few. A precondition for deference to the wisdom of the crowd—a large number of independent judgments—is absent.

Group polarization. There is a related point, with particular importance for Justice Condorcet's thinking. Through the process of *group polarization*, deliberation tends to move people to a more extreme position in line with their predeliberation tendencies.[11] Imagine, for example, that like-minded citizens are speaking together about a decision of the Supreme Court, and that they begin with a significant level of disapproval; their discussions may well increase mere disapproval to outrage. When deliberation leads juries to greater levels of outrage, group polarization is often responsible.[12] Much of the time, intense feelings and even outrage are a product of the kinds of social influences that produce group polarization.

It follows that if the public is outraged by a Supreme Court decision, group polarization may be responsible. Deliberating with one another, citizens may become quite stirred up, even though few would have reacted strongly on their own. To the extent that this is so, Justice Condorcet will likely conclude that outrage lacks epistemic credentials, because it is not a product of the independent judgments that can make large groups wise.

HESITATION AND HUMILITY WITHOUT THE JURY THEOREM

Even without worrying about a systematic bias or social influences, Condorcet will want to ask himself: Is it really the case that many or most members of the public are more likely than not to provide correct answers

---

[11] See David Schkade et al., What Happened on Deliberation Day? 95 *Cal. L. Rev.* 915 (2007).
[12] See id.

to legally relevant questions of fact and morality? If morality is pertinent to constitutional adjudication, Condorcet might be puzzled by the suggestion that most people will answer the key questions correctly. Suppose that Condorcet is exploring some constitutional question associated with racial segregation, free speech in a time of war, the establishment clause, or discrimination on grounds of sexual orientation. Why—Condorcet might wonder—should I believe that most people are more than 50 percent likely to provide the right answer to the underlying question?

If Condorcet cannot answer this question, and hence finds the Jury Theorem irrelevant, it remains possible that he will hesitate on many minds grounds before rejecting the views of the majority. He might believe that the issue is comparative: Is the public more likely, or less likely, to be right than are federal judges? Does the answer to this question change if the public is genuinely outraged? If Condorcet is an originalist, he will be confident that the public's views do not much matter. If he thinks that judges have a unique ability to discern evolving values, he will not be greatly interested in what the public thinks. Here again we can find a temporary epistemic alliance (truce?), in rejecting the views of the public, between originalists and many of those who believe that the Constitution's meaning evolves over time.

But Condorcet might observe that the Court consists of nine lawyers— mostly white, mostly male, mostly wealthy, and mostly old (or at least not young). In light of that fact, he might believe that judges are at an epistemic disadvantage in answering some important questions—perhaps because of their relative lack of diversity, perhaps because they are the ones who are likely to suffer from a systematic bias. If Condorcet thinks in this way, and if he believes that judgments of fact or morality bear on constitutional meaning, he might well be interested in the widely held views of the public.

PRACTICAL PROBLEMS

In theory, these points are straightforward. In practice, they create serious problems for those who invoke many minds arguments for considering public outrage. Suppose that Condorcet is a humble judge, alert to his own fallibility, who wants to consider the views of others on any relevant proposition unless there is a systematic bias, a cascade effect, or group polarization. Condorcet must decide whether a bias, a cascade, or polarization is at work. Suppose, first, that he has unerring tools for making that decision. If so, there is no particular problem; he knows when the circumstances are right for consulting the public's view. But if Condorcet really does have such tools, he probably knows a great deal, and he might well be able to rely on his own judgment. If so, he need not worry about what other people think.

Suppose, as is far more realistic, that he lacks such tools. To know whether the public suffers from a relevant bias or thinks as it does because of a cascade or polarization, Condorcet has to answer some hard questions—conceptual, normative, and empirical. As a judge, he will likely lack the tools to answer them well. Realistically, his own views about the merits, in cases 1A–1F, will undoubtedly influence his answers. If most people disagree with him, he is likely to conclude that they do, in fact, suffer from some kind of bias. There is a pervasive risk that any judge, asking whether the preconditions for collective wisdom are met, will answer the question affirmatively only when he already agrees with what people think.

Let us imagine that Condorcet can overcome this problem and approach the underlying questions in an acceptably neutral way. Is it possible for him to know when a bias, a cascade, or polarization is at work? In the abstract, we can imagine how he might make progress on that question. Perhaps his theory of interpretation permits him to consider certain judgments to be "biases" in a constitutionally relevant sense. Perhaps he believes that if most people oppose racial intermarriage or same-sex marriage on moral grounds, those very grounds are illicit under the proper theory of (say) the equal protection clause. Perhaps the public is split along lines that suggest some kind of bias. If a relatively weak group is not outraged, and if an identifiably powerful group is outraged, Condorcet might conclude that a bias is likely to be at work. Perhaps the existence of outrage among powerful groups, whose interests are conspicuously at stake, does not have much epistemic value, because of the risk of bias.[13] With respect to cascade effects and polarization, Condorcet must inquire into the social and political dynamics by which the public thinks as it does.

---

[13] Condorcet has to be careful here. What groups count as powerful, and what groups count as powerless, is not only a mere question of fact; it has a normative component as well. See Bruce Ackerman,

Perhaps Condorcet would like to consult the wisdom of the crowd to obtain an answer to the meta-question whether there is a bias, a cascade, or polarization, but on the meta-question, a bias, a cascade, or polarization may also be at work (and so too on the meta-meta-question). Perhaps Condorcet can work with presumptions of one or another kind. If he is particularly humble, he will find a bias or suspect a cascade or polarization only if he is very firmly convinced that one or the other is present.

Condorcet's Conclusions

All in all, the many minds argument for considering intensely held public convictions emerges as intelligible but fragile—more so than the consequentialist argument. For the many minds argument to have any force at all, the public must have a view on some proposition of fact or value that bears on the legal conclusion. Even if it does so, the public's view may be a product of a systematic bias. Even if it is not, it may be a result of the kinds of social influence involved in cascades and polarization. Judges lack good tools for investigating these questions.

If there is a consensus within the relevant community on a question of law, or on a question that bears on the right answer to a question of law, then judges should pay attention to that consensus. But in hard constitutional cases, a consensus will be rare, and judges will in any case be unlikely to want to rule in a way that rejects it.

Beyond Outrage (Again)

To take the many minds argument seriously, I have focused on intense public reactions and even outrage. But I have also said that outrage is simply an extreme point along a continuum of disapproval, starting with mild disagreement and culminating in outrage. Under the Jury Theorem, what matters is numerosity, not intensity. Suppose that 90 percent of the public believes that the Court would be wrong to strike down bans on same-sex marriages, or to rule that the president lacks the authority to commit troops to combat an apparent threat. At first glance, outrage is not important. What matters is whether the underlying judgment is widely held.

Beyond *Carolene Products*, 98 *Harv. L. Rev.* 713 (1985). And if a powerful group is large, Condorcet might hesitate before rejecting its view, notwithstanding its power.

As I have noted, the Court's decision to invalidate a ban on same-sex sodomy seemed to have a great deal to do with a belief that invalidation fit with emerging social values. Thus the Court said that "[i]n the United States criticism of *Bowers* [upholding a ban on same-sex sexual relations] has been substantial and continuing, disapproving of its reasoning in all respects,"[14] and the Court emphasized "an emerging awareness that liberty gives substantial protection to adult persons in deciding how to conduct their private lives."[15] And if nonjudicial actors would disagree with a decision, that point might seem relevant too, even if their disagreement is much milder than outrage. Armed with an understanding of some of the arguments thus far, we can better appreciate some time-honored views about the appropriate role of the judiciary in American government.

Return in this light to the view associated with James Bradley Thayer, which asks judges to defer to any plausible understanding of the Constitution. There is an unmistakable Condorcetian dimension to Thayer's own argument for the view that courts should uphold government decisions unless they are unconstitutional "beyond a reasonable doubt."[16] If the public and its representatives, who have their own duty of fidelity to the document, have understood a constitutional provision in a certain way, then the Court should pay respectful attention to their views. At the very least, a point of this kind provides a plausible reason for the Court to take account of the constitutional conclusions of other branches of the national government,[17] and perhaps of the constitutional judgments of the high courts of other nations (see chapter 8). If other branches have focused squarely on the constitutional question, and reached a consensus in favor of one or another view, the Court might well pay attention for epistemic reasons.

On an alternative view, the Court should pay close attention to existing social commitments, not always in order to uphold whatever legislatures have done, but sometimes in order to strike down legislation. Indeed, some of the most aggressive invalidations by the Court have been defended on the ground that the Court is reflecting widespread social judgments—by, for example, banning sex discrimination and recognizing a right of privacy

---

[14] *Lawrence*, 539 U.S. at 576.

[15] Id. at 572.

[16] Id.

[17] See, e.g., Rostker v. Goldberg, 453 U.S. 57, 64 (1981) (holding that when Congress has specifically considered the question of an act's constitutionality the "customary deference accorded the judgments of Congress are certainly appropriate").

within marriage.[18] In some cases, the Court has explicitly referred to social judgments as a basis for invalidating legislation. At first glance, it is puzzling to suggest that the Supreme Court should strike statutes down on this ground; if a statute is inconsistent with public commitments, it is likely to be changed or repealed in any event. But some statutes, especially at the state level, may reflect judgments of fact or morality that are not in line with the views of the public at large. If this is so, and if the Court can reliably measure public convictions, there is a plausible Condorcetian justification for taking them into account, at least on a certain view of constitutional interpretation.

Interesting debates might be imagined between two camps: Thayerians, reluctant to invalidate legislation on epistemic grounds, and those who are willing to do so on those same grounds. Thayerians would be tempted to emphasize the lack of good tools by which judges might measure public convictions. Their adversaries would respond that it is extravagant and even foolish to identify any particular statute, especially at the state level, with the will of the public. What is of interest here is that both sides are likely to raise a simple question: What makes outrage distinctive, if the many minds argument is the governing one?

It is not clear that a good answer exists. If it does, the answer is that outrage suggests a degree of both confidence and intensity, in a way that strengthens the epistemic credentials of the public judgment. Recall that under the Jury Theorem, a successful answer from a large group can be expected if most people are at least more that 50 percent likely to be right. The key point is that if most people are confident that they are right, we might be able to find that the conditions for a correct group answer are more likely to be present. When people are less confident of a position, their views tend to moderate;[19] and it is hard to be outraged without a degree of confidence. Moreover, confidence is correlated with accuracy.[20] Of course confident people are often wrong. But confidence has been

---

[18] See, e.g., Klarman, *Jim Crow* (defending *Brown* on such grounds); Richard A. Posner, *Sex and Reason* (Cambridge: Harvard University Press, 1994) (defending *Griswold* on such grounds); Harry Wellington, Common Law Rules and Constitutional Double Standards: Some Notes on Adjudication, 83 *Yale L.J.* 221 (1973) (defending *Roe* on such grounds).

[19] See Robert S. Baron et al., Social Corroboration and Opinion Extremity, 32 *J. Experimental Soc. Psychol.* 537, 538 (1996).

[20] See Reid Hastie, Review Essay: Experimental Evidence of Group Accuracy, in *Information Pooling and Group Decision Making* 129, 133–46 (Bernard Grofman and Guillermo Owen eds.) (Greenwich: JAI Press, 1983).

found to be "associated with correctness for both individual and group performance."[21] We might therefore think that when the public is outraged, it is more likely to be confident and hence its members are more likely to be right.

These points must be taken with many grains of salt. People might be confident about some highly technical issue of law, but they might not be outraged if judges give the wrong answer, simply because the issue is highly technical and little might turn on its resolution. People might be confident and outraged but entirely wrong, especially when the Court is rejecting their prejudices. Alternatively, people might be outraged even though they are not entirely confident, simply because the stakes are so high. Perhaps outrage, when it exists, is associated with a systematic bias or a cascade effect or polarization. Certainly it is plausible to say that those who have been polarized are more likely to be outraged. Hence outrage is a highly imperfect proxy for confidence, just as confidence is a highly imperfect proxy for accuracy.

It follows that if Justice Condorcet is humble, he might well pay attention to widely held public convictions even if outrage is not involved—at least if there is no systematic bias and if many people are making up their minds independently.

Beyond Courts: Bentham and Condorcet in the Democratic Branches

My emphasis throughout has been on the question of whether judges should attend to public opinion. In this section, I explore two related questions. The first is the relationship between popular constitutionalism and the arguments thus far; the second involves the implications of the argument for elected officials.

We the People

We have seen that many people have expressed interest in popular constitutionalism—in the view, with some roots in the founding period, that the meaning of the Constitution should be ultimately resolved by We the Peo-

---

[21] See id. at 148.

ple, not by the federal judiciary. On this view, the interpretations of the Supreme Court lack finality; the public is entitled to have the ultimate say, not because it has ratified any constitutional amendment, but because it has settled on its own view about how the document is best understood. A related but more modest position emphasizes that other branches of government have an independent duty to be faithful to the Constitution, and that this independent duty calls for a degree of interpretive independence on their part.[22]

On a prominent version of this view, for example, courts systematically "underenforce" the Constitution, because of their awareness of their own institutional limitations.[23] It follows that whatever the Supreme Court has said, the president and Congress might disapprove of (say) affirmative action or bans on same-sex marriage on constitutional grounds, and take their own steps to prevent, and in a sense to invalidate, those same practices. When elected officials read the Constitution more expansively than the Court does, they might be acting perfectly legitimately. Elected officials do not face the same limitations that the Court does, and hence they are entitled to be more aggressive with it. It is not difficult to find examples of situations in which public officials, animated by their own views of constitutional commands, extended constitutional barriers in ways that the Supreme Court refused to do. In the domain of property rights and federalism, Presidents Reagan and George W. Bush have insisted on a broader understanding of constitutional limits than that of the Supreme Court.[24]

Perhaps intense public reactions to constitutional rulings can be seen as an especially dramatic exercise in popular constitutionalism, not least when it is likely to have concrete consequences. And when the political branches express disapproval of what the Court does, they may well be exercising their own independent interpretive authority, especially when they ask for more severe constitutional barriers than the Court has proved willing to erect. If we emphasize the many minds argument for judicial attention to outrage, we might see that argument as embodying, even calling for, a

---

[22] See Fleming, *Securing Constitutional Democracy.*

[23] See Lawrence Sager, Fair Measure: The Legal Status of Underenforced Constitutional Norms, 91 *Harv. L. Rev.* 1212 (1978).

[24] Note, for example, President Reagan's executive orders on federalism and takings. Exec. Order No. 12,612, 3 C.F.R. 252 (1987) (requiring that executive agencies follow certain enumerated principles of federalism and consult states to the extent practicable before pursuing policies that would limit state "policymaking discretion"); Exec. Order No. 12,630, 53 Fed. Reg. 8859 (March 15, 1988), reprinted in

kind of popular constitutionalism, or at least attention to the independent interpretive judgments of other branches.

I do not mean to speak directly here to the controversies over popular constitutionalism and the distribution of interpretive authority among the branches of government. Let us simply notice that when there is popular "backlash," a great deal depends on its grounds, at least if the goal is to assess the question of whether it can be seen as an exercise in popular constitutionalism. Perhaps the public's judgment is not in any sense rooted in a judgment about constitutional meaning. Perhaps its outrage is a reflection of some kind of policy-driven, constitution-blind opprobrium. We have seen that if a cascade or group polarization is at work, the many minds argument loses much of its force; so too if there is a systemic bias. On the other hand, "backlash" might legitimately be seen as constitutionally relevant insofar as it reflects a widespread and considered judgment about the merits of the constitutional issue. Here, as elsewhere, that question cannot be resolved without an account of constitutional interpretation and some information about what, exactly, lies beneath public disapproval.

ELECTED OFFICIALS

The discussion thus far has implications for the decisions of many public officials, including presidents, legislators, governors, and mayors. If such officials anticipate intense disapproval or outrage in reaction to their decisions, they will often be deterred, even if they think that the outrage is unjustified or worse. Of course there is a large debate about whether representatives should make independent judgments or instead follow the views of those whom they represent.[25] Return in this light to cases 1A–1D; suppose now that the president of the United States holds the relevant views as a matter either of constitutional interpretation or of fundamental principle. He might hesitate to press those views for either of the two now-familiar reasons. He might believe that if he acts in accordance with his convictions, he will produce bad consequences. Alternatively, he might be-

---

5 U.S.C. § 601 (2000) (requiring executive agencies to conduct takings impact assessments when making regulatory decisions that may impact private property rights).

[25] See Hannah Pitkin, *The Concept of Representation* (Berkeley and Los Angeles: University of California Press, 1965).

lieve that his own judgments are unreliable, simply because so many people disagree with him.

Suppose, for example, that an American president concludes that same-sex marriages should be permitted. He believes that there is no good reason to ban such marriages, and indeed he thinks that existing bans are a reflection of unjustified prejudice and hostility. He might nonetheless hesitate before pressing his view in public or through legislation. He might proceed slowly and cautiously, fearing that such an insistence would compromise the ultimate goal of producing same-sex marriage. Perhaps an evolutionary process, involving a high degree of social learning, is the best way of achieving his preferred end. Perhaps his own aggressive efforts would have a helpful influence on that process, but perhaps they would compromise his other important goals, including those relating to environmental protection, national security, energy independence, and income tax reform.

Whether or not a court should be concerned about its limited political "capital," a national leader certainly has to decide whether and when to spend that capital. If a president has an assortment of projects, he might well hesitate before pressing a commitment that will generate public outrage. President Clinton's early effort to allow gays and lesbians to serve in the military produced a firestorm of protest, in a way that had serious adverse effects on his first year in office.[26] Perhaps it would have been better, in light of President Clinton's own goals, for him to have proceeded more slowly or not at all.

Return in this connection to Abraham Lincoln's practices with respect to slavery, mentioned in chapter 5. As we saw, Lincoln always insisted that slavery was wrong, but the fact that slavery was wrong did not mean that it had to be eliminated immediately. In Lincoln's view, the feeling of "the great mass of white people" would not permit this result.[27] Recall Lincoln's most striking declaration: "A universal feeling, whether well or ill-founded, can not be safely disregarded."[28] Evidently Lincoln believed that efforts to create immediate social change in this especially sensitive area could have

---

[26] See Janet Halley, *Don't: A Reader's Guide to the Military Anti-Gay Policy* (Durham, NC: Duke University Press, 1999).

[27] Bickel, *The Least Dangerous Branch*, at 66 (quoting Abraham Lincoln, speech at Peoria, Illinois (October 16, 1854)), in *Collected Works*, 2:256.

[28] Id.

unintended consequences or backfire, even if those efforts were founded on entirely sound principle. It was necessary first to educate people about the reasons for the change. Passions had to be cooled. Important interests had to be accommodated or persuaded to join the cause. Issues of timing were crucial. For Lincoln, rigidity about the principle was combined with caution and care about the means by which the right outcome would be achieved. It is easy to imagine why many elected officials might think in the same general terms suggested by Lincoln.

Alternatively, a high-level official might think that if most people do see a good reason for some social practice, their views are entitled to respect. Indeed, an elected official may well have stronger epistemic reasons to consider the views of the public and the prospect of outrage than do judges, simply because the views of the public are far more likely to bear on the particular questions that concern the official. Suppose that an official believes that affirmative action should be abolished tomorrow, or that abortion should be banned, but that a strong majority of the public disagrees. The official might conclude that the public has relevant information on questions of both fact and value, and that she should hesitate before acting in a way that violates public convictions.

Here as well, however, the risks of systematic bias, cascade effects, and polarization introduce important cautionary notes for political leaders no less than for judges. A conscientious official will inquire into the relevant risks in deciding whether to consider public commitments and the possibility of outrage. The most general point is that an understanding of the consequentialist and many minds arguments helps to illuminate long-standing debates over the concept of representation: Should politicians attempt to implement the public will, or should they understand themselves as having considerable discretion to depart from it? Those who are skeptical about official discretion, and want to cabin it, might have an epistemic point in mind. Perhaps the public is likely, on some or many questions, to know a great deal more than the relevant officials. Alternatively, they might believe, with Lincoln, that in certain domains, the consequences would be very bad if officials diverged too sharply from the public will. An appreciation of the epistemic and consequentialist arguments should help to show when, and why, the diverging models of representation have particular force.

My general focus, however, has been on the behavior of courts. In the general run of constitutional cases, public opinion and even outrage are indeed irrelevant; the rule-consequentialist objection is convincing. In rare but important circumstances, however, judges legitimately consider intensely held public convictions because and to the extent that consequences matter, and because and to the extent that those convictions provide information about the best interpretation of the Constitution.

PART IV

Cosmopolitanism

CHAPTER 8

~

What Other Nations Do

The practice of consulting "foreign precedents" has received a great deal of attention in connection with several controversial decisions of the Supreme Court.[1] In those decisions, the Court has referred to the law of other nations in deciding whether a state practice—banning sexual relations between people of the same sex, calling for execution of juveniles or the mentally retarded—violates the United States Constitution.[2] It is an understatement to say that many people have been disturbed by those references. Why should the meaning of the American Constitution turn on the views of judges (and others) in Germany, France, Italy, and the United Kingdom? When the Court refers to the practices of other nations, might it not be yielding a measure of American sovereignty? Might it not be saying,

---

[1] See Roger P. Alford, Misusing International Sources to Interpret the Constitution, 98 *Am. J. Int'l L.* 57 (2004); Mark Tushnet, The Possibilities of Comparative Constitutional Law, 108 *Yale L.J.* 1225 (1999); Mark Tushnet, Transnational/Domestic Constitutional Law, 37 *Loy. L.A. L. Rev.* 239 (2003); Ernest A. Young, The Supreme Court, 2004 Term—Comment: Foreign Law and the Denominator Problem, 119 *Harv. L. Rev.* 148 (2005); Vicki C. Jackson, The Supreme Court, 2004 Term—Comment: Constitutional Comparisons: Convergence, Resistance, Engagement, 119 *Harv. L. Rev.* 109 (2005); Jeremy Waldron, The Supreme Court, 2004 Term—Comment: Foreign Law and the Modern Ius Gentium, 119 *Harv. L. Rev.* 129 (2005); Eugene Kontorovich, Disrespecting the "Opinions of Mankind": International Law in Constitutional Interpretation, 8 Green Bag 2d 261 (2005); Kenneth Anderson, Foreign Law and the U.S. Constitution, *Pol'y Rev.*, June–July 2005, at 33; Steven G. Calabresi and Stephanie Dotson Zimdahl, The Supreme Court and Foreign Sources of Law: Two Hundred Years of Practice and the Juvenile Death Penalty Decision, 47 *Wm. & Mary L. Rev.* (2005); Sanford Levinson, Looking Abroad When Interpreting the U.S. Constitution: Some Reflections, 39 *Tex. Int'l L.J.* 353 (2004); Rex Glensy, Which Countries Count? *Lawrence v. Texas* and the Selection of Foreign Persuasive Authority, 45 *Va. J. Int'l L.* 357 (2005). A bill in the House would forbid courts to rely on foreign law, see Reaffirmation of American Independence Resolution, H.R. Res. 568, 108th Cong. (2004).

[2] In the last decade, the Court has referred to foreign precedents on several occasions. See Lawrence v. Texas, 539 U.S. 558, 568–74 (2003); Roper v. Simmons, 543 U.S. 551 (2005); Grutter v. Bollinger, 539 U.S. 306, 342 (2003) (Ginsburg, J., concurring); Printz v. United States, 521 U.S. 898, 977 (1997) (Breyer, J., dissenting); Planned Parenthood of Southeastern Pa. v. Casey, 505 U.S. 833, 945 n. 1 (1992) (Rehnquist, C.J., concurring in part, dissenting in part); Foster v. Florida, 537 U.S. 990, 992–93 (2002) (Breyer, J., dissenting); Elledge v. Florida, 525 U.S. 944, 944–45 (1998) (Breyer, J., dissenting from

effectively, that foreign countries are permitted to alter the interpretation of the nation's founding document? How can that be appropriate?

These are legitimate questions. They have been pressed with particular urgency by conservatives on the bench and in the nation, who think that the meaning of the Constitution cannot possibly depend on what other nations do. Justice Antonin Scalia argues that foreign legal materials are "never" relevant to a judgment about the Constitution's meaning, and that use of such materials is part of a product of revising the Constitution rather than construing it.[3] Prominent legislators have even suggested that Congress should take steps to bar courts from considering foreign legal materials—and that the Constitution itself should be amended to impose that bar.

While conservative opposition has been particularly fierce, many moderates and liberals have been both puzzled and disturbed by judicial consultation of the practices of foreign countries. Most nations give less protection to speech and to religious liberty than the United States does; should constitutional protection in the United States be diluted because of what other nations do? If censorship of dissent amidst wartime is the usual practice in most of the world, should the United States allow censorship? Many nations do not believe in equality on the basis of sex; should the United States follow their lead?

These are legitimate questions. But if we broaden the viewscreen, we will be able to obtain a better perspective. In some ways, it is quite standard for courts to refer to the decisions of other jurisdictions, and the debate over the references of the United States Supreme Court can be understood only in the context of the standard practice of *constitutional cosmopolitanism*.

Outside of the United States, national courts regularly consult "foreign precedents" in deciding on the meaning of their own constitutions.[4] Between 1994 and 1998, South African Supreme Court and Constitutional Court decisions made no fewer than 1,258 references to American, Cana-

---

denial of certiorari); Washington v. Glucksberg, 521 U.S. 702, 734 (1997); Atkins v. Virginia, 536 U.S. 304, 316 n. 21 (2002); Raines v. Byrd, 521 U.S. 811 (1997).

[3] Antonin Scalia, Keynote Address: Foreign Legal Authority in the Federal Courts, 98 *Am. Society Int'l L. Proc.* 305, 307–9 (2004).

[4] See, e.g., S. v. Mamabolo, 2001 (1) SACR 686 (CC) (S.Afr.). A great deal of relevant information can be found in *The Use of Comparative Law by Courts* (Ulrich Drobnig and Sjef van Erp eds.) (Boston: Kluwer, 1997). An illuminating theoretical overview, with many references, can be found in Sujit Choudhry, Globalization in Search of Justification: Toward a Theory of Comparative Constitutional Interpretation, 74 *Ind. L. J.* 819 (1999).

dian, British, German, European, and Indian courts.[5] The Supreme Court of Ireland cites foreign law with great frequency.[6] The Supreme Court of Israel makes heavy use of foreign law in multiple domains.[7] German courts consult foreign courts as well,[8] and Swiss and Austrian practice makes a regular appearance.[9] Canadian courts hardly restrict themselves to Canadian precedents,[10] and Australian courts reach far and wide.[11] Use of foreign law occurs, if tacitly, in Italy and France.[12] In Britain the practice is common, and it appears to be growing over time.[13] Constitutional cosmopolitanism seems to be the wave of the future. The legal world is, in a sense, becoming smaller and more transparent, and consultation of foreign judgments is therefore inevitable—especially but not only in young nations.

Indeed, consultation of international practice is sometimes obligatory. The South African Constitution requires its constitutional court to take international law into account. All of the forty-six member-states of the Council of Europe require their courts to take into account the judgments of the European Court of Human Rights. All twenty-seven nations of the European Union have to follow both European Union law and the decisions of the European Court of Justice.

It is simple to identify a many minds argument on behalf of constitutional cosmopolitanism. Indeed, the argument is closely analogous to those that generate interest in traditions and in popular constitutionalism. Here, as elsewhere, the goal is to enlarge the set of views that are being consulted, with the hope of producing more information about what is right and what

[5] See Basil Markesinis and Jorg Fedke, The Judge as Comparativist, 80 *Tul. L. Rev.* 11, 57–58 n. 158 (2005); in the same general vein, see Hoyt Webb, The Constitutional Court of South Africa: Rights Interpretation and Comparative Constitutional Law, 1 *U. Pa. J. Const. L.* 205 (1998).

[6] See Bruce Carolan, The Search for Coherence in the Use of Foreign Court Judgments by the Supreme Court of Ireland, 12 *Tulsa J. Comp. & Int'l L.* 123 (Fall 2004).

[7] See Renee Sanilevici, The Use of Comparative Law by Israeli Courts, in Drobnig and van Erp, *Use of Comparative Law*, 197–221.

[8] Markesinis and Fedke, The Judge as Comparativist, at 35–45.

[9] Ulrich Drobnig, The Use of Foreign Law by German Courts, in Drobnig and van Erp, *Use of Comparative Law*, 127, 134–135.

[10] See S. Ian Bushnell, The Use of American Cases, 35 *University of New Brunswick L.J.* 157 (1986); J. M. MacIntyre, The Use of American Cases in Canadian Courts, 2 *U. British Columbia L. Rev.* 478 (1966); H. Patrick Glenn, Persuasive Authority, 32 *McGill L.J.* 261 (1987); Peter McCormick, Judicial Authority and the Provincial Courts of Appeal: A Statistical Investigation of Citation Practices, 22 *Man. L.J.* 286 (1993).

[11] See Russell Smyth, What Do Intermediate Appellate Courts Cite? A Quantitative Study of the Citation Practice of Australian State Supreme Court, 21 *Adelaide L. Rev.* 51 (1999).

[12] See Markesinis and Fedke, The Judge as Comparativist, at 26–31 (noting that Italian and French courts do not cite foreign sources but extrinsic evidence suggests they are influenced by them).

[13] Id. at 31–35.

is true. Suppose, for example, that the South African Constitutional Court is deciding whether to adopt principle A or instead principle B. Suppose that the vast majority of nations have adopted principle A. If we assume that each nation is more likely than not to make the right decision, then there is good reason to believe that the South African Constitutional Court should, in fact, adopt principle A. When states are deciding on appropriate policies, it is at least reasonable to assume that each is, or most are, likely to do better than random, which is an adequate basis for analyzing the question in terms of the Jury Theorem.

Of course there is a significant difference between this kind of many minds argument and those arguments that call for attention to tradition and to public opinion. The difference has to do with membership in a political community. If the South African Constitutional Court consults the views of South Africans, it is consulting people who are unquestionably relevant. If the U.S. Supreme Court examines local traditions in the domain of religious freedom, it is considering the practices of Americans, not foreigners. It might seem wrong to take account of the views of those who cannot vote in national elections and have not been elected by the relevant people. If the U.S. Supreme Court consults precedents from France and Germany, it might even be seen to have given up American sovereignty.

Suppose, however, that in hard cases, the U.S. Supreme Court consults French and German precedents in the same way that American doctors might, in hard cases, consult the work of French and German doctors. The purpose of the consultation is to obtain relevant information, not to yield anything. If French and German courts have chosen principle A, and indeed if almost all nations have done so, perhaps the U.S. Supreme Court should do so as well, not out of deference to the authority of foreigners, but out of a sense that they might be correct.

As in the context of traditionalism and populism, this argument is easiest to accept if we can assume that there is a right answer to the question of whether a nation should prefer principle A or principle B. If the court is focusing on a factual question, and if a majority of nations has answered that question a certain way, the court has some reason to believe that the majority view is correct. We might therefore arrive at a simple conclusion, suitable for most nations if not for all: *Where the choice of legal rule turns on an answer to a disputed question of fact, the practice of a substantial majority of nations deserves careful attention.*

It is imaginable, for example, that the right answer to a question about sexual relationships between people of the same sex depends, in part, on whether children will be harmed by permitting such relationships. Or suppose that the legitimacy of capital punishment for juveniles depends, in part, on whether such punishment has a significant deterrent effect on juveniles. The practices of most nations might be taken to provide some evidence on these questions. If one answer commands a consensus or receives widespread support, the likelihood that it is right might appear to be very high.

Suppose, however, that the question is not simply or largely one of fact. Perhaps it is a moral question; perhaps the nation wants to know whether it is morally acceptable to ban same-sex sexual relationships, to refuse to protect an asserted right to housing or health care, or to execute juveniles. For consultation of foreign law, the same remains true as for consultation of traditions and public opinion: If we are not skeptics, and if we believe that moral questions do have right answers, then it makes sense to consult the majority's view.

This, then, is the core of a many minds argument for consulting the law of other nations. Because we have explored that kind of argument in detail in other contexts, the investigation can be significantly briefer here. In the end, the argument is more convincing in some nations than in others. It is most plausible in new democracies, attempting to produce constitutional doctrine without much in the way of established precedents. In European nations, with their high degree of integration, constitutional cosmopolitanism has a great deal to recommend it; courts in Germany and France are likely to learn a great deal, in hard cases, by asking what is done in Ireland, Italy, and Spain. By contrast, the argument fails to produce a persuasive defense of constitutional cosmopolitanism in the United States. Such consultation increases the burdens of decisions for both judges and litigants; the question is whether the additional information is likely to improve decisions. If a court is required to ask about foreign practices, it will have far more work to do, and lawyers will face greater burdens still—arguing about the nature and relevance of conclusions in the United Kingdom and Portugal, Israel and Hungary, Poland and Brazil. Is it worthwhile to do all this work? Most of the time, the gain will not justify the effort.

In addition, assessment of international practice may turn out to be opportunistic rather than objective—a matter of looking for friendly precedents, rather than for some kind of consensus. There is a pervasive risk that judges will consult foreign law only to the extent that it supports their antecedent convictions. For example, those who favor consultation of foreign law rarely do so in order to call for greater restrictions on libelous speech, obscenity, or incitement to violence, even though the United States offers unusual levels of protection to such speech. If other nations engage in practices that strike Americans as abhorrent, it is most unlikely that the U.S. Supreme Court will consult foreign practice in deciding on the meaning of the U.S. Constitution. And if this is true, a degree of opportunism is probably inevitable—with foreign precedents being used to prop up a conclusion reached on other grounds.

WHO VOTES AND OTHER PUZZLES

There is an initial question, involving the *Who votes?* problem. Suppose that a court seeks to determine whether some law, X, has some desirable effect, Y. The court observes that most other nations have enacted law X, but it also discovers that, in the aggregate, more legislators oppose X than support it—in the states with X, a bare majority of legislators voted in favor of the law, while in states without X, nearly all legislators voted against the law. Should the court count the states with law X or the legislators who voted for X? Or suppose that polls show that the majority of populations in all states oppose X while the majority of legislators voted for X. Should the court count the legislators or instead the people? Similarly, should courts that look at outcomes in other courts count the number of judge-votes or the number of court-votes? These complications can be multiplied.

In principle, the *Who votes?* question is easy to answer. From the Condorcetian perspective, the court should focus on the people who have the best information, and who are therefore most likely to be right. Suppose that foreign legislators focus on the deterrent effect of the juvenile death penalty; foreign populations focus on its moral permissibility; and foreign courts focus on its consistency with local law. If so, then an American court that cares only about the deterrence issue should count the legislators rather than the other agents. In practice, however, it will be difficult for courts to make such fine distinctions. The motives of legislators, the thinking of populations, and the workings of government are sufficiently opaque to foreigners that it is probably appropriate to rely only on the authoritative outcomes—duly enacted legislation, judicial opinions—and ignore the rest.

The more fundamental point is that for the Condorcetian argument to work, it is necessary to explore the three questions that should now be familiar. First, the judgments of foreign states must bear on a relevant proposition. Second, each state, or most states, must be more likely than not to make the right choice. Third, the law of the foreign states must reflect an independent judgment; it must not be a matter of merely following other nations. To the extent that nations are participating in cascades, they are undermining a key assumption on which consultation of foreign law depends.

For a preliminary sense of these points, consider the question faced by the Supreme Court in the *Roper* case, which was whether the juvenile death penalty is "cruel and unusual."[14] The issue is whether the abolition of the juvenile death penalty in most other countries is relevant information for the Supreme Court of the United States. Suppose, first, that the Court wants to know whether the juvenile death penalty deters juvenile crime. Can the Court plausibly conclude that nearly all other nations have expressed an independent judgment that the juvenile death penalty does not deter crime—and that therefore the probability that the juvenile death penalty deters crime is very low, perhaps close to zero?

If deterrence is the question, it seems clear that the Court should ignore states that abolished the juvenile death penalty for explicitly moral, religious, or ideological reasons independent of any juvenile crime problem. The reason is that the abolition of the penalty did not reflect a judgment about the relevant issue, which is whether the juvenile death penalty deters. In addition, the Court should ignore states whose judgments are unreliable for one or another reason. Finally, the Court should ignore states that abolished the juvenile death penalty merely because other nations abolished the juvenile death penalty.

Let us now consider these points in more detail.

[14] See *Roper*, 543 U.S. at 573.

INFORMATION AND VOTES

The Jury Theorem requires that the voter make a judgment of some kind and then vote sincerely on the basis of it. There are two points here. First, the voter must have private information. Second, the voter must sincerely reveal this information. How do these considerations apply to nations?

The first point is that the voter (here the foreign state) must have private information. For example, Germany might have abolished the juvenile death penalty because the government had information, not available to other countries (or the United States), about the juvenile death penalty. The type of information depends on context. As we have seen, the Supreme Court might want to look at German law for relevant facts (whether the juvenile death penalty deters), including "moral facts" (whether the juvenile death penalty is immoral). The requirement of private information should not be taken too literally. The deterrent effect of the juvenile death penalty in Germany is in some sense public; the German legislature must base its decision on an assessment of facts that must be widely available within Germany. The point is only that an American court will often be able to determine these facts more easily and reliably by consulting German law than by doing its own research about the facts on which German law is based. When this is not the case, of course, then the argument for consulting foreign law is much weaker. If the U.S. Supreme Court has direct and unmediated access to the facts, it should consult the facts, rather than another nation's assessment of the facts.

This problem leads to the second inquiry, which is whether the state is "sincere." In the standard application of the Jury Theorem, sincerity requires the voter's vote to be based on her private information, and she must not vote "strategically," that is, in an effort to achieve some other end. As an example, consider the application of the Jury Theorem to an ordinary jury. A juror votes sincerely if her vote reflects her assessment about the defendant's guilt. A juror votes insincerely if her vote reflects some other purpose—for example, to ensure that deliberations end quickly, or to impress other jurors, or to show other jurors that she is a contrarian or has an independent mind.

For present purposes, the sincerity requirement can be understood as mandating that the state's political system produces laws (or its legal system produces judicial decisions) that accurately reflect the "private" facts or values. The question is whether the foreign government adopted the law or ruling at issue because of the relevant private information or because of political dynamics of no concern to the American court. Suppose that Germany lacks the juvenile death penalty because of the disproportionate influence of an interest group, one that does not much care about the relevant facts or moral principles. The influence of the interest group muddies the informational value of the vote.

States are not people, and some may find it odd to label a state law as "sincere" or not. What is important is not sincerity in the psychological sense but whether the laws of other nations, including judicial decisions, reflect a political or legal process that incorporates information that is private to the state—in the sense that government officials have that information as a result of their own research, their own local knowledge, or their ability to aggregate the information, judgments, and values of the mass of citizens. Political and legal systems may be defective in various ways. The laws might reflect the choices of a tiny ruling elite; so might the judicial opinions. In these cases, it would be wise for the American court to ignore or discount the law of the other state.

WHAT PROPOSITION? (I) OF RELATIVISM

As we have seen throughout, a central question is whether the views of other nations bear on the proposition that concerns the Supreme Court. The absence of a juvenile death penalty in a nation like Switzerland, with little violent crime among juveniles, may provide no information on any relevant proposition. Perhaps Switzerland has never had to confront the question of whether to have a juvenile death penalty because no one thinks there is a juvenile crime problem. If the practices of other nations are being consulted because of the implications of those practices for a factual question, it is necessary to be clear about what factual question is actually in question.

Cultural relativism? The relevance of the Jury Theorem when moral judgments are at issue is both more interesting and more complex. To use the Jury Theorem, it is necessary to reject any strong form of cultural relativism, according to which the appropriate moral rules are culture-dependent, so that the moral requirements that are suitable for one culture need not be suitable for another culture. If they are not suitable, the moral proposition supported by most nations may not be relevant to the judgments of other nations. For those who are committed to cultural relativism, consultation of foreign law will make little sense. Perhaps the appropriate domain of privacy greatly differs across cultures. Perhaps certain forms of sex discrimination are utterly unacceptable in some societies, but essentially unobjectionable in others.

Whether or not the essentials of morality are subject to cultural variation, perhaps we can agree that the nature and scope of certain rights can vary significantly across place and time. For example, Germany might ban hate speech, because of the salience of the Holocaust; perhaps the United States should not. A practice that is common in Europe may not be suitable to Canada, and vice versa, simply because of strongly held and legitimately different social norms.

Constitutional relativism? Many questions might be raised about various forms of cultural relativism. If cultural relativists intend to reject the general idea of universal rights, their position seems to me preposterous; but I cannot defend that judgment here.[15] However those questions are answered, it remains possible to accept a form of cultural relativism with respect to constitutional law in particular. Even if human rights are not relative in any interesting sense, constitutional law might be, because texts and principles of interpretation might lead constitutional courts in South Africa, Germany, and Hungary to results that make no sense for Canada, Brazil, or the United States. We might even be able to imagine an incompletely theorized agreement against reliance on foreign law—an agreement joined by people with disparate positions on foundational questions.

Of course constitutional texts differ, and textual differences should be expected to produce different outcomes, whatever one's approach to interpretation. Thayerians, committed to judicial restraint, will be reluctant to strike down statutes simply because they are inconsistent with practices in other democracies. And on a standard understanding of originalism, the practices of other nations are generally irrelevant, because the interpretive goal is to recover the original understanding of the relevant provision. For

[15] For relevant discussion, see Martha C. Nussbaum, *Women and Human Development: The Capabilities Approach* (New York: Oxford University Press, 2002).

originalists, the meaning of the founding document will rarely if ever depend on what other nations do. So too for traditionalists, who are likely to believe that local traditions are what matter. Minimalists of all stripes might conclude that inquiring into those practices is more trouble than it is worth—and inconsistent with the minimalist enterprise.

If any one of these positions is accepted, of course, a degree of cultural relativism is appropriate in the domain of constitutional law. When some nations consult comparative law, it is because their own interpretive practices justify the consultation; there is no reason to think that every nation must follow the same such practices. Young democracies, trying to generate constitutional doctrine essentially from scratch, will naturally take account of what other nations do. Under the approach in South Africa, for example, the constitutionality of certain laws does turn, in part, on the views of other nations; those views provide information, and here the Condorcet Jury Theorem helps to explain why the South African practice is hardly senseless. The United States and Germany might be different; how their courts should proceed depends on a judgment about the right theory of constitutional interpretation for those nations.

Moral readings? Suppose, however, that we accept a view of constitutional interpretation that calls for attention to what is required by the right approach to morality and politics. As we have seen, those who endorse "moral readings" of the Constitution ask judges to consider what morality actually requires. Suppose too that many or most nations endorse the same approach to a particular question. As long as those nations allow free and open debate, the very fact that different societies have come to the same conclusion increases one's confidence that the norms are genuinely universal and transcend merely historical or institutional differences. Here is a sense in which differences, rather than similarities, among societies strengthen the case for consulting foreign materials. If the overwhelming majority of nations agrees that there is a right to free speech, and also agrees on a particular entailment of that right, we have some reason for confidence in their view, at least if it is supposed that all or most are at least 50 percent likely to be correct.

Indeed, the Universal Declaration of Human Rights was produced through a self-conscious effort to build on widespread understandings, in a way that is highly relevant to the debate over consultation of foreign law.[16] The basic enterprise operated by surveying the behavior of most nations, and by building a "universal declaration" on the basis of shared practices. A philosophers' group involved in the project "began its work by sending a questionnaire to statesmen and scholars around the world."[17] At a key stage, the people involved in drafting the declaration produced "a list of forty-eight items that represented . . . the common core of" a wide range of documents and proposals, including judgments from "Arabic, British, Canadian, Chinese, French, pre-Nazi German, Italian, Latin American, Polish, Soviet Russian and Spanish" nations and cultures.[18] The Universal Declaration of Human Rights emerged directly from this process.

Thus Jacques Maritain, a philosopher closely involved in the process that produced the Universal Declaration, famously said, "Yes, we agree about the rights, but on condition no one asks us why."[19] Notably, the judgment in favor of the Universal Declaration reflected not an abstract theory but the views of many minds. If it is plausible to take account of those views, it is because most of them are more likely than not to be right, or at least because most of them are likely to do better than any person, or small group, that attempts to develop an account of its own.

Consider as well the International Covenant on Civil and Political Rights, a treaty that refines and establishes as law many of the civil and political rights in the Universal Declaration.[20] The basic rights recognized by the ICCPR include many that Americans take for granted, including prohibitions on slavery (Art. 8) arbitrary arrest (Art. 9), freedom of movement (Art. 12), and freedom of conscience (Art. 18). But for many countries emerging from authoritarian regimes in the 1980s and 1990s, the fact that this treaty existed, and reflected the judgments of numerous diverse countries, must have provided good reason for believing that the rights recognized in the treaty ought to be respected in their countries as well. Note that at least one country, Egypt, states in a declaration that the ICCPR was not inconsistent with the Sharia. The ratification of the ICCPR by other Muslim-dominated states might be similarly inter-

---

[16] See Mary Ann Glendon, *A World Made Anew* (New York: Random House, 2001)
[17] Id. at 51.
[18] Id. at 57.
[19] Id. at 77 (citing Maritain).
[20] Universal Declaration of Human Rights, G.A. Res. 217 A, U.N. GAOR, 3d Sess., art. 1, U.N. Doc. A/810 (1948).

preted.[21] These facts suggest that people from different social and political systems may recognize that some norms transcend their differences—and that the very pervasiveness of a moral commitment is reason to accept it.

By contrast, most states have refused to ratify the second optional protocol to the ICCPR, which bans the death penalty.[22] This refusal shows that judgments about the effectiveness or desirability of the death penalty are more diverse, and that therefore a state deciding whether to eliminate the death penalty may learn relatively less from the judgments of other nations.[23]

In general, courts must take account of two points here. First, some human rights norms are abstractions, subject to competing interpretations. A ban on "torture" might be specified in several different ways; people disagree on what, exactly, counts as torture. Second, there is a difference between "law on the books" and "law in action." Nations might be publicly committed to norms that they simultaneously violate. It is a nice question whether a cosmopolitan judge, interested in taking account of international practice, should focus on public commitments or actual practice. If the question is really a Condorcetian one, there is a good argument that practice is what matters, and that the commitment provides merely a clue about the nature of the practice.

The conclusions of this brief if somewhat unruly discussion are straightforward. Cultural and constitutional relativists will be skeptical of the idea that the practices of other nations should help determine the practices of another, because the proposition supported by the general practice does not bear on the issue at hand, which is the appropriate practice for the nation in question. Constitutional relativism is especially plausible, because texts differ, and because many different approaches to interpretation might converge on that form of relativism. On the other hand, those who believe in moral readings of constitutional texts might well be interested in what other nations do, because their practices help inform the right moral readings. As we shall see, this point has special power for young nations.

---

[21] International Covenant on Civil and Political Rights, opened for signature December 16, 1966, art. 1, S. Exec. Doc E, 95–2 (1978), 999 U.N.T.S. 171 (entered into force March 23, 1976).

[22] Second Optional Protocol to the International Covenant on Civil and Political Rights, Aiming at the Abolition of the Death Penalty (adopted by UNGA Res. 44/128 of December 15, 1989).

[23] As of January 2006, 155 states had ratified the ICCPR; only 56 had ratified the second optional protocol.

WHAT PROPOSITION?
(II) LEGAL AND INSTITUTIONAL DIFFERENCES

Let us put the most important forms of relativism to one side. More particular legal and institutional differences may make the Jury Theorem irrelevant, again because the proposition endorsed by other nations may not bear
on the proposition that is in dispute. A good example is Justice Breyer's
reliance on German law in making arguments about the meaning of American federalism.[24] German federalism allows the German states to enforce
national law; so (Justice Breyer asks) why not in America, when mandatory
enforcement is challenged as inconsistent with federalism? The question
makes sense if the practice of Germany is informative on some question
of relevance to American law. The problem with the argument is that in
Germany, the states play a far greater role in creating national law than
American states do, and this institutional difference may well make German law uninformative on the questions that concern Americans.

Justice Breyer meant to suggest that the German practice helps to show
what the American practice ought to be, or might legitimately or reasonably be; perhaps he erred in ignoring institutional differences between the
two systems. Justice Breyer might therefore have been wrong to rely on
German institutions, because they do not bear on the proposition at hand.
His best counterargument would be pragmatic: The institutional provisions
of the U.S. Constitution should be construed, where ambiguous, in a way
that makes pragmatic sense, and the German experience provides information on that question. For those who think that Justice Breyer was wrong,
it should be noted that courts commonly appeal to British laws and institutions—notwithstanding the fact that the British parliamentary system is
radically different from the American system, indeed more so than the
various presidential systems in Latin America and elsewhere that are mod-
eled on the American system. Consider this explanation of Justice Scalia,
a sharp critic of Supreme Court reliance on foreign law:

> I don't use British law for everything. I use British law for those
> elements of the Constitution that were taken from Britain. The
> phrase "the right to be confronted with witnesses against him"—what
> did confrontation consist of in England? It had a meaning to the

---

[24] *Printz*, 521 U.S. at 976.

American colonists, all of whom were intimately familiar with my friend Blackstone. And what they understood when they ratified this Constitution was that they were affirming the rights of Englishmen. So to know what the Constitution meant at the time, you have to know what English law was at the time. And that isn't so for every provision of the Constitution.[25]

On originalist grounds, Justice Scalia's assumption that the criminal defendant's confrontation right had the same understanding in the United States as in Britain is plausible, and his reliance on British law is therefore reasonable. But note that the implicit assumption here is that eighteenth century Americans believed that the confrontation right should exist in America as it did in Britain, despite the enormous institutional differences between the two countries—Britain was a constitutional monarchy and America a republic. One could imagine someone arguing in the eighteenth century (or today) that because the United States was a republic, it did not need to grant as generous protections to criminal defendants as Britain did, for politically motivated prosecutions would be punished at the polls (as they indeed were, in the election of 1800).[26] If this argument is correct, the confrontation right in the United States should be understood more narrowly than the confrontation right in Britain. The contrary view, which has prevailed, is that politically motivated or otherwise unfair prosecutions could be a serious problem in a republic as well as in a monarchy.

The more general point is that large institutional differences greatly matter; they suggest that a many minds argument, based on practices around the globe, will be unconvincing in a nation with distinctive institutional arrangements. An obvious example involves the question whether the executive can use military force without a congressional declaration of war. On the more sensible view, the practice in the United Kingdom and other nations is irrelevant, because the American republic rests on principles radically different from those that underlie the British monarchy.[27] It

[25] See Transcript of Scalia-Breyer Debate on Foreign Law, American University, January 13, 2005, available at: http://www.freerepublic.com/focus/f-news/1352357/posts.

[26] James Morton Smith, *Freedom's Fetters: The Alien and Sedition Laws and American Civil Liberties* (Ithaca: Cornell University Press, 1956).

[27] See, e.g., James Wilson, Legislative Department, Lectures on Law, in 3 *The Founders Constitution* 94–95 (Philip Kurland and Ralph Lerner eds.) (Chicago: University of Chicago Press, 1987); Remarks of Pierce Butler, South Carolina Legislature, in id. at 94.

follows that even if the king can initiate wars on his own, it hardly follows that the president can as well.

Return now to the juvenile death penalty. Is it relevant that this penalty was abolished in countries with different political systems? It might be irrelevant if we think that those political systems do not aggregate values and information well; but this seems highly unlikely, at least as a claim about the extremely wide range of systems that have abolished the death penalty. It might also be irrelevant if we adopt a particular understanding of constitutional interpretation, in accordance with which the Eighth Amendment contains a fixed category of prohibitions, or a category of prohibitions that, if not fixed, evolves with changing values and practices in the United States alone. Perhaps what counts as "cruel and unusual" is a function of the views of Americans, not of the world as a whole. If so, consultation of the practices of other nations is a blunder, because those practices do not bear on any proposition that is involved in the interpretation of the American Constitution. But if interpretation depends on some kind of moral judgment, the practices of other nations, if universal or nearly so, may indeed be informative.

SYSTEMATIC BIAS AND LIBERAL DEMOCRACIES

As we have seen throughout, a key question for many minds arguments is whether the general practice reflects a systematic bias. To understand the point in the context at hand, imagine that there is a parallel Earth, in which almost all nations are authoritarian. Imagine too that of two hundred nations, merely three have embarked on an experiment in self-government. Should those three hesitate to do so, on the ground that their practice is so unusual? If the question seems fanciful, consider the fact that for most of the world's history, democratic self-government was indeed exceptional.

It would certainly be possible for the three emerging democracies to conclude that systematic biases are responsible for antidemocratic practices, which therefore deserve little attention. In a similar vein, a nation that is interested in banning slavery, or discrimination on the basis of race or sex, might not be much deterred if, at the relevant moment, slavery, race discrimination, and sex discrimination are pervasive.

If many minds arguments are taken seriously here, and if we want to attend to the need for widespread assent and the risk of systematic biases, we might be able to draw some relevant lines. As we have seen, authoritarian nations cannot claim the epistemic credentials that Burke saw for traditions. To the extent that many minds matter, democracies are the most relevant nations to consider, because the outcomes of democratic processes reflect the judgments of many minds. And if one group of people has repressed another, the repression is not easily defended on the ground that it is pervasive.

From these points, it might seem to follow that American courts should consult the legal materials only of liberal democracies. It may well be that democracies, because they are democratic, are more likely to incorporate information about what is true or right. Compare nations that are dictatorships, inclined to oppress their people; perhaps we will believe that the practices of dictatorships are less than 50 percent likely to be right. But for two reasons, the argument for restricting consultation to liberal democracies seems vulnerable, at least in its crudest forms.

First, many countries that are not liberal democracies nonetheless have some good laws and institutions. There is no reason to think that a nondemocracy enacts only bad laws; the leaders of most nondemocracies want the public to be satisfied as long as the leaders can accomplish this goal without undermining their own ends. Indeed, public satisfaction is often helpful to the achievement of those ends. Much ordinary law—criminal law, contract law, and so forth—is relatively constant across both democracies and nondemocracies. For the purpose of comparative constitutionalism, relying on foreign legal materials is not meant to express approval of all aspects of the foreign country; it is simply a way of taking advantage of unexploited mines of information.

Second, the very fact that nondemocratic nations recognize a particular norm may show that the norm is exceptionally strong. For example, we are accustomed to think that nondemocracies are less tolerant of crime than democracies, and therefore have stricter criminal penalties. Thus, the fact that the vast majority of authoritarian states do not have the juvenile death penalty was frequently cited as evidence that the penalty violates a significant moral norm—a norm so widely accepted that even crime-obsessed authoritarian states cannot ignore it.

As a general matter, however, it is true that democracies are a more reliable source of information about both facts and norms, simply because democratic governments are open and accountable, and more tightly constrained by public opinion and values. Political competition gives parties an incentive to gauge popular attitudes, and itself generates information when elections reveal that a particular program is not as popular as one might have thought. But this is a matter of degree, and there is no reason in principle to doubt that successful authoritarian governments maintain power by catering to the interests of the public to some degree.[28] It follows that an ideal exercise in comparative constitutionalism would survey all countries, democracies and nondemocracies alike; place far more weight on the legal materials, including judicial decisions, of democracies than on those of nondemocracies; but consider the latter as well. At the same time, the constraints of feasibility may require courts to limit their inquiry to a small number of countries, in which case they should focus on democracies, which do provide more reliable information.

INDEPENDENCE AND CASCADES

We have seen that for the Jury Theorem to be applicable, the decision of each state must be at least partly independent of the decisions of other nations. Suppose, for example, that former colonies of the United Kingdom adopted certain British laws and institutions just because they were British—not because the former colonies had made an independent judgment in favor of those laws and institutions. In that event, the existence of identical British-derived legal rules in dozens of nations provides no more information about the value of the rules than if they existed in only one nation, Britain itself. We might imagine that some newly independent nations adopt many laws and institutions because they do not have the time and resources to study the legal systems of other nations, and so maintaining existing laws and institutions is simply the path of least resistance.[29]

---

[28] An inconclusive literature debates whether dictators who seek to maximize their power would choose laws that the public desires, except where they directly interfere with the dictator's monopoly on power (for example, electoral laws), or would choose laws that are frequently undesirable. Compare Casey B. Mulligan, Ricard Gil, and Xavier Sala-i-Martin, Do Democracies Have Different Public Policies Than Nondemocracies? 18 *J. Econ. Perspectives* 51 (2004) (taking the former view) and Mancur Olson, *Power and Prosperity: Outgrowing Communist and Capitalist Dictatorships* 111–34 (New York: Basic 2000) (taking the latter view).

[29] See Alan Watson, *Legal Transplants: An Approach to Comparative Law* (Athens: University of Georgia Press, 2nd ed. 1993). As Watson shows, some countries, such as Japan, carefully studied the legal systems of other nations before reforming their own; others did not.

Nations themselves participate in cascades. If two nations have adopted a law, a third may do so, not because of any kind of independent judgment, but because it is following its predecessors. And if three nations have made the same decision, a cascade might be starting to form. The problem is that subsequent nations might assume that decisions have been made independently, even though most have been following the crowd. The general idea of "policy diffusion" can be understand as a reflection of cascade effects across nations.[30] Much of the time, the diffusion of policies from one nation to another is a product of an informational cascade.

Reputational pressures also play a large role at the level of nations. Some nations follow others, not because of private information, but because of those pressures. Consider a domestic analogy and assume that a number of states within the United States have adopted some version of Megan's Law—a statute requiring registration of sex offenders.[31] Additional states might follow the first group, not because they believe the statute is a good idea, but because its supporters are able to impose reputational pressure by pointing to the practice of prior states. The international analogy should be clear. If a nation adopts some new environmental regulation, or bans nuclear power, or deregulates, or forbids the death penalty, it might be attempting to obtain some kind of reputational benefit. When this is so, its decisions fail to provide additional information.

The cascade model provides an important warning about using the Condorcet Jury Theorem to justify reliance on the view of a majority of nations. If all nations have the same law, the fact is no more informative than if only one or two nations had the same law if it turns out that later nations imitated earlier nations—as they should, under the analysis thus far! In this sense, use of the Jury Theorem, to justify reference to the law of other nations, turns out to be self-defeating; it undermines its own precondition.

This odd implication should not, however, be taken too seriously. The objection would be convincing only if enough nations did in fact merely imitate and fail to make independent judgments. To be sure, they might sometimes—especially in the important but narrow case where new nations

---

[30] See the illuminating treatment of Kurt Weyland, *Bounded Rationality and Policy Diffusion* (Princeton: Princeton University Press, 2007).

[31] See Linda Greenhouse, The Supreme Court: Sex Offenders; Justices Reject Challenges to Megan's Laws, *New York Times*, March 6, 2003, at A29 (discussing legal challenges to Megan's Law).

adopt or inherit wholesale foreign legal systems, which is known as "legal transplant." But in the usual case, nations imitate laws and policies of other nations only after going through a process of deliberation, one that takes account of local conditions and differences between the earlier adopters and the nation in question. In this case, the "vote" is only partially dependent, and thus reveals some information about the general desirability of the laws and policies at issue.

Judicial Competence and a Framework

The Jury Theorem implicitly assumes that the person who implements the policy chosen by the jury will adequately interpret the jurors' votes. Can judges reliably interpret foreign materials, so that they can tell whether a particular law or decision should be considered a "vote" in favor of some moral norm, fact, or policy? More generally, can they assess the relevant conditions?

The analysis so far might seem to suggest that the proper use of foreign materials requires such exhaustive information about foreign norms and institutions that judges could not possibly use foreign materials properly. Here, it seems, is an especially strong argument against the use of comparative materials, to the effect that the best inquiry is so complex, so unlikely to be helpful, and so likely to produce error, that it should not be undertaken at all. If so, an interesting mystery would remain, which is why so many courts, interpreting their own constitutions, do cite the practices of other nations. The pervasiveness of the practice suggests that the enterprise may not be so daunting after all. Of course, it may make more sense for some nations than for others—but that is a separate point.

If international practice is to be consulted, the best approach would be to develop a framework that simplifies the analysis. Consider a few possibilities. These are designed for any English-speaking high court, but they could easily be adapted by courts of many different kinds.

- The Jury Theorem teaches that the informational value of an additional vote declines rapidly after a certain number of votes have been registered. In other words, surveying 10 countries is much more important than surveying 5; but surveying 190 countries adds little beyond a survey of 185. Perhaps, then, judges should survey the legal materials of 10 or 20 other (relevant) countries, and not try to survey the legal materials of all 190 or so countries. This will allow them to spend more time avoiding errors, and will reduce the aggregate information by very little. This point strengthens the idea that the U.S. Supreme Court should restrict itself to the practices of other democracies.

- The value of using foreign legal materials depends on their being an accurate gauge of the sentiments and judgments of the population. This point suggests that judges should not survey the legal materials of foreign nations that have highly authoritarian or dysfunctional institutions. For similar reasons, there is little reason to consult the legal materials of nations with small populations, which are the overwhelming majority.
- English-speaking judges should consult nations whose legal materials are translated into English and adequately understood in the English-speaking world.
- Judges should favor recent sources over old sources, because recent sources are more likely to reflect modern conditions.
- Judges should be alert to cascades, which are most likely when uniform legal change occurs rapidly without much debate or deliberation across different countries.

Taken together, these principles suggest that English-speaking courts should probably confine themselves to only about twenty or thirty countries, including the Western liberal democracies, plus countries such as India, Japan, Brazil, Israel, and South Korea. The precise set of countries might appropriately be constant across cases (a bright-line rule), or it might be better to have the set depend on the type of case. If courts are to take constitutional cosmopolitanism seriously, they should be required to go through each of the countries in the relevant set and describe explicitly in the opinion whether the outcomes in those countries are consistent and support the constitutional interpretation advanced by the court.

It may be that this level of care is unnecessary in most cases. But when the Supreme Court of Ireland, the Constitutional Court of South Africa, or the Supreme Court of Australia is consulting foreign practices, principles of these kinds should help to discipline and systematize the inquiry. In most cases, the analysis should be relatively straightforward. Where foreign law is most useful, it is because there is a consensus or strong majority on one or another side, and it is usually simple to establish that fact.

Because the legitimate sources of American constitutional law are sharply disputed, many people will reject the claim that a framework of this sort should be used in the United States. But some of these principles already exist, in nascent form, in those U.S. Supreme Court opinions that rely on foreign legal materials. Although *Atkins* too casually claimed that the "world community" rejected capital punishment of the mentally retarded,[32] and *Roper* also referred to the rejection of the juvenile death penalty by nearly the entire world,[33] *Lawrence* limited itself to western Europe,[34] and so did other, earlier cases.[35]

If the various strands of the analysis are drawn together, we might accept the following formulation. In difficult cases, courts in young nations, or nations without much in the way of constitutional precedent, should be willing to consider using foreign legal materials to interpret constitutional provisions when the proper interpretation requires factual or moral information that is contained in those materials. Such materials are likely to be useful when (1) they are relatively uniform; (2) they are the result of legislative or judicial judgments in the foreign states; (3) the problems addressed by those materials are relatively similar; and (4) the foreign legal materials reflect relatively independent judgments.

The analysis for courts in nations with developed constitutional traditions is different, because consideration of foreign materials may impose significant burdens without improving reasoning or results. But if such courts are to consider foreign law, they should first discard the legal materials of the foreign nations that do not meet conditions (2), (3), and (4), and then should determine whether the remaining legal materials are uniform, and occur in a nontrivial number of nations (say, five or more). Some useful proxies may further narrow discretion. A court might simplify its task by considering only relatively recent laws and decisions (under point 2), by considering the laws of only nations that have similar problems along the relevant dimension (under point 3), and by considering only laws that appear to be the result of substantial legislative process or litigation (under point 4).

[32] *Atkins*, 536 U.S. at 316 n. 21

[33] *Roper*, 543 U.S. at 562.

[34] *Lawrence*, 539 U.S. at 576. For accuracy, note that some members of the ECHR are not in western Europe.

[35] E.g., Thompson v. Oklahoma, 487 U.S. 815, 830–31 (1988).

Yes and No

For nations that have recently been attempting to create a new constitutional order, such as Canada, South Africa, Hungary, and Poland, consultation of other nations' practices is entirely sensible and legitimate, simply because those practices provide valuable information. Dealing with vague constitutional provisions, and often lacking a firmly developed body of precedent, constitutional courts might well do best to ask what other nations do. For new nations, the benefits of constitutional cosmopolitanism are especially likely to be high.

By contrast, American constitutional law has a large stock of precedents on which to draw, and its traditions are both developed and distinctive. Even with the simplifying framework set out here, consultation of foreign practices might well add new complexity without clearly producing better decisions. There is also a pervasive risk of opportunistic use of foreign law: Because the number of relevant jurisdictions is large, it is possible to use international practice selectively, or to characterize that practice in a certain way even though an objective reading would suggest otherwise.

Much of the discussion here is meant to help to explain the conclusion that for some nations, it is not worthwhile, all things considered, to consult foreign practices. To put the point another way, such consultation increases the burdens of decisions, for litigants and courts alike, and it may do so without producing better outcomes. Whether better outcomes are likely depends partly on judicial capacities and partly on the prevailing theory of interpretation. One of my main goals has been to show that both American and international practices closely follow the logic of many minds arguments. It follows that if there is a convincing justification for judicial consultation of foreign law, in the United States and elsewhere, it rests on the likely wisdom of many independent minds. And if the justification for consulting foreign law is not convincing, it is because the many minds argument fails for one or more of the now-familiar reasons.

Afterword

Americans revere their Constitution. But what, exactly, is their Constitution?

The most obvious answer is the written text, most of it well over two hundred years old. But the Constitution was hardly completed by the drafters and ratifiers in the eighteenth century. Formal amendments have been exceedingly important; they have altered the document in fundamental ways. But those amendments are merely a part of the set of processes that have produced existing understandings of the founding document.

Our Many Founders

If we are speaking of the Constitution's founders, we must include not merely Madison and Hamilton and their compatriots, but also Abraham Lincoln, Susan B. Anthony, Franklin Delano Roosevelt, Martin Luther King, Lyndon Baines Johnson, Barry Goldwater, Ronald Reagan, Gloria Steinem, and countless other public figures in and out of government. Ordinary citizens have played a crucial role, certainly insofar as their judgments of both fact and value have helped to motivate fresh interpretations of the document. History has rejected Jefferson's plea for formal rethinking of the Constitution through active engagement by citizens. But the content of the American Constitution has significantly changed as a result of citizens' beliefs and commitments, developing over time. Americans celebrate the stability of their Constitution. But generational change is a fact of constitutional life.

At its best, the American tradition has refused to engage in ancestor worship, and for one simple reason: Our ancestors knew much less than we do. Bentham was right to mock those who would celebrate the "wisdom of the cradle." As Pascal wrote, those now living are the real ancients, because our stock of experience is so much greater than that of those who preceded us. Our children will soon be our elders.

From its inception, the American constitutional tradition has doubted the private wisdom supposedly held by any individual; we know that isolated people, however powerful and learned, may know far too little. Skepticism about the judgments of the Supreme Court starts with this question: Why should Americans trust the moral judgments of a small group of lawyers in Washington, DC? The answer depends, in large part, on noticing that when things are going well, the Court's conclusions rest on something other than the idiosyncratic judgments of its nine members.

Traditionalism, Populism, Cosmopolitanism

Traditionalists, populists, and cosmopolitans all use many minds arguments. They ask: If many people have settled on some practice or proposition, shouldn't we, or the Supreme Court, pay careful attention to the settlement? The nature and force of the argument greatly differs across the three different contexts. But the structure of the argument is identical.

We have seen that traditions greatly matter to constitutional meaning. When Congress and the president have settled on a certain understanding of the separation of powers, the settlement is likely to stick. The permissible relationship between church and state is hardly determined by consulting history, but long-standing practices are entitled to a great deal of weight, and most justices are reluctant to disturb those practices. In deciding on the content of "liberty" under the due process clause, the Court gives careful attention to traditions. More generally, Burkean minimalists reject originalism on the ground that an abstract theory ought not to be used as a kind of bomb with which to explode practices that have stood the test of time. For the same reason, Burkeans reject perfectionist approaches that would authorize judges to understand constitutional provisions by reference to ambitious theories about our rights and our institutions.

It is often believed that the duty of the Court is to say what the law is, without the slightest regard to public opinion. How can public convictions bear on the meaning of the Constitution? The standard view is more right than wrong, because constitutional law should not involve opinion polls;

but it neglects two key facts. First, consequences matter, and if the consequences of a decision would be very bad, the Court legitimately takes account of that fact. If the public is likely to be outraged by a decision, the consequences may indeed be bad. Second, the Court might lack confidence that its own view is correct, and an intensely held public conviction might deserve respectful attention. We can imagine times and places in which judges properly take account of a widespread conviction that their own views are false or objectionable. In a nation in which constitutional meaning turns on moral or political arguments, and in which judges are comparatively bad at resolving those arguments, it would be best to adopt a large measure of popular constitutionalism.

The Court's occasional references to the law of other nations have produced intense public disapproval, but a many minds argument underlies those references as well. The Universal Declaration of Human Rights owes its origins to a worldwide effort to elicit the views of many minds; those who drafted the Universal Declaration showed an implicit but unmistakable Condorcetian logic. It should not be surprising to find that all over the world, constitutional courts resolve difficult questions only after exploring what other nations do. If most nations, or most relevant nations, believe that it is wrong to impose capital punishment on mentally retarded people, or that same-sex sexual relationships should not be criminalized, their views seem to deserve attention.

We have also seen that many minds arguments run into three pervasive problems. First, it is important to specify the proposition on which many people have converged. If circumstances have changed, there may be no support for the proposition in dispute. Perhaps the view of the public, or of most nations, has no relevance to the question on which constitutional meaning turns. Second, many minds may suffer from a systematic bias. If so, their views are entitled to less respect, not more, as their numbers increase. Third, a widely held view may reflect far less in the way of independent judgment than first appears. Many people may be following the crowd, depriving the collective wisdom of its epistemic credentials. Human beings often bow before the weight of numbers, not realizing that the numbers are as high as they are only because others have bowed as well.

These three problems create genuine difficulties for reliance on traditions, public opinion, and the law of other nations. In constitutional law, the most serious of these difficulties arise in the face of an equal protection problem. When there has been pervasive discrimination against one or another group, traditions are an unreliable guide, and public opinion may be the problem, not the solution. Discrimination on the basis of race, religion, sex, sexual orientation, and disability is not properly defended on the grounds that discriminatory practices are time-honored.

The most general point is that once we are armed with an understanding of many minds arguments and their characteristic weaknesses, we can make progress in identifying the domains in which those arguments make most sense. It is readily apparent that Burkean approaches have little appeal in authoritarian societies, in which relatively few people have helped to produce the rules by which citizens are governed. Burke's arguments about the wisdom of traditions have force only when many people have been able to decide, freely, whether and how much to follow a long-standing practice.

I have suggested that in the areas of separation of powers and gun rights, traditionalism deserves a great deal of support. The picture is much less clear for substantive due process, where rationalist minimalism is better, on reasonable assumptions about judicial capacities. The establishment clause presents an intermediate case. On the one hand, courts should be inclined to respect agreed-upon accommodations among diverse religious groups. When practices (say, the use of the words "under God" in the Pledge of Allegiance) have persisted for many years, they do seem to have been agreeable to most or all. On the other hand, some of those accommodations might amount, in practice, to the imposition of a practice on those who have lacked the power to resist it.

With respect to public opinion, we need to make a sharp distinction between consequentialist arguments, stressing the risk of harm, and epistemic arguments, stressing the possibility that the public's view offers valuable lessons about constitutional meaning. In rare but important cases, the Court rightly invokes the passive virtues or minimalism so as to avoid the harmful effects of an aggressive ruling. On consequentialist grounds, the Court should not now rule that states must recognize same-sex marriage, even it believes that the Constitution requires that result as a matter of principle. By contrast, the epistemic grounds for deference to the public are usually fragile. The public's judgment often bears on no relevant proposition; that judgment may well reflect a systematic bias; and "meaning entrepreneurs" often create cascade effects. But it is easy to imagine circumstances in which humble judges rightly hesitate to impose their own views on the nation. In any event, society's judgments inevitably influence the judges' judgments, if only because judges live in society.

For new countries, attempting to establish constitutional democracies, it is extremely sensible to attend to what other constitutional democracies do. In South Africa, Israel, and Hungary, a kind of cosmopolitanism, in the form of attention to foreign practices, is an excellent way to do constitutional law. Contrary to a widespread view, it is hardly outrageous or bizarre for American judges to conclude that those practices provide useful information. But most of the time, the relevant inquiries are likely to increase the burdens of decisions without improving them.

Is it possible to compare and to rank the three kinds of many minds arguments? For the United States, I have suggested that traditions are likely to provide the strongest basis for constitutional law, and that international practices provide the weakest. Public convictions are in the middle. We have also seen that the three arguments have intriguingly different political valences. Arguments from traditions have had considerable appeal to conservatives and less to liberals. Arguments from international practice have had considerable appeal to liberals, but are widely disapproved of by conservatives. During the period of the Warren Court, conservatives embraced a kind of popular constitutionalism, which was championed by many liberals in the New Deal era and which has enjoyed an unmistakable rise in popularity among liberals in recent years.

My most important goal has been less to specify particular uses and outcomes than to understand why, exactly, specific conclusions might be embraced. We could easily imagine a nation—say, a post-Soviet democracy—in which traditions were largely irrelevant and in which international practice was entitled to a great deal of weight. We could also imagine a nation with a well-functioning democracy and a poorly functioning court system, in which judges should be most reluctant to act in defiance of firmly held public convictions.

Beyond Many Minds—and Visionaries

I have referred to a serious problem with traditionalism. Judges who defer to long-standing practices seem timid, even frightened—more fearful about getting things wrong than determined to get things right. On one view of constitutional law, the best understanding of the founding document licenses judges to engage in a degree of critical reflection, not constrained by what others have done before. Constitutional visionaries see the document as setting forth large ideals that point toward a more just future. If the Constitution is seen in this way, we would raise equally serious questions about populism. Suppose that many people think that racial segregation is acceptable or that it is fine to discriminate on grounds of sexual orientation and disability; so what? What if their views are based on errors of fact or value? The same questions might be raised about cosmopolitanism. Suppose that most nations engage in some abhorrent practice. Shouldn't judges feel free to rethink that practice?

The simplest response is that sensible answers to these questions must depend on some comparative judgments. How much can we trust the relevant traditions? How much can we trust the judges? But a fuller answer must acknowledge the importance of constitutional visionaries. At least in the United States, it is worthwhile to insist that judges should sometimes attempt a degree of depth, and need not always struggle to root their decisions in what other people already think. Of course judges are not going to rule in a social vacuum; they live in the world. But those who live in the world sometimes do best if they ask, with some seriousness, whether a challenged practice really is justified, not whether most people like it.

Beyond Constitutional Law

I have focused throughout on constitutional law and judicial behavior, but I hope that the discussion has broader implications. Minimalism is a political phenomenon, not merely a legal one. Political leaders sometimes prize both narrowness and shallowness—sometimes for pragmatic reasons, sometimes for reasons of principle. It may not be prudent to take on the fundamental commitments of a significant percentage of one's fellow citizens; doing so may be a form of electoral suicide. Where disagreement is reasonable, it is not merely reasonable but also respectful to bracket disagreement. The linked virtues of humility and respect can be found in a form of political minimalism, practiced by leaders all over the globe. Indeed, minimalism can also be a kind of charity, in which political actors go out of their way to acknowledge the legitimacy of competing views on the deepest questions. But like judicial minimalism, political minimalism has serious limitations. Sometimes it is necessary, and best, to bite the bullet, and to take on the most fundamental issues. America's greatest presidents—Abraham Lincoln and Franklin Delano Roosevelt—did exactly that.

Many minds arguments can be found in countless domains. If officials in Washington, Paris, or London are deciding how to deal with terrorism, or how to think about climate change, or how to reform occupational safety and health law, they might want to ask about the practices of other nations. If officials in Germany are choosing among air pollution policies, they might ask about what other nations do, and give serious consideration to the majority's practice. If a computer company is deciding what product to market, it might consult a large group of (relevant) employees and follow the majority's answer. Both public and private institutions often accept many minds arguments—sometimes intuitively, sometimes with a committed belief that numerous people are unlikely to be wrong.

In all of these cases, those who are interested in such arguments would do well to identify the relevant proposition, to inquire into the possibility of a systematic bias, and to investigate whether there have been cascade effects. With an understanding of these points, we should be able to specify when many minds arguments deserve respectful attention—and when they should be rejected. That specification will have implications in turn for the proper approach not only to constitutional law, but also to markets, political representation, and democracy itself.

ACKNOWLEDGMENTS

My greatest debt is to Martha Nussbaum, Eric Posner, Richard Posner, and Adrian Vermeule for many conversations and valuable comments over the years. Special thanks to all four, and also to Adam Samaha, for comments on the manuscript as a whole; special thanks as well to Eric Posner for permission to draw heavily on our joint essay, The Law of Other States, 53 *Stan. L. Rev.* 131 (2006), for chapter 8. Thanks too to three anonymous reviewers for valuable comments and to Chuck Myers for superb suggestions, general support, and wise counsel.

I have drawn here from a number of previously published essays, though the exposition has been greatly changed and in some cases the basic argument is significantly different. The essays include Second-Order Perfectionism, 75 *Fordham L. Rev.* 2867 (2007); Burkean Minimalism, 105 *Mich. L. Rev.* 353 (2006); Due Process Traditionalism, 106 *Mich. L. Rev.* 2017 (2008); If People Would Be Outraged by Their Decisions, Should Judges Care? 60 *Stan. L. Rev.* 155 (2007); The Law of Other States, 53 *Stan. L. Rev.* 131 (2006). Many thanks to the editors of these journals for permission to reprint materials here and for valuable help of multiple kinds.

Index

Ackerman, Bruce, 5

aggregative account of many minds traditionalism: bias and prejudice, problem of, 101–2; Burke's statement of, 94–95; due process traditionalism and, 97–107, 120; force of for the Court and in social life, 96–97; independent judgments, problem of, 102–6; social cascades, problem of, 103–6; tradition and proposition, problem of linking, 97–100

Alito, Samuel, 11

Anthony, Susan B., 210

Atkins v. Virginia, 208

Australia, 189

authoritarianism, 102–3, 202–4

backlash: bad consequences that could occur from, 152; the Condorcet Jury Theorem and judicial attention to, 136; contextual assumptions in addressing the question of, 126–27, 138–39; Court rulings and, the question of, 12, 125–27; defined, 125; democracy, judicial deference in a, 136–38; elected officials and, 181–84; group polarization and, 173; Jeffersonian justification of considering, 135–36; judicial error, likelihood of and the need to consider, 133–36 (*see also* judicial humility); legal channels for public disapproval and, 138; Lincoln's consideration of the potential for, 128–29; Olympian judges' refusal to consider, 127–30; originalist judges' refusal to consider except in extreme cases, 131–33; popular con-

stitutionalism, as an exercise in, 180–81 (*see also* popular constitutionalism). *See also* public opinion

Bentham, Jeremy, 40, 83, 211

bias. *See* prejudice

Bickel, Alexander, 127–30, 139, 150

Brennan, William, 10–11

Breyer, Stephen, 10–11, 21, 47, 63, 200

Britain, 189, 200–1

Brown v. Board of Education, 28–29, 40–41, 74, 152

Burke, Edmund: aggregative account of the many minds argument, 94; authority of the past for, 70; Bentham and, opposition between, 40; common law, valuing of, 52–53; constitutional traditionalism and, 10; democracy and the thought of, 68, 103, 111; prejudice, favoring of, 49–51, 101; tradition, social change as emerging from, 67; tradition as a reflection of many minds, belief in, 88; traditions and the Condorcet Jury Theorem, 51–52

Burkean minimalism: approaches to, social practices and judicial decisions as, 47–49; best case for, 40–41; cases illustrating, 35–36; consequentialist defense of, need for, 69–72, 87–88; conservative alternatives to, 37–39; constitutional law, applicability to, 83–85; context, significance of, 75–77; the dilemma of, 85–87; domains favorable for, specification of, 89–90; due process and (*see* due process; due process traditionalism); experience as guide, critics' use of argument for, 80–83; foundations of, 87–88; judicial